P9-DWP-199

2020 EDITION

MODEL RULES
OF
PROFESSIONAL
CONDUCT

AMERICAN**BAR**ASSOCIATION

Center for Professional
Responsibility

Cover design by ABA Design/ABA Publishing.

The ABA Model Rules of Professional Conduct, including Preamble, Scope and Comment, were adopted by the ABA House of Delegates on August 2, 1983, and amended in 1987, 1989, 1990, 1991, 1992, 1993, 1994, 1995, 1997, 1998, 2000, 2002, 2003, 2007, 2008, 2009, 2012, 2013, 2016, and 2018.

Nothing contained herein is to be considered as the rendering of legal advice for specific cases, and readers are responsible for obtaining such advice from their own legal counsel. This book is intended for educational and informational purposes only.

©2020 American Bar Association. All rights reserved.

No part of this publication may be reproduced, stored in a retrieval system, or transmitted in any form or by any means, electronic, mechanical, photocopying, recording, or otherwise, without the prior written permission of the publisher. For permission contact the ABA Copyrights & Contracts Department, copyright@americanbar.org, or complete the online form at http://www.americanbar.org/utility/reprint.html.

Printed in the United States of America.

24 23 22 21 20   5 4 3 2 1

ISBN: 978-1-64105-649-6
e-ISBN: 978-1-64105-650-2

Discounts are available for books ordered in bulk. Special consideration is given to state bars, CLE programs, and other bar-related organizations. Inquire at Book Publishing, ABA Publishing, American Bar Association, 321 N. Clark Street, Chicago, Illinois 60654-7598.

www.ShopABA.org

AMERICAN BAR ASSOCIATION
CENTER FOR PROFESSIONAL RESPONSIBILITY

The Center for Professional Responsibility is the American Bar Association's "home" for lawyers who are interested in professionalism, ethics, client protection, discipline, and regulation. The Center has served as locus for many ABA initiatives, including those of the Commission on Multidisciplinary Practice, the Commission on Multijurisdictional Practice, the Commission on Evaluation of the Rules of Professional Conduct (Ethics 2000), the Joint Commission to Evaluate the Model Code of Judicial Conduct, and the Commission on Ethics 20/20. The Center comprises numerous committees and publishes various works relating to professional responsibility law. In addition, the Center:

- Develops rules of lawyer and judicial ethics, professional discipline, and client protection that serve as the model for jurisdictions throughout the country;
- Produces numerous publications including *Annotated Model Rules of Professional Conduct*, *Annotated Model Code of Judicial Conduct*, *The Paralegal's Guide to Professional Responsibility*, model lawyer, judicial, and client protection rules, and, in partnership with Bloomberg BNA, the *ABA/BNA Lawyers' Manual on Professional Conduct*;
- Issues formal opinions to resolve questions about applying ethics rules;
- Operates the National Lawyer Regulatory Data Bank, the only national repository of information relating to lawyers who have received public disciplinary sanctions;
- Offers on-site consultations to individual jurisdictions reviewing their discipline systems; and
- Presents the annual National Conference on Professional Responsibility, National Forum on Client Protection, National Legal Malpractice Conference, and numerous CLE webinars.

Center membership is open to ABA lawyer, associate, and law student members in all practice settings. Benefits include steep discounts on publications and CLE events.

Find out more about the Center at http://ambar.org/CPRHome or contact the Center at cpr@americanbar.org.

ABA Standing Committee on Ethics and Professional Responsibility
2019–2020

BARBARA S. GILLERS, *Chair*
New York, NY

MICHAEL H. RUBIN
Baton Rouge, LA

LONNIE T. BROWN
Athens, GA

LYNDA C. SHELY
Scottsdale, AZ

ROBERT HIRSHON
Ann Arbor, MI

NORMAN W. SPAULDING
Stanford, CA

HON. GOODWIN LIU
San Francisco, CA

ELIZABETH C. TARBERT
Tallahassee, FL

THOMAS B. MASON
Washington, DC

LISA DEITSCH TAYLOR
Parsippany, NJ

Board of Governors Liaison
CHARLES J. VIGIL
Albuquerque, NM

American Bar Association
Center for Professional Responsibility

Director
TERESA SCHMID

Dedicated to the memory of
Jeanne P. Gray
Director, ABA Center for Professional Responsibility,
1982–2013

CONTENTS

PUBLIC SERVICE

INFORMATION ABOUT LEGAL SERVICES

MAINTAINING THE INTEGRITY OF THE PROFESSION

APPENDICES

PREFACE

For more than one hundred years, the American Bar Association has provided leadership in legal ethics and professional responsibility through the adoption of professional standards that serve as models of the regulatory law governing the legal profession.

On August 27, 1908, the Association adopted the original Canons of Professional Ethics. These were based principally on the Code of Ethics adopted by the Alabama Bar Association in 1887, which in turn had been borrowed largely from the lectures of Judge George Sharswood, published in 1854 as Professional Ethics, and from the fifty resolutions included in David Hoffman's A Course of Legal Study (2d ed. 1836). Piecemeal amendments to the Canons occasionally followed.

In 1913, the Standing Committee on Professional Ethics of the American Bar Association was established to keep the Association informed about state and local bar activities concerning professional ethics. In 1919 the name of the Committee was changed to the Committee on Professional Ethics and Grievances; its role was expanded in 1922 to include issuing opinions "concerning professional conduct, and particularly concerning the application of the tenets of ethics thereto." In 1958 the Committee on Professional Ethics and Grievances was separated into two committees: a Committee on Professional Grievances, with authority to review issues of professional misconduct, and a Committee on Professional Ethics with responsibility to express its opinion concerning proper professional and judicial conduct. The Committee on Professional Grievances was discontinued in 1971. The name of the Committee on Professional Ethics was changed to the Committee on Ethics and Professional Responsibility in 1971 and remains so.

In 1964, at the request of President Lewis F. Powell Jr., the House of Delegates of the American Bar Association created a Special Committee on Evaluation of Ethical Standards (the "Wright Committee") to assess whether changes should be made in the then-current Canons of Professional Ethics. In response, the Committee produced the Model Code of Professional Responsibility. The Model Code was adopted by the House of Delegates on August 12, 1969, and subsequently by the vast majority of state and federal jurisdictions.

In 1977, the American Bar Association created the Commission on Evaluation of Professional Standards to undertake a comprehensive rethinking of the ethical premises and problems of the legal profession. Upon evaluating the Model Code and determining that amendment of the Code would not achieve a comprehensive statement of the law governing the legal profession, the Commission commenced a six-year study and drafting process that produced the Model Rules of Professional Conduct. The Model Rules were adopted by the House of Delegates of the American Bar Association on August 2, 1983.

Between 1983 and 2002, the House amended the Rules and Comments on fourteen different occasions. In 1997, the American Bar Association created the Commission on Evaluation of the Rules of Professional Conduct ("Ethics 2000 Commission") to comprehensively review the Model Rules and propose amendments as deemed appropriate. On February 5, 2002 the House of Delegates adopted a series of amendments that arose from this process.

In 2000, the American Bar Association created the Commission on Multijurisdictional Practice to research, study and report on the application of current ethics and bar admission rules to the multijurisdictional practice of law. On August 12, 2002 the House of Delegates adopted amendments to Rules 5.5 and 8.5 as a result of the Commission's work and recommendations.

In 2002, the American Bar Association created the Task Force on Corporate Responsibility to examine systemic issues relating to corporate responsibility arising out of the unexpected and traumatic bankruptcy of Enron and other Enron-like situations that had shaken confidence in the effectiveness of the governance and disclosure systems applicable to public companies in the United States. In August 11-12, 2003, the House of Delegates adopted amendments to Rules 1.6 and 1.13 as a result of the Task Force's work and recommendations.

In 2009, the American Bar Association created the Commission on Ethics 20/20 to perform a thorough review of the ABA Model Rules of Professional Conduct and the U.S. system of lawyer regulation in the context of advances in technology and global legal practice developments. On August 6, 2012 and February 11, 2013 the House of Delegates adopted a series of amendments to the Rules and Comments as a result of the Commission's work and recommendations.

In February 2016, the Section on International Law recommended amending Model Rule of Professional Conduct 5.5 and the ABA Model Rule for Registration of In-House Counsel to include language specifying that the court of highest appellate jurisdiction may, in its discretion, allow foreign in-house lawyers who do not meet the ABA definition of foreign lawyer because they cannot be "members of the bar" to be able to practice as in-house counsel in the United States and to be so registered. On February 8, 2016, the House of Delegates adopted the suggested amendments with further revisions.

In August 2016, the Standing Committee on Ethics and Professional Responsibility brought to the House of Delegates amendments to Model Rule 8.4, Misconduct. Proposed new paragraph (g) prohibited lawyers from discrimination and harassment in conduct related to the practice of law. On August 8, 2016, the House of Delegates adopted the recommended amendments.

In 2018, the Standing Committee on Ethics and Professional Responsibility suggested amendments to the Model Rules regulating lawyer advertising with the goal of simplifying and making those rules more uniform. On August 6, 2018, the House of Delegates adopted the suggested amendments.

The American Bar Association continues to pursue its goal of assuring the highest standards of professional competence and ethical conduct. The Standing Committee on Ethics and Professional Responsibility, charged with interpreting the professional standards of the Association and recommending appropriate amendments and clarifications, issues opinions interpreting the Model Rules of Professional Conduct and the Model Code of Judicial Conduct. The opinions of the Committee are published by the American Bar Association in a series of bound volumes containing opinions from 1924 through 2013 and as individual PDFs starting with the 1984 opinions.

Requests that the Committee issue opinions on particular questions of professional and judicial conduct should be directed to the American Bar Association, Center for Professional Responsibility, 321 N. Clark Street, Chicago, Illinois 60654.

ABA Commission on Evaluation of Professional Standards (1977–1983)

ROBERT W. MESERVE, *Chair*
Boston, Massachusetts

MARVIN E. FRANKEL
New York, New York

RICHARD H. SINKFIELD
Atlanta, Georgia

ALAN BARTH
Washington, D.C.

LOIS C. HARRISON
Lakeland, Florida

WILLIAM B. SPANN, JR.
Atlanta, Georgia

ARNO H. DENECKE
Salem, Oregon

ROBERT O. HETLAGE
St. Louis, Missouri

SAMUEL D. THURMAN
Salt Lake City, Utah

THOMAS EHRLICH
Washington, D.C.

ROBERT B. McKAY
New York, New York

ROBERT J. KUTAK
Omaha, Nebraska
Former Chair

JANE FRANK-HARMAN
Washington, D.C.

L. CLAIR NELSON
Washington, D.C.

Liaisons

MICHAEL FRANCK
Lansing, Michigan
*Standing Committee on
Professional Discipline*

JOHN C. DEACON
Jonesboro, Arkansas
Board of Governors

H. WILLIAM ALLEN
Little Rock, Arkansas
*Standing Committee on
Ethics and Professional
Responsibility*

THOMAS Z. HAYWARD, JR.
Chicago, Illinois

Consultants

BETTY B. FLETCHER
Seattle, Washington

L. RAY PATTERSON
Atlanta, Georgia

JOHN F. SUTTON, JR.
Austin, Texas

Reporter

GEOFFREY C. HAZARD, JR.
New Haven, Connecticut

Assistant Reporters

THOMAS J. McCORMICK
Washington, D.C.

DANIEL S. REYNOLDS
DeKalb, Illinois

Commission on Evaluation of Professional Standards
Chair's Introduction

The Commission on Evaluation of Professional Standards was appointed in the summer of 1977 by former ABA President William B. Spann, Jr. Chaired by Robert J. Kutak until his death in early 1983, the Commission was charged with evaluating whether existing standards of professional conduct provided comprehensive and consistent guidance for resolving the increasingly complex ethical problems in the practice of law. For the most part, the Commission looked to the former ABA Model Code of Professional Responsibility, which served as a model for the majority of state ethics codes. The Commission also referred to opinions of the ABA Standing Committee on Ethics and Professional Responsibility, as well as to decisions of the United States Supreme Court and of state supreme courts. After thoughtful study, the Commission concluded that piecemeal amendment of the Model Code would not sufficiently clarify the profession's ethical responsibilities in light of changed conditions. The Commission therefore commenced a drafting process that produced numerous drafts, elicited voluminous comment, and launched an unprecedented debate on the ethics of the legal profession.

On January 30, 1980, the Commission presented its initial suggestions to the bar in the form of a Discussion Draft of the proposed Model Rules of Professional Conduct. The Discussion Draft was subject to the widest possible dissemination and interested parties were urged to offer comments and suggestions. Public hearings were held around the country to provide forums for expression of views on the draft.

In the year following the last of these public hearings, the Commission conducted a painstaking analysis of the submitted comments and attempted to integrate into the draft those which seemed consistent with its underlying philosophy. The product of this analysis and integration was presented on May 31, 1981, as the proposed Final Draft of the Model Rules of Professional Conduct. This proposed Final Draft was submitted in two formats. The first format, consisting of blackletter Rules and accompanying Comments in the so-called restatement format, was submitted with the Commission's recommendation that it be adopted. The alternative format was patterned after the Model Code and consisted of Canons, Ethical Considerations, and Disciplinary Rules. In February 1982, the House of Delegates by substantial majority approved the restatement format of the Model Rules.

The proposed Final Draft was submitted to the House of Delegates for debate and approval at the 1982 Annual Meeting of the Association in San Francisco. Many organizations and interested parties offered their comments in the form of proposed amendments to the Final Draft. In the time allotted on its agenda, however, the House debated only proposed amendments to Rule 1.5. Consideration of the remainder of the document was deferred until the 1983 Midyear Meeting in New Orleans. The proposed Final Draft, as amended by the House in San Francisco, was reprinted in the November 1982 issue of the *ABA Journal*.

At the 1983 Midyear Meeting the House resumed consideration of the Final Draft. After two days of often vigorous debate, the House completed its review of the proposed amendments to the blackletter Rules. Many amendments, particularly in the area of confidentiality, were adopted. Debate on a Preamble, Scope, Terminology, and Comments, rewritten to reflect the New Orleans amendments, was deferred until the 1983 Annual Meeting in Atlanta, Georgia.

On March 11, 1983, the text of the blackletter Rules as approved by the House in February, together with the proposed Preamble, Scope, Terminology, and Comments, was circulated to members of the House, Section and Committee chairs, and all other interested parties. The text of the Rules reflected the joint efforts of the Commission and the House Drafting Committee to incorporate the changes approved by the House and to ensure stylistic continuity and uniformity. Recipients of the draft were again urged to submit comments in the form of proposed amendments. The House Committees on Drafting and Rules and Calendar met on May 23, 1983, to consider all of the proposed amendments that had been submitted in response to this draft. In addition, discussions were held among concerned parties in an effort to reach accommodation of the various positions. On July 11, 1983, the final version of the Model Rules was again circulated.

The House of Delegates commenced debate on the proposed Preamble, Scope, Terminology, and Comments on August 2, 1983. After four hours of debate, the House completed its consideration of all the proposed amendments and, upon motion of the Commission, the House voted to adopt the Model Rules of Professional Conduct, together with the ancillary material as amended. The task of the Commission had ended and it was discharged with thanks.

Throughout the drafting process, active participants included not only the members of the Commission but also the Sections and Committees of the American Bar Association and national, state, and local bar organizations. The work of the Commission was subject to virtually continuous scrutiny by academicians, practicing lawyers, members of the press, and the judiciary. Consequently, every provision of the Model Rules reflects the thoughtful consideration and hard work of many dedicated professionals. Because of their input, the Model Rules are truly national in derivation. The Association can take immense pride in its continued demonstration of leadership in the area of professional responsibility.

The Model Rules of Professional Conduct are intended to serve as a national framework for implementation of standards of professional conduct. Although the Commission endeavored to harmonize and accommodate the views of all the participants, no set of national standards that speaks to such a diverse constituency as the legal profession can resolve each issue to the complete satisfaction of every affected party. Undoubtedly there will be those who take issue with one or another of the Rules' provisions. Indeed, such dissent from individual provisions is expected. And the Model Rules, like all model legislation, will be subject to modification at the level of local implementation. Viewed as a whole, however, the Model Rules represent a responsible approach to the ethical practice of law and are consistent with professional obligations imposed by other law, such as constitutional, corporate, tort, fiduciary, and agency law.

I should not end this report without speaking of the Commission's debt to many people who have aided us in our deliberations, and have devoted time, energy, and goodwill to the advancement of our work over the last six years. It would probably be impossible to name each of the particular persons whose help was significant to us, and it surely would be unfortunate if the name of anyone were omitted from the list. We are, and shall remain, deeply grateful to the literally hundreds of people who aided us with welcome and productive suggestions. We think the bar should be grateful to each of them, and to our deceased members, Alan Barth of the District of Columbia, who we hardly had time to know, Bill Spann, who became a member after the conclusion of his presidential term, and our original chair, Bob Kutak.

The long work of the Commission and its resulting new codification of the ethical rules of practice demonstrate, it is submitted, the commitment of the American lawyer to his or her profession and to achievement of the highest standards.

Robert W. Meserve
September 1983

ABA Commission on Evaluation of the Rules of Professional Conduct (1997–2002)

HON. E. NORMAN VEASEY, *Chair*
Wilmington, Delaware

MARGARET C. LOVE
Washington, D.C.

LAWRENCE J. FOX
Philadelphia, Pennsylvania

SUSAN R. MARTYN
Toledo, Ohio

ALBERT C. HARVEY
Memphis, Tennessee

DAVID T. MCLAUGHLIN
New London, New Hampshire

GEOFFREY C. HAZARD, JR.
Swarthmore, Pennsylvania

RICHARD E. MULROY
Ridgewood, New Jersey

HON. PATRICK E. HIGGINBOTHAM
Dallas, Texas

LUCIAN T. PERA
Memphis, Tennessee

W. LOEBER LANDAU
New York, New York

HON. HENRY RAMSEY, JR. (Ret.)
Berkeley, California

HON. LAURIE D. ZELON
Los Angeles, California

Liaisons

JAMES B. LEE
Salt Lake City, Utah
Board of Governors

SETH ROSNER
Greenfield Center, New York
Board of Governors

Reporters

NANCY J. MOORE
Boston, Massachusetts
Chief Reporter

THOMAS D. MORGAN (1998–1999)
Washington, D.C.

CARL A. PIERCE
Knoxville, Tennessee

Center for Professional Responsibility

JEANNE P. GRAY
Chicago, Illinois
Director

CHARLOTTE K. STRETCH, *Counsel*
Chicago, Illinois

SUSAN M. CAMPBELL, *Paralegal*
Chicago, Illinois

COMMISSION ON EVALUATION OF THE
RULES OF PROFESSIONAL CONDUCT ("ETHICS 2000")

CHAIR'S INTRODUCTION

In mid-1997, ABA President Jerome J. Shestack, his immediate predecessor, N. Lee Cooper, and his successor, Philip S. Anderson had the vision to establish the "Ethics 2000" Commission. These three leaders persuaded the ABA Board of Governors that the Model Rules adopted by the ABA House of Delegates in 1983 needed comprehensive review and some revision, and this project was launched. Though some might have thought it premature to reopen the Model Rules to such a rigorous general reassessment after only fourteen years, the evaluation process has proven that the ABA leadership was correct.

One of the primary reasons behind the decision to revisit the Model Rules was the growing disparity in state ethics codes. While a large majority of states and the District of Columbia had adopted some version of the Model Rules (then thirty-nine, now forty-two), there were many significant differences among the state versions that resulted in an undesirable lack of uniformity—a problem that had been exacerbated by the approximately thirty amendments to the Model Rules between 1983 and 1997. A few states had elected to retain some version of the 1969 Model Code of Professional Responsibility, and California remained committed to an entirely separate system of lawyer regulation.

But it was not only the patchwork pattern of state regulation that motivated the ABA leaders of 1997 to take this action. There were also new issues and questions raised by the influence that technological developments were having on the delivery of legal services. The explosive dynamics of modern law practice and the anticipated developments in the future of the legal profession lent a sense of urgency as well as a substantive dimension to the project. These developments were underscored by the work then underway on the American Law Institute's *Restatement of the Law Governing Lawyers*.

There was also a strong countervailing sense that there was much to be valued in the existing concepts and articulation of the Model Rules. The Commission concluded early on that these valuable aspects of the Rules should not be lost or put at risk in our revision effort. As a result, the Commission set about to be comprehensive, but at the same time conservative, and to recommend change only where necessary. In balancing the need to preserve the good with the need for improvement, we were mindful of Thomas Jefferson's words of nearly 185 years ago, in a letter concerning the Virginia Constitution, that "moderate imperfections had better be borne with; because, when once known, we accommodate ourselves to them, and find practical means of correcting their ill effects."

Thus, we retained the basic architecture of the Model Rules. We also retained the primary disciplinary function of the Rules, resisting the temptation to preach aspirationally about "best practices" or professionalism concepts. Valuable as the profession might find such guidance, it would not have—and should not be misperceived as having—a regulatory dimension. We were, however, always conscious of the educational role of the Model Rules. Finally, we tried to keep our changes to a minimum: when a particular provision was found not to be "broken" we did not try to "fix" it. Even so, as the reader will note, the Commission ended up making a large number of changes: some are relatively innocuous and nonsubstantive, in the nature of editorial or stylistic changes; others are substantive but not particularly controversial; and a few are both substantive and controversial.

The deliberations of the Commission did not take place in a vacuum and our determinations are not being pronounced *ex cathedra*. Rather, they are products of thorough research, scholarly analysis, and thoughtful consideration. Of equal importance, they have been influenced by the views of practitioners, scholars, other members of the legal profession, and the public. All these constituencies have had continual access to and considerable—and proper—influence upon the deliberations of the Commission throughout this process.

I must pause to underscore the openness of our process. We held over fifty days of meetings, all of which were open, and ten public hearings at regular intervals over a four-and-a-half-year period. There were a large number of interested observers at our meetings, many of whom were members of our Advisory Council of 250-plus persons, to offer comments and suggestions. Those observations were very helpful and influential in shaping the Report. Our public discussion drafts, minutes, and Report were available on our website for the world to see and comment upon. As a consequence, we received an enormous number of excellent comments and suggestions, many of which were adopted in the formulation of our Report.

Moreover, we encouraged state and local bar associations, ABA sections and divisions, other professional organizations, and the judiciary to appoint specially designated committees to work with and counsel the Commission. This effort was successful, and the Commission benefitted significantly from the considered views of these groups.

In heeding the counsel of these advisors, we were constantly mindful of substantial and high-velocity changes in the legal profession, particularly over the past decade. These changes have been highlighted by increased public scrutiny of lawyers and an awareness of their influential role in the formation and implementation of public policy; persistent concerns about lawyer honesty, candor, and civility; external competitive and technological pressures on the legal profession; internal pressures on law firm organization and management raised by sheer size, as well as specialization and lawyer mobility; jurisdictional and governance issues, such as multidisciplinary and multijurisdictional practice; special concerns of lawyers in nontraditional practice settings, such as government lawyers and in-house counsel; and the need to enhance public trust and confidence in the legal profession.

At the end of the day, our goal was to develop Rules that are comprehensible to the public and provide clear guidance to the practitioner. Our desire was to preserve all that is valuable and enduring about the existing Model Rules, while at the same time adapting them to the realities of modern law practice and the limits of professional discipline. We believe our product is a balanced blend of traditional precepts and forward-looking provisions that are responsive to modern developments. Our process has been thorough, painstaking, open, scholarly, objective, and collegial.

It is impossible here to go into detail about the changes proposed by the Commission. The changes recommended by the Commission clarified and strengthened a lawyer's duty to communicate with the client; clarified and strengthened a lawyer's duty to clients in certain specific problem areas; responded to the changing organization and structure of modern law practice; responded to new issues and questions raised by the influence that technological developments are having on the delivery of legal services; clarified existing Rules to provide better guidance and explanation to lawyers; clarified and strengthened a lawyer's obligations to the tribunal and to the justice system; responded to the need for changes in the delivery of legal services to low- and middle-income persons; and increased protection of third parties.

The ABA House of Delegates began consideration of the Commission's Report at the August 2001 Annual Meeting in Chicago and completed its review at the February 2002 Midyear Meeting in Philadelphia.

At the August 2002 Annual Meeting in Washington, D.C., the ABA House of Delegates considered and adopted additional amendments to the Model Rules sponsored by the ABA Commission on Multijurisdictional Practice and the ABA Standing Committee on Ethics and Professional Responsibility. As state supreme courts consider implementation of these newly revised Rules, it is our fervent hope that the goal of uniformity will be the guiding beacon.

In closing, the Commission expresses its gratitude to the law firm of Drinker Biddle & Reath, whose generous contribution helped make possible the continued, invaluable support of the Commission's Chief Reporter. I also want to express personally my gratitude to and admiration for my colleagues. The chemistry, goodwill, good humor, serious purpose, collegiality, and hard work of the Commission members, Reporters, and ABA staff have been extraordinary. The profession and the public have been enriched beyond measure by their efforts. It has been a pleasure and a privilege for me to work with all of them.

Hon. E. Norman Veasey
August 2002

PREAMBLE AND SCOPE

PREAMBLE:
A LAWYER'S RESPONSIBILITIES

[1] A lawyer, as a member of the legal profession, is a representative of clients, an officer of the legal system and a public citizen having special responsibility for the quality of justice.

[2] As a representative of clients, a lawyer performs various functions. As advisor, a lawyer provides a client with an informed understanding of the client's legal rights and obligations and explains their practical implications. As advocate, a lawyer zealously asserts the client's position under the rules of the adversary system. As negotiator, a lawyer seeks a result advantageous to the client but consistent with requirements of honest dealings with others. As an evaluator, a lawyer acts by examining a client's legal affairs and reporting about them to the client or to others.

[3] In addition to these representational functions, a lawyer may serve as a third-party neutral, a nonrepresentational role helping the parties to resolve a dispute or other matter. Some of these Rules apply directly to lawyers who are or have served as third-party neutrals. See, e.g., Rules 1.12 and 2.4. In addition, there are Rules that apply to lawyers who are not active in the practice of law or to practicing lawyers even when they are acting in a nonprofessional capacity. For example, a lawyer who commits fraud in the conduct of a business is subject to discipline for engaging in conduct involving dishonesty, fraud, deceit or misrepresentation. See Rule 8.4.

[4] In all professional functions a lawyer should be competent, prompt and diligent. A lawyer should maintain communication with a client concerning the representation. A lawyer should keep in confidence information relating to representation of a client except so far as disclosure is required or permitted by the Rules of Professional Conduct or other law.

[5] A lawyer's conduct should conform to the requirements of the law, both in professional service to clients and in the lawyer's business and personal affairs. A lawyer should use the law's procedures only for legitimate purposes and not to harass or intimidate others. A lawyer should demonstrate respect for the legal system and for those who serve it, including judges, other lawyers and public officials. While it is a law-

yer's duty, when necessary, to challenge the rectitude of official action, it is also a lawyer's duty to uphold legal process.

[6] As a public citizen, a lawyer should seek improvement of the law, access to the legal system, the administration of justice and the quality of service rendered by the legal profession. As a member of a learned profession, a lawyer should cultivate knowledge of the law beyond its use for clients, employ that knowledge in reform of the law and work to strengthen legal education. In addition, a lawyer should further the public's understanding of and confidence in the rule of law and the justice system because legal institutions in a constitutional democracy depend on popular participation and support to maintain their authority. A lawyer should be mindful of deficiencies in the administration of justice and of the fact that the poor, and sometimes persons who are not poor, cannot afford adequate legal assistance. Therefore, all lawyers should devote professional time and resources and use civic influence to ensure equal access to our system of justice for all those who because of economic or social barriers cannot afford or secure adequate legal counsel. A lawyer should aid the legal profession in pursuing these objectives and should help the bar regulate itself in the public interest.

[7] Many of a lawyer's professional responsibilities are prescribed in the Rules of Professional Conduct, as well as substantive and procedural law. However, a lawyer is also guided by personal conscience and the approbation of professional peers. A lawyer should strive to attain the highest level of skill, to improve the law and the legal profession and to exemplify the legal profession's ideals of public service.

[8] A lawyer's responsibilities as a representative of clients, an officer of the legal system and a public citizen are usually harmonious. Thus, when an opposing party is well represented, a lawyer can be a zealous advocate on behalf of a client and at the same time assume that justice is being done. So also, a lawyer can be sure that preserving client confidences ordinarily serves the public interest because people are more likely to seek legal advice, and thereby heed their legal obligations, when they know their communications will be private.

[9] In the nature of law practice, however, conflicting responsibilities are encountered. Virtually all difficult ethical problems arise from conflict between a lawyer's responsibilities to clients, to the legal system and to the lawyer's own interest in remaining an ethical person while earning a satisfactory living. The Rules of Professional Conduct often prescribe terms for resolving such conflicts. Within the framework of these Rules,

however, many difficult issues of professional discretion can arise. Such issues must be resolved through the exercise of sensitive professional and moral judgment guided by the basic principles underlying the Rules. These principles include the lawyer's obligation zealously to protect and pursue a client's legitimate interests, within the bounds of the law, while maintaining a professional, courteous and civil attitude toward all persons involved in the legal system.

[10] The legal profession is largely self-governing. Although other professions also have been granted powers of self-government, the legal profession is unique in this respect because of the close relationship between the profession and the processes of government and law enforcement. This connection is manifested in the fact that ultimate authority over the legal profession is vested largely in the courts.

[11] To the extent that lawyers meet the obligations of their professional calling, the occasion for government regulation is obviated. Self-regulation also helps maintain the legal profession's independence from government domination. An independent legal profession is an important force in preserving government under law, for abuse of legal authority is more readily challenged by a profession whose members are not dependent on government for the right to practice.

[12] The legal profession's relative autonomy carries with it special responsibilities of self-government. The profession has a responsibility to assure that its regulations are conceived in the public interest and not in furtherance of parochial or self-interested concerns of the bar. Every lawyer is responsible for observance of the Rules of Professional Conduct. A lawyer should also aid in securing their observance by other lawyers. Neglect of these responsibilities compromises the independence of the profession and the public interest which it serves.

[13] Lawyers play a vital role in the preservation of society. The fulfillment of this role requires an understanding by lawyers of their relationship to our legal system. The Rules of Professional Conduct, when properly applied, serve to define that relationship.

SCOPE

[14] The Rules of Professional Conduct are rules of reason. They should be interpreted with reference to the purposes of legal representation and of the law itself. Some of the Rules are imperatives, cast in the terms "shall" or "shall not." These define proper conduct for purposes of professional discipline. Others, generally cast in the term "may," are

permissive and define areas under the Rules in which the lawyer has discretion to exercise professional judgment. No disciplinary action should be taken when the lawyer chooses not to act or acts within the bounds of such discretion. Other Rules define the nature of relationships between the lawyer and others. The Rules are thus partly obligatory and disciplinary and partly constitutive and descriptive in that they define a lawyer's professional role. Many of the Comments use the term "should." Comments do not add obligations to the Rules but provide guidance for practicing in compliance with the Rules.

[15] The Rules presuppose a larger legal context shaping the lawyer's role. That context includes court rules and statutes relating to matters of licensure, laws defining specific obligations of lawyers and substantive and procedural law in general. The Comments are sometimes used to alert lawyers to their responsibilities under such other law.

[16] Compliance with the Rules, as with all law in an open society, depends primarily upon understanding and voluntary compliance, secondarily upon reinforcement by peer and public opinion and finally, when necessary, upon enforcement through disciplinary proceedings. The Rules do not, however, exhaust the moral and ethical considerations that should inform a lawyer, for no worthwhile human activity can be completely defined by legal rules. The Rules simply provide a framework for the ethical practice of law.

[17] Furthermore, for purposes of determining the lawyer's authority and responsibility, principles of substantive law external to these Rules determine whether a client-lawyer relationship exists. Most of the duties flowing from the client-lawyer relationship attach only after the client has requested the lawyer to render legal services and the lawyer has agreed to do so. But there are some duties, such as that of confidentiality under Rule 1.6, that attach when the lawyer agrees to consider whether a client-lawyer relationship shall be established. See Rule 1.18. Whether a client-lawyer relationship exists for any specific purpose can depend on the circumstances and may be a question of fact.

[18] Under various legal provisions, including constitutional, statutory and common law, the responsibilities of government lawyers may include authority concerning legal matters that ordinarily reposes in the client in private client-lawyer relationships. For example, a lawyer for a government agency may have authority on behalf of the government to decide upon settlement or whether to appeal from an adverse judgment. Such authority in various respects is generally vested in the attorney

general and the state's attorney in state government, and their federal counterparts, and the same may be true of other government law officers. Also, lawyers under the supervision of these officers may be authorized to represent several government agencies in intragovernmental legal controversies in circumstances where a private lawyer could not represent multiple private clients. These Rules do not abrogate any such authority.

[19] Failure to comply with an obligation or prohibition imposed by a Rule is a basis for invoking the disciplinary process. The Rules presuppose that disciplinary assessment of a lawyer's conduct will be made on the basis of the facts and circumstances as they existed at the time of the conduct in question and in recognition of the fact that a lawyer often has to act upon uncertain or incomplete evidence of the situation. Moreover, the Rules presuppose that whether or not discipline should be imposed for a violation, and the severity of a sanction, depend on all the circumstances, such as the willfulness and seriousness of the violation, extenuating factors and whether there have been previous violations.

[20] Violation of a Rule should not itself give rise to a cause of action against a lawyer nor should it create any presumption in such a case that a legal duty has been breached. In addition, violation of a Rule does not necessarily warrant any other nondisciplinary remedy, such as disqualification of a lawyer in pending litigation. The Rules are designed to provide guidance to lawyers and to provide a structure for regulating conduct through disciplinary agencies. They are not designed to be a basis for civil liability. Furthermore, the purpose of the Rules can be subverted when they are invoked by opposing parties as procedural weapons. The fact that a Rule is a just basis for a lawyer's self-assessment, or for sanctioning a lawyer under the administration of a disciplinary authority, does not imply that an antagonist in a collateral proceeding or transaction has standing to seek enforcement of the Rule. Nevertheless, since the Rules do establish standards of conduct by lawyers, a lawyer's violation of a Rule may be evidence of breach of the applicable standard of conduct.

[21] The Comment accompanying each Rule explains and illustrates the meaning and purpose of the Rule. The Preamble and this note on Scope provide general orientation. The Comments are intended as guides to interpretation, but the text of each Rule is authoritative.

RULE 1.0: TERMINOLOGY

(a) "Belief" or "believes" denotes that the person involved actually supposed the fact in question to be true. A person's belief may be inferred from circumstances.

(b) "Confirmed in writing," when used in reference to the informed consent of a person, denotes informed consent that is given in writing by the person or a writing that a lawyer promptly transmits to the person confirming an oral informed consent. See paragraph (e) for the definition of "informed consent." If it is not feasible to obtain or transmit the writing at the time the person gives informed consent, then the lawyer must obtain or transmit it within a reasonable time thereafter.

(c) "Firm" or "law firm" denotes a lawyer or lawyers in a law partnership, professional corporation, sole proprietorship or other association authorized to practice law; or lawyers employed in a legal services organization or the legal department of a corporation or other organization.

(d) "Fraud" or "fraudulent" denotes conduct that is fraudulent under the substantive or procedural law of the applicable jurisdiction and has a purpose to deceive.

(e) "Informed consent" denotes the agreement by a person to a proposed course of conduct after the lawyer has communicated adequate information and explanation about the material risks of and reasonably available alternatives to the proposed course of conduct.

(f) "Knowingly," "known," or "knows" denotes actual knowledge of the fact in question. A person's knowledge may be inferred from circumstances.

(g) "Partner" denotes a member of a partnership, a shareholder in a law firm organized as a professional corporation, or a member of an association authorized to practice law.

(h) "Reasonable" or "reasonably" when used in relation to conduct by a lawyer denotes the conduct of a reasonably prudent and competent lawyer.

(i) "Reasonable belief" or "reasonably believes" when used in reference to a lawyer denotes that the lawyer believes the matter in question and that the circumstances are such that the belief is reasonable.

(j) "Reasonably should know" when used in reference to a lawyer denotes that a lawyer of reasonable prudence and competence would ascertain the matter in question.

(k) "Screened" denotes the isolation of a lawyer from any participation in a matter through the timely imposition of procedures within a firm that are reasonably adequate under the circumstances to protect information that the isolated lawyer is obligated to protect under these Rules or other law.

(l) "Substantial" when used in reference to degree or extent denotes a material matter of clear and weighty importance.

(m) "Tribunal" denotes a court, an arbitrator in a binding arbitration proceeding or a legislative body, administrative agency or other body acting in an adjudicative capacity. A legislative body, administrative agency or other body acts in an adjudicative capacity when a neutral official, after the presentation of evidence or legal argument by a party or parties, will render a binding legal judgment directly affecting a party's interests in a particular matter.

(n) "Writing" or "written" denotes a tangible or electronic record of a communication or representation, including handwriting, typewriting, printing, photostating, photography, audio or videorecording, and electronic communications. A "signed" writing includes an electronic sound, symbol or process attached to or logically associated with a writing and executed or adopted by a person with the intent to sign the writing.

Comment

Confirmed in Writing

[1] If it is not feasible to obtain or transmit a written confirmation at the time the client gives informed consent, then the lawyer must obtain or transmit it within a reasonable time thereafter. If a lawyer has obtained a client's informed consent, the lawyer may act in reliance on that consent so long as it is confirmed in writing within a reasonable time thereafter.

Firm

[2] Whether two or more lawyers constitute a firm within paragraph (c) can depend on the specific facts. For example, two practitioners who share office space and occasionally consult or assist each other ordinarily would not be regarded as constituting a firm. However, if they present themselves to the public in a way that suggests that they are a firm or conduct themselves as a firm, they should be regarded as a firm for purposes of the Rules. The terms of any formal agreement between associated lawyers are relevant in determining whether they are a firm, as

is the fact that they have mutual access to information concerning the clients they serve. Furthermore, it is relevant in doubtful cases to consider the underlying purpose of the Rule that is involved. A group of lawyers could be regarded as a firm for purposes of the Rule that the same lawyer should not represent opposing parties in litigation, while it might not be so regarded for purposes of the Rule that information acquired by one lawyer is attributed to another.

[3] With respect to the law department of an organization, including the government, there is ordinarily no question that the members of the department constitute a firm within the meaning of the Rules of Professional Conduct. There can be uncertainty, however, as to the identity of the client. For example, it may not be clear whether the law department of a corporation represents a subsidiary or an affiliated corporation, as well as the corporation by which the members of the department are directly employed. A similar question can arise concerning an unincorporated association and its local affiliates.

[4] Similar questions can also arise with respect to lawyers in legal aid and legal services organizations. Depending upon the structure of the organization, the entire organization or different components of it may constitute a firm or firms for purposes of these Rules.

Fraud

[5] When used in these Rules, the terms "fraud" or "fraudulent" refer to conduct that is characterized as such under the substantive or procedural law of the applicable jurisdiction and has a purpose to deceive. This does not include merely negligent misrepresentation or negligent failure to apprise another of relevant information. For purposes of these Rules, it is not necessary that anyone has suffered damages or relied on the misrepresentation or failure to inform.

Informed Consent

[6] Many of the Rules of Professional Conduct require the lawyer to obtain the informed consent of a client or other person (e.g., a former client or, under certain circumstances, a prospective client) before accepting or continuing representation or pursuing a course of conduct. See, e.g., Rules 1.2(c), 1.6(a) and 1.7(b). The communication necessary to obtain such consent will vary according to the Rule involved and the circumstances giving rise to the need to obtain informed consent. The lawyer must make reasonable efforts to ensure that the client or other person

possesses information reasonably adequate to make an informed decision. Ordinarily, this will require communication that includes a disclosure of the facts and circumstances giving rise to the situation, any explanation reasonably necessary to inform the client or other person of the material advantages and disadvantages of the proposed course of conduct and a discussion of the client's or other person's options and alternatives. In some circumstances it may be appropriate for a lawyer to advise a client or other person to seek the advice of other counsel. A lawyer need not inform a client or other person of facts or implications already known to the client or other person; nevertheless, a lawyer who does not personally inform the client or other person assumes the risk that the client or other person is inadequately informed and the consent is invalid. In determining whether the information and explanation provided are reasonably adequate, relevant factors include whether the client or other person is experienced in legal matters generally and in making decisions of the type involved, and whether the client or other person is independently represented by other counsel in giving the consent. Normally, such persons need less information and explanation than others, and generally a client or other person who is independently represented by other counsel in giving the consent should be assumed to have given informed consent.

[7] Obtaining informed consent will usually require an affirmative response by the client or other person. In general, a lawyer may not assume consent from a client's or other person's silence. Consent may be inferred, however, from the conduct of a client or other person who has reasonably adequate information about the matter. A number of Rules require that a person's consent be confirmed in writing. See Rules 1.7(b) and 1.9(a). For a definition of "writing" and "confirmed in writing," see paragraphs (n) and (b). Other Rules require that a client's consent be obtained in a writing signed by the client. See, e.g., Rules 1.8(a) and (g). For a definition of "signed," see paragraph (n).

Screened

[8] This definition applies to situations where screening of a personally disqualified lawyer is permitted to remove imputation of a conflict of interest under Rules 1.10, 1.11, 1.12 or 1.18.

[9] The purpose of screening is to assure the affected parties that confidential information known by the personally disqualified lawyer remains protected. The personally disqualified lawyer should acknowledge

the obligation not to communicate with any of the other lawyers in the firm with respect to the matter. Similarly, other lawyers in the firm who are working on the matter should be informed that the screening is in place and that they may not communicate with the personally disqualified lawyer with respect to the matter. Additional screening measures that are appropriate for the particular matter will depend on the circumstances. To implement, reinforce and remind all affected lawyers of the presence of the screening, it may be appropriate for the firm to undertake such procedures as a written undertaking by the screened lawyer to avoid any communication with other firm personnel and any contact with any firm files or other information, including information in electronic form, relating to the matter, written notice and instructions to all other firm personnel forbidding any communication with the screened lawyer relating to the matter, denial of access by the screened lawyer to firm files or other information, including information in electronic form, relating to the matter and periodic reminders of the screen to the screened lawyer and all other firm personnel.

[10] In order to be effective, screening measures must be implemented as soon as practical after a lawyer or law firm knows or reasonably should know that there is a need for screening.

CLIENT-LAWYER RELATIONSHIP

RULE 1.1: COMPETENCE

A lawyer shall provide competent representation to a client. Competent representation requires the legal knowledge, skill, thoroughness and preparation reasonably necessary for the representation.

Comment
Legal Knowledge and Skill

[1] In determining whether a lawyer employs the requisite knowledge and skill in a particular matter, relevant factors include the relative complexity and specialized nature of the matter, the lawyer's general experience, the lawyer's training and experience in the field in question, the preparation and study the lawyer is able to give the matter and whether it is feasible to refer the matter to, or associate or consult with, a lawyer of established competence in the field in question. In many instances, the

required proficiency is that of a general practitioner. Expertise in a particular field of law may be required in some circumstances.

[2] A lawyer need not necessarily have special training or prior experience to handle legal problems of a type with which the lawyer is unfamiliar. A newly admitted lawyer can be as competent as a practitioner with long experience. Some important legal skills, such as the analysis of precedent, the evaluation of evidence and legal drafting, are required in all legal problems. Perhaps the most fundamental legal skill consists of determining what kind of legal problems a situation may involve, a skill that necessarily transcends any particular specialized knowledge. A lawyer can provide adequate representation in a wholly novel field through necessary study. Competent representation can also be provided through the association of a lawyer of established competence in the field in question.

[3] In an emergency a lawyer may give advice or assistance in a matter in which the lawyer does not have the skill ordinarily required where referral to or consultation or association with another lawyer would be impractical. Even in an emergency, however, assistance should be limited to that reasonably necessary in the circumstances, for ill-considered action under emergency conditions can jeopardize the client's interest.

[4] A lawyer may accept representation where the requisite level of competence can be achieved by reasonable preparation. This applies as well to a lawyer who is appointed as counsel for an unrepresented person. See also Rule 6.2.

Thoroughness and Preparation

[5] Competent handling of a particular matter includes inquiry into and analysis of the factual and legal elements of the problem, and use of methods and procedures meeting the standards of competent practitioners. It also includes adequate preparation. The required attention and preparation are determined in part by what is at stake; major litigation and complex transactions ordinarily require more extensive treatment than matters of lesser complexity and consequence. An agreement between the lawyer and the client regarding the scope of the representation may limit the matters for which the lawyer is responsible. See Rule 1.2(c).

Retaining or Contracting With Other Lawyers

[6] Before a lawyer retains or contracts with other lawyers outside the lawyer's own firm to provide or assist in the provision of legal services to a client, the lawyer should ordinarily obtain informed consent

from the client and must reasonably believe that the other lawyers' services will contribute to the competent and ethical representation of the client. See also Rules 1.2 (allocation of authority), 1.4 (communication with client), 1.5(e) (fee sharing), 1.6 (confidentiality), and 5.5(a) (unauthorized practice of law). The reasonableness of the decision to retain or contract with other lawyers outside the lawyer's own firm will depend upon the circumstances, including the education, experience and reputation of the nonfirm lawyers; the nature of the services assigned to the nonfirm lawyers; and the legal protections, professional conduct rules, and ethical environments of the jurisdictions in which the services will be performed, particularly relating to confidential information.

[7] When lawyers from more than one law firm are providing legal services to the client on a particular matter, the lawyers ordinarily should consult with each other and the client about the scope of their respective representations and the allocation of responsibility among them. See Rule 1.2. When making allocations of responsibility in a matter pending before a tribunal, lawyers and parties may have additional obligations that are a matter of law beyond the scope of these Rules.

Maintaining Competence

[8] To maintain the requisite knowledge and skill, a lawyer should keep abreast of changes in the law and its practice, including the benefits and risks associated with relevant technology, engage in continuing study and education and comply with all continuing legal education requirements to which the lawyer is subject.

Definitional Cross-References

"Reasonably" *See* Rule 1.0(h)

RULE 1.2: SCOPE OF REPRESENTATION AND ALLOCATION OF AUTHORITY BETWEEN CLIENT AND LAWYER

(a) Subject to paragraphs (c) and (d), a lawyer shall abide by a client's decisions concerning the objectives of representation and, as required by Rule 1.4, shall consult with the client as to the means by which they are to be pursued. A lawyer may take such action on behalf of the client as is impliedly authorized to carry out the representation. A lawyer shall abide by a client's decision

whether to settle a matter. In a criminal case, the lawyer shall abide by the client's decision, after consultation with the lawyer, as to a plea to be entered, whether to waive jury trial and whether the client will testify.

(b) A lawyer's representation of a client, including representation by appointment, does not constitute an endorsement of the client's political, economic, social or moral views or activities.

(c) A lawyer may limit the scope of the representation if the limitation is reasonable under the circumstances and the client gives informed consent.

(d) A lawyer shall not counsel a client to engage, or assist a client, in conduct that the lawyer knows is criminal or fraudulent, but a lawyer may discuss the legal consequences of any proposed course of conduct with a client and may counsel or assist a client to make a good faith effort to determine the validity, scope, meaning or application of the law.

Comment

Allocation of Authority between Client and Lawyer

[1] Paragraph (a) confers upon the client the ultimate authority to determine the purposes to be served by legal representation, within the limits imposed by law and the lawyer's professional obligations. The decisions specified in paragraph (a), such as whether to settle a civil matter, must also be made by the client. See Rule 1.4(a)(1) for the lawyer's duty to communicate with the client about such decisions. With respect to the means by which the client's objectives are to be pursued, the lawyer shall consult with the client as required by Rule 1.4(a)(2) and may take such action as is impliedly authorized to carry out the representation.

[2] On occasion, however, a lawyer and a client may disagree about the means to be used to accomplish the client's objectives. Clients normally defer to the special knowledge and skill of their lawyer with respect to the means to be used to accomplish their objectives, particularly with respect to technical, legal and tactical matters. Conversely, lawyers usually defer to the client regarding such questions as the expense to be incurred and concern for third persons who might be adversely affected. Because of the varied nature of the matters about which a lawyer and client might disagree and because the actions in question may implicate the interests of a tribunal or other persons, this Rule does not prescribe how

such disagreements are to be resolved. Other law, however, may be applicable and should be consulted by the lawyer. The lawyer should also consult with the client and seek a mutually acceptable resolution of the disagreement. If such efforts are unavailing and the lawyer has a fundamental disagreement with the client, the lawyer may withdraw from the representation. See Rule 1.16(b)(4). Conversely, the client may resolve the disagreement by discharging the lawyer. See Rule 1.16(a)(3).

[3] At the outset of a representation, the client may authorize the lawyer to take specific action on the client's behalf without further consultation. Absent a material change in circumstances and subject to Rule 1.4, a lawyer may rely on such an advance authorization. The client may, however, revoke such authority at any time.

[4] In a case in which the client appears to be suffering diminished capacity, the lawyer's duty to abide by the client's decisions is to be guided by reference to Rule 1.14.

Independence from Client's Views or Activities

[5] Legal representation should not be denied to people who are unable to afford legal services, or whose cause is controversial or the subject of popular disapproval. By the same token, representing a client does not constitute approval of the client's views or activities.

Agreements Limiting Scope of Representation

[6] The scope of services to be provided by a lawyer may be limited by agreement with the client or by the terms under which the lawyer's services are made available to the client. When a lawyer has been retained by an insurer to represent an insured, for example, the representation may be limited to matters related to the insurance coverage. A limited representation may be appropriate because the client has limited objectives for the representation. In addition, the terms upon which representation is undertaken may exclude specific means that might otherwise be used to accomplish the client's objectives. Such limitations may exclude actions that the client thinks are too costly or that the lawyer regards as repugnant or imprudent.

[7] Although this Rule affords the lawyer and client substantial latitude to limit the representation, the limitation must be reasonable under the circumstances. If, for example, a client's objective is limited to securing general information about the law the client needs in order to handle a common and typically uncomplicated legal problem, the lawyer and

client may agree that the lawyer's services will be limited to a brief telephone consultation. Such a limitation, however, would not be reasonable if the time allotted was not sufficient to yield advice upon which the client could rely. Although an agreement for a limited representation does not exempt a lawyer from the duty to provide competent representation, the limitation is a factor to be considered when determining the legal knowledge, skill, thoroughness and preparation reasonably necessary for the representation. See Rule 1.1.

[8] All agreements concerning a lawyer's representation of a client must accord with the Rules of Professional Conduct and other law. See, e.g., Rules 1.1, 1.8 and 5.6.

Criminal, Fraudulent and Prohibited Transactions

[9] Paragraph (d) prohibits a lawyer from knowingly counseling or assisting a client to commit a crime or fraud. This prohibition, however, does not preclude the lawyer from giving an honest opinion about the actual consequences that appear likely to result from a client's conduct. Nor does the fact that a client uses advice in a course of action that is criminal or fraudulent of itself make a lawyer a party to the course of action. There is a critical distinction between presenting an analysis of legal aspects of questionable conduct and recommending the means by which a crime or fraud might be committed with impunity.

[10] When the client's course of action has already begun and is continuing, the lawyer's responsibility is especially delicate. The lawyer is required to avoid assisting the client, for example, by drafting or delivering documents that the lawyer knows are fraudulent or by suggesting how the wrongdoing might be concealed. A lawyer may not continue assisting a client in conduct that the lawyer originally supposed was legally proper but then discovers is criminal or fraudulent. The lawyer must, therefore, withdraw from the representation of the client in the matter. See Rule 1.16(a). In some cases, withdrawal alone might be insufficient. It may be necessary for the lawyer to give notice of the fact of withdrawal and to disaffirm any opinion, document, affirmation or the like. See Rule 4.1.

[11] Where the client is a fiduciary, the lawyer may be charged with special obligations in dealings with a beneficiary.

[12] Paragraph (d) applies whether or not the defrauded party is a party to the transaction. Hence, a lawyer must not participate in a transaction to effectuate criminal or fraudulent avoidance of tax liability. Paragraph (d) does not preclude undertaking a criminal defense incident to a

general retainer for legal services to a lawful enterprise. The last clause of paragraph (d) recognizes that determining the validity or interpretation of a statute or regulation may require a course of action involving disobedience of the statute or regulation or of the interpretation placed upon it by governmental authorities.

[13] If a lawyer comes to know or reasonably should know that a client expects assistance not permitted by the Rules of Professional Conduct or other law or if the lawyer intends to act contrary to the client's instructions, the lawyer must consult with the client regarding the limitations on the lawyer's conduct. See Rule 1.4(a)(5).

Definitional Cross-References

"Fraudulent" *See* Rule 1.0(d)
"Informed consent" *See* Rule 1.0(e)
"Knows" *See* Rule 1.0(f)
"Reasonable" *See* Rule 1.0(h)

RULE 1.3: DILIGENCE

A lawyer shall act with reasonable diligence and promptness in representing a client.

Comment

[1] A lawyer should pursue a matter on behalf of a client despite opposition, obstruction or personal inconvenience to the lawyer, and take whatever lawful and ethical measures are required to vindicate a client's cause or endeavor. A lawyer must also act with commitment and dedication to the interests of the client and with zeal in advocacy upon the client's behalf. A lawyer is not bound, however, to press for every advantage that might be realized for a client. For example, a lawyer may have authority to exercise professional discretion in determining the means by which a matter should be pursued. See Rule 1.2. The lawyer's duty to act with reasonable diligence does not require the use of offensive tactics or preclude the treating of all persons involved in the legal process with courtesy and respect.

[2] A lawyer's work load must be controlled so that each matter can be handled competently.

[3] Perhaps no professional shortcoming is more widely resented than procrastination. A client's interests often can be adversely affected

by the passage of time or the change of conditions; in extreme instances, as when a lawyer overlooks a statute of limitations, the client's legal position may be destroyed. Even when the client's interests are not affected in substance, however, unreasonable delay can cause a client needless anxiety and undermine confidence in the lawyer's trustworthiness. A lawyer's duty to act with reasonable promptness, however, does not preclude the lawyer from agreeing to a reasonable request for a postponement that will not prejudice the lawyer's client.

[4] Unless the relationship is terminated as provided in Rule 1.16, a lawyer should carry through to conclusion all matters undertaken for a client. If a lawyer's employment is limited to a specific matter, the relationship terminates when the matter has been resolved. If a lawyer has served a client over a substantial period in a variety of matters, the client sometimes may assume that the lawyer will continue to serve on a continuing basis unless the lawyer gives notice of withdrawal. Doubt about whether a client-lawyer relationship still exists should be clarified by the lawyer, preferably in writing, so that the client will not mistakenly suppose the lawyer is looking after the client's affairs when the lawyer has ceased to do so. For example, if a lawyer has handled a judicial or administrative proceeding that produced a result adverse to the client and the lawyer and the client have not agreed that the lawyer will handle the matter on appeal, the lawyer must consult with the client about the possibility of appeal before relinquishing responsibility for the matter. See Rule 1.4(a)(2). Whether the lawyer is obligated to prosecute the appeal for the client depends on the scope of the representation the lawyer has agreed to provide to the client. See Rule 1.2.

[5] To prevent neglect of client matters in the event of a sole practitioner's death or disability, the duty of diligence may require that each sole practitioner prepare a plan, in conformity with applicable rules, that designates another competent lawyer to review client files, notify each client of the lawyer's death or disability, and determine whether there is a need for immediate protective action. Cf. Rule 28 of the American Bar Association Model Rules for Lawyer Disciplinary Enforcement (providing for court appointment of a lawyer to inventory files and take other protective action in absence of a plan providing for another lawyer to protect the interests of the clients of a deceased or disabled lawyer).

Definitional Cross-References

"Reasonable" *See* Rule 1.0(h)

RULE 1.4: COMMUNICATION

(a) A lawyer shall:

(1) promptly inform the client of any decision or circumstance with respect to which the client's informed consent, as defined in Rule 1.0(e), is required by these Rules;

(2) reasonably consult with the client about the means by which the client's objectives are to be accomplished;

(3) keep the client reasonably informed about the status of the matter;

(4) promptly comply with reasonable requests for information; and

(5) consult with the client about any relevant limitation on the lawyer's conduct when the lawyer knows that the client expects assistance not permitted by the Rules of Professional Conduct or other law.

(b) A lawyer shall explain a matter to the extent reasonably necessary to permit the client to make informed decisions regarding the representation.

Comment

[1] Reasonable communication between the lawyer and the client is necessary for the client effectively to participate in the representation.

Communicating with Client

[2] If these Rules require that a particular decision about the representation be made by the client, paragraph (a)(1) requires that the lawyer promptly consult with and secure the client's consent prior to taking action unless prior discussions with the client have resolved what action the client wants the lawyer to take. For example, a lawyer who receives from opposing counsel an offer of settlement in a civil controversy or a proffered plea bargain in a criminal case must promptly inform the client of its substance unless the client has previously indicated that the proposal will be acceptable or unacceptable or has authorized the lawyer to accept or to reject the offer. See Rule 1.2(a).

[3] Paragraph (a)(2) requires the lawyer to reasonably consult with the client about the means to be used to accomplish the client's objectives. In some situations—depending on both the importance of the action under consideration and the feasibility of consulting with the client —this duty will require consultation prior to taking action. In other cir-

cumstances, such as during a trial when an immediate decision must be made, the exigency of the situation may require the lawyer to act without prior consultation. In such cases the lawyer must nonetheless act reasonably to inform the client of actions the lawyer has taken on the client's behalf. Additionally, paragraph (a)(3) requires that the lawyer keep the client reasonably informed about the status of the matter, such as significant developments affecting the timing or the substance of the representation.

[4] A lawyer's regular communication with clients will minimize the occasions on which a client will need to request information concerning the representation. When a client makes a reasonable request for information, however, paragraph (a)(4) requires prompt compliance with the request, or if a prompt response is not feasible, that the lawyer, or a member of the lawyer's staff, acknowledge receipt of the request and advise the client when a response may be expected. A lawyer should promptly respond to or acknowledge client communications.

Explaining Matters

[5] The client should have sufficient information to participate intelligently in decisions concerning the objectives of the representation and the means by which they are to be pursued, to the extent the client is willing and able to do so. Adequacy of communication depends in part on the kind of advice or assistance that is involved. For example, when there is time to explain a proposal made in a negotiation, the lawyer should review all important provisions with the client before proceeding to an agreement. In litigation a lawyer should explain the general strategy and prospects of success and ordinarily should consult the client on tactics that are likely to result in significant expense or to injure or coerce others. On the other hand, a lawyer ordinarily will not be expected to describe trial or negotiation strategy in detail. The guiding principle is that the lawyer should fulfill reasonable client expectations for information consistent with the duty to act in the client's best interests, and the client's overall requirements as to the character of representation. In certain circumstances, such as when a lawyer asks a client to consent to a representation affected by a conflict of interest, the client must give informed consent, as defined in Rule 1.0(e).

[6] Ordinarily, the information to be provided is that appropriate for a client who is a comprehending and responsible adult. However, fully informing the client according to this standard may be impracticable, for example, where the client is a child or suffers from diminished capacity.

See Rule 1.14. When the client is an organization or group, it is often impossible or inappropriate to inform every one of its members about its legal affairs; ordinarily, the lawyer should address communications to the appropriate officials of the organization. See Rule 1.13. Where many routine matters are involved, a system of limited or occasional reporting may be arranged with the client.

Withholding Information

[7] In some circumstances, a lawyer may be justified in delaying transmission of information when the client would be likely to react imprudently to an immediate communication. Thus, a lawyer might withhold a psychiatric diagnosis of a client when the examining psychiatrist indicates that disclosure would harm the client. A lawyer may not withhold information to serve the lawyer's own interest or convenience or the interests or convenience of another person. Rules or court orders governing litigation may provide that information supplied to a lawyer may not be disclosed to the client. Rule 3.4(c) directs compliance with such rules or orders.

Definitional Cross-References

"Informed consent" *See* Rule 1.0(e)
"Knows" *See* Rule 1.0(f)
"Reasonably" *See* Rule 1.0(h)

RULE 1.5: FEES

(a) A lawyer shall not make an agreement for, charge, or collect an unreasonable fee or an unreasonable amount for expenses. The factors to be considered in determining the reasonableness of a fee include the following:

(1) the time and labor required, the novelty and difficulty of the questions involved, and the skill requisite to perform the legal service properly;

(2) the likelihood, if apparent to the client, that the acceptance of the particular employment will preclude other employment by the lawyer;

(3) the fee customarily charged in the locality for similar legal services;

(4) the amount involved and the results obtained;

(5) the time limitations imposed by the client or by the circumstances;

(6) the nature and length of the professional relationship with the client;

(7) the experience, reputation, and ability of the lawyer or lawyers performing the services; and

(8) whether the fee is fixed or contingent.

(b) The scope of the representation and the basis or rate of the fee and expenses for which the client will be responsible shall be communicated to the client, preferably in writing, before or within a reasonable time after commencing the representation, except when the lawyer will charge a regularly represented client on the same basis or rate. Any changes in the basis or rate of the fee or expenses shall also be communicated to the client.

(c) A fee may be contingent on the outcome of the matter for which the service is rendered, except in a matter in which a contingent fee is prohibited by paragraph (d) or other law. A contingent fee agreement shall be in a writing signed by the client and shall state the method by which the fee is to be determined, including the percentage or percentages that shall accrue to the lawyer in the event of settlement, trial or appeal; litigation and other expenses to be deducted from the recovery; and whether such expenses are to be deducted before or after the contingent fee is calculated. The agreement must clearly notify the client of any expenses for which the client will be liable whether or not the client is the prevailing party. Upon conclusion of a contingent fee matter, the lawyer shall provide the client with a written statement stating the outcome of the matter and, if there is a recovery, showing the remittance to the client and the method of its determination.

(d) A lawyer shall not enter into an arrangement for, charge, or collect:

(1) any fee in a domestic relations matter, the payment or amount of which is contingent upon the securing of a divorce or upon the amount of alimony or support, or property settlement in lieu thereof; or

(2) a contingent fee for representing a defendant in a criminal case.

(e) A division of a fee between lawyers who are not in the same firm may be made only if:

(1) the division is in proportion to the services performed by each lawyer or each lawyer assumes joint responsibility for the representation;

(2) the client agrees to the arrangement, including the share each lawyer will receive, and the agreement is confirmed in writing; and

(3) the total fee is reasonable.

Comment

Reasonableness of Fee and Expenses

[1] Paragraph (a) requires that lawyers charge fees that are reasonable under the circumstances. The factors specified in (1) through (8) are not exclusive. Nor will each factor be relevant in each instance. Paragraph (a) also requires that expenses for which the client will be charged must be reasonable. A lawyer may seek reimbursement for the cost of services performed in-house, such as copying, or for other expenses incurred in-house, such as telephone charges, either by charging a reasonable amount to which the client has agreed in advance or by charging an amount that reasonably reflects the cost incurred by the lawyer.

Basis or Rate of Fee

[2] When the lawyer has regularly represented a client, they ordinarily will have evolved an understanding concerning the basis or rate of the fee and the expenses for which the client will be responsible. In a new client-lawyer relationship, however, an understanding as to fees and expenses must be promptly established. Generally, it is desirable to furnish the client with at least a simple memorandum or copy of the lawyer's customary fee arrangements that states the general nature of the legal services to be provided, the basis, rate or total amount of the fee and whether and to what extent the client will be responsible for any costs, expenses or disbursements in the course of the representation. A written statement concerning the terms of the engagement reduces the possibility of misunderstanding.

[3] Contingent fees, like any other fees, are subject to the reasonableness standard of paragraph (a) of this Rule. In determining whether a particular contingent fee is reasonable, or whether it is reasonable to charge any form of contingent fee, a lawyer must consider the factors that are relevant under the circumstances. Applicable law may impose limitations on contingent fees, such as a ceiling on the percentage allowable, or

may require a lawyer to offer clients an alternative basis for the fee. Applicable law also may apply to situations other than a contingent fee, for example, government regulations regarding fees in certain tax matters.

Terms of Payment

[4] A lawyer may require advance payment of a fee, but is obliged to return any unearned portion. See Rule 1.16(d). A lawyer may accept property in payment for services, such as an ownership interest in an enterprise, providing this does not involve acquisition of a proprietary interest in the cause of action or subject matter of the litigation contrary to Rule 1.8 (i). However, a fee paid in property instead of money may be subject to the requirements of Rule 1.8(a) because such fees often have the essential qualities of a business transaction with the client.

[5] An agreement may not be made whose terms might induce the lawyer improperly to curtail services for the client or perform them in a way contrary to the client's interest. For example, a lawyer should not enter into an agreement whereby services are to be provided only up to a stated amount when it is foreseeable that more extensive services probably will be required, unless the situation is adequately explained to the client. Otherwise, the client might have to bargain for further assistance in the midst of a proceeding or transaction. However, it is proper to define the extent of services in light of the client's ability to pay. A lawyer should not exploit a fee arrangement based primarily on hourly charges by using wasteful procedures.

Prohibited Contingent Fees

[6] Paragraph (d) prohibits a lawyer from charging a contingent fee in a domestic relations matter when payment is contingent upon the securing of a divorce or upon the amount of alimony or support or property settlement to be obtained. This provision does not preclude a contract for a contingent fee for legal representation in connection with the recovery of post-judgment balances due under support, alimony or other financial orders because such contracts do not implicate the same policy concerns.

Division of Fee

[7] A division of fee is a single billing to a client covering the fee of two or more lawyers who are not in the same firm. A division of fee facilitates association of more than one lawyer in a matter in which neither alone could serve the client as well, and most often is used when the fee

is contingent and the division is between a referring lawyer and a trial specialist. Paragraph (e) permits the lawyers to divide a fee either on the basis of the proportion of services they render or if each lawyer assumes responsibility for the representation as a whole. In addition, the client must agree to the arrangement, including the share that each lawyer is to receive, and the agreement must be confirmed in writing. Contingent fee agreements must be in a writing signed by the client and must otherwise comply with paragraph (c) of this Rule. Joint responsibility for the representation entails financial and ethical responsibility for the representation as if the lawyers were associated in a partnership. A lawyer should only refer a matter to a lawyer whom the referring lawyer reasonably believes is competent to handle the matter. See Rule 1.1.

[8] Paragraph (e) does not prohibit or regulate division of fees to be received in the future for work done when lawyers were previously associated in a law firm.

Disputes over Fees

[9] If a procedure has been established for resolution of fee disputes, such as an arbitration or mediation procedure established by the bar, the lawyer must comply with the procedure when it is mandatory, and, even when it is voluntary, the lawyer should conscientiously consider submitting to it. Law may prescribe a procedure for determining a lawyer's fee, for example, in representation of an executor or administrator, a class or a person entitled to a reasonable fee as part of the measure of damages. The lawyer entitled to such a fee and a lawyer representing another party concerned with the fee should comply with the prescribed procedure.

Definitional Cross-References

"Confirmed in writing" *See* Rule 1.0(b)
"Firm" *See* Rule 1.0(c)
"Writing" and "Written" and "Signed" *See* Rule 1.0(n)

RULE 1.6: CONFIDENTIALITY OF INFORMATION

(a) A lawyer shall not reveal information relating to the representation of a client unless the client gives informed consent, the disclosure is impliedly authorized in order to carry out the representation or the disclosure is permitted by paragraph (b).

(b) A lawyer may reveal information relating to the

representation of a client to the extent the lawyer reasonably believes necessary:

(1) to prevent reasonably certain death or substantial bodily harm;

(2) to prevent the client from committing a crime or fraud that is reasonably certain to result in substantial injury to the financial interests or property of another and in furtherance of which the client has used or is using the lawyer's services;

(3) to prevent, mitigate or rectify substantial injury to the financial interests or property of another that is reasonably certain to result or has resulted from the client's commission of a crime or fraud in furtherance of which the client has used the lawyer's services;

(4) to secure legal advice about the lawyer's compliance with these Rules;

(5) to establish a claim or defense on behalf of the lawyer in a controversy between the lawyer and the client, to establish a defense to a criminal charge or civil claim against the lawyer based upon conduct in which the client was involved, or to respond to allegations in any proceeding concerning the lawyer's representation of the client;

(6) to comply with other law or a court order; or

(7) to detect and resolve conflicts of interest arising from the lawyer's change of employment or from changes in the composition or ownership of a firm, but only if the revealed information would not compromise the attorney-client privilege or otherwise prejudice the client.

(c) A lawyer shall make reasonable efforts to prevent the inadvertent or unauthorized disclosure of, or unauthorized access to, information relating to the representation of a client.

Comment

[1] This Rule governs the disclosure by a lawyer of information relating to the representation of a client during the lawyer's representation of the client. See Rule 1.18 for the lawyer's duties with respect to information provided to the lawyer by a prospective client, Rule 1.9(c)(2) for the lawyer's duty not to reveal information relating to the lawyer's prior representation of a former client and Rules 1.8(b) and 1.9(c)(1) for the lawyer's duties with respect to the use of such information to the disadvantage of clients and former clients.

[2] A fundamental principle in the client-lawyer relationship is that, in the absence of the client's informed consent, the lawyer must not reveal information relating to the representation. See Rule 1.0(e) for the definition of informed consent. This contributes to the trust that is the hallmark of the client-lawyer relationship. The client is thereby encouraged to seek legal assistance and to communicate fully and frankly with the lawyer even as to embarrassing or legally damaging subject matter. The lawyer needs this information to represent the client effectively and, if necessary, to advise the client to refrain from wrongful conduct. Almost without exception, clients come to lawyers in order to determine their rights and what is, in the complex of laws and regulations, deemed to be legal and correct. Based upon experience, lawyers know that almost all clients follow the advice given, and the law is upheld.

[3] The principle of client-lawyer confidentiality is given effect by related bodies of law: the attorney-client privilege, the work product doctrine and the rule of confidentiality established in professional ethics. The attorney-client privilege and work product doctrine apply in judicial and other proceedings in which a lawyer may be called as a witness or otherwise required to produce evidence concerning a client. The rule of client-lawyer confidentiality applies in situations other than those where evidence is sought from the lawyer through compulsion of law. The confidentiality rule, for example, applies not only to matters communicated in confidence by the client but also to all information relating to the representation, whatever its source. A lawyer may not disclose such information except as authorized or required by the Rules of Professional Conduct or other law. See also Scope.

[4] Paragraph (a) prohibits a lawyer from revealing information relating to the representation of a client. This prohibition also applies to disclosures by a lawyer that do not in themselves reveal protected information but could reasonably lead to the discovery of such information by a third person. A lawyer's use of a hypothetical to discuss issues relating to the representation is permissible so long as there is no reasonable likelihood that the listener will be able to ascertain the identity of the client or the situation involved.

Authorized Disclosure

[5] Except to the extent that the client's instructions or special circumstances limit that authority, a lawyer is impliedly authorized to make disclosures about a client when appropriate in carrying out the represen-

tation. In some situations, for example, a lawyer may be impliedly authorized to admit a fact that cannot properly be disputed or to make a disclosure that facilitates a satisfactory conclusion to a matter. Lawyers in a firm may, in the course of the firm's practice, disclose to each other information relating to a client of the firm, unless the client has instructed that particular information be confined to specified lawyers.

Disclosure Adverse to Client

[6] Although the public interest is usually best served by a strict rule requiring lawyers to preserve the confidentiality of information relating to the representation of their clients, the confidentiality rule is subject to limited exceptions. Paragraph (b)(1) recognizes the overriding value of life and physical integrity and permits disclosure reasonably necessary to prevent reasonably certain death or substantial bodily harm. Such harm is reasonably certain to occur if it will be suffered imminently or if there is a present and substantial threat that a person will suffer such harm at a later date if the lawyer fails to take action necessary to eliminate the threat. Thus, a lawyer who knows that a client has accidentally discharged toxic waste into a town's water supply may reveal this information to the authorities if there is a present and substantial risk that a person who drinks the water will contract a life-threatening or debilitating disease and the lawyer's disclosure is necessary to eliminate the threat or reduce the number of victims.

[7] Paragraph (b)(2) is a limited exception to the rule of confidentiality that permits the lawyer to reveal information to the extent necessary to enable affected persons or appropriate authorities to prevent the client from committing a crime or fraud, as defined in Rule 1.0(d), that is reasonably certain to result in substantial injury to the financial or property interests of another and in furtherance of which the client has used or is using the lawyer's services. Such a serious abuse of the client-lawyer relationship by the client forfeits the protection of this Rule. The client can, of course, prevent such disclosure by refraining from the wrongful conduct. Although paragraph (b)(2) does not require the lawyer to reveal the client's misconduct, the lawyer may not counsel or assist the client in conduct the lawyer knows is criminal or fraudulent. See Rule 1.2(d). See also Rule 1.16 with respect to the lawyer's obligation or right to withdraw from the representation of the client in such circumstances, and Rule 1.13(c), which permits the lawyer, where the client is an organization, to reveal information relating to the representation in limited circumstances.

[8] Paragraph (b)(3) addresses the situation in which the lawyer does not learn of the client's crime or fraud until after it has been consummated. Although the client no longer has the option of preventing disclosure by refraining from the wrongful conduct, there will be situations in which the loss suffered by the affected person can be prevented, rectified or mitigated. In such situations, the lawyer may disclose information relating to the representation to the extent necessary to enable the affected persons to prevent or mitigate reasonably certain losses or to attempt to recoup their losses. Paragraph (b)(3) does not apply when a person who has committed a crime or fraud thereafter employs a lawyer for representation concerning that offense.

[9] A lawyer's confidentiality obligations do not preclude a lawyer from securing confidential legal advice about the lawyer's personal responsibility to comply with these Rules. In most situations, disclosing information to secure such advice will be impliedly authorized for the lawyer to carry out the representation. Even when the disclosure is not impliedly authorized, paragraph (b)(4) permits such disclosure because of the importance of a lawyer's compliance with the Rules of Professional Conduct.

[10] Where a legal claim or disciplinary charge alleges complicity of the lawyer in a client's conduct or other misconduct of the lawyer involving representation of the client, the lawyer may respond to the extent the lawyer reasonably believes necessary to establish a defense. The same is true with respect to a claim involving the conduct or representation of a former client. Such a charge can arise in a civil, criminal, disciplinary or other proceeding and can be based on a wrong allegedly committed by the lawyer against the client or on a wrong alleged by a third person, for example, a person claiming to have been defrauded by the lawyer and client acting together. The lawyer's right to respond arises when an assertion of such complicity has been made. Paragraph (b)(5) does not require the lawyer to await the commencement of an action or proceeding that charges such complicity, so that the defense may be established by responding directly to a third party who has made such an assertion. The right to defend also applies, of course, where a proceeding has been commenced.

[11] A lawyer entitled to a fee is permitted by paragraph (b)(5) to prove the services rendered in an action to collect it. This aspect of the rule expresses the principle that the beneficiary of a fiduciary relationship may not exploit it to the detriment of the fiduciary.

[12] Other law may require that a lawyer disclose information about a client. Whether such a law supersedes Rule 1.6 is a question of law beyond the scope of these Rules. When disclosure of information relating to the representation appears to be required by other law, the lawyer must discuss the matter with the client to the extent required by Rule 1.4. If, however, the other law supersedes this Rule and requires disclosure, paragraph (b)(6) permits the lawyer to make such disclosures as are necessary to comply with the law.

Detection of Conflicts of Interest

[13] Paragraph (b)(7) recognizes that lawyers in different firms may need to disclose limited information to each other to detect and resolve conflicts of interest, such as when a lawyer is considering an association with another firm, two or more firms are considering a merger, or a lawyer is considering the purchase of a law practice. See Rule 1.17, Comment [7]. Under these circumstances, lawyers and law firms are permitted to disclose limited information, but only once substantive discussions regarding the new relationship have occurred. Any such disclosure should ordinarily include no more than the identity of the persons and entities involved in a matter, a brief summary of the general issues involved, and information about whether the matter has terminated. Even this limited information, however, should be disclosed only to the extent reasonably necessary to detect and resolve conflicts of interest that might arise from the possible new relationship. Moreover, the disclosure of any information is prohibited if it would compromise the attorney-client privilege or otherwise prejudice the client (e.g., the fact that a corporate client is seeking advice on a corporate takeover that has not been publicly announced; that a person has consulted a lawyer about the possibility of divorce before the person's intentions are known to the person's spouse; or that a person has consulted a lawyer about a criminal investigation that has not led to a public charge). Under those circumstances, paragraph (a) prohibits disclosure unless the client or former client gives informed consent. A lawyer's fiduciary duty to the lawyer's firm may also govern a lawyer's conduct when exploring an association with another firm and is beyond the scope of these Rules.

[14] Any information disclosed pursuant to paragraph (b)(7) may be used or further disclosed only to the extent necessary to detect and resolve conflicts of interest. Paragraph (b)(7) does not restrict the use of information acquired by means independent of any disclosure pursu-

ant to paragraph (b)(7). Paragraph (b)(7) also does not affect the disclosure of information within a law firm when the disclosure is otherwise authorized, see Comment [5], such as when a lawyer in a firm discloses information to another lawyer in the same firm to detect and resolve conflicts of interest that could arise in connection with undertaking a new representation.

[15] A lawyer may be ordered to reveal information relating to the representation of a client by a court or by another tribunal or governmental entity claiming authority pursuant to other law to compel the disclosure. Absent informed consent of the client to do otherwise, the lawyer should assert on behalf of the client all nonfrivolous claims that the order is not authorized by other law or that the information sought is protected against disclosure by the attorney-client privilege or other applicable law. In the event of an adverse ruling, the lawyer must consult with the client about the possibility of appeal to the extent required by Rule 1.4. Unless review is sought, however, paragraph (b)(6) permits the lawyer to comply with the court's order.

[16] Paragraph (b) permits disclosure only to the extent the lawyer reasonably believes the disclosure is necessary to accomplish one of the purposes specified. Where practicable, the lawyer should first seek to persuade the client to take suitable action to obviate the need for disclosure. In any case, a disclosure adverse to the client's interest should be no greater than the lawyer reasonably believes necessary to accomplish the purpose. If the disclosure will be made in connection with a judicial proceeding, the disclosure should be made in a manner that limits access to the information to the tribunal or other persons having a need to know it and appropriate protective orders or other arrangements should be sought by the lawyer to the fullest extent practicable.

[17] Paragraph (b) permits but does not require the disclosure of information relating to a client's representation to accomplish the purposes specified in paragraphs (b)(1) through (b)(6). In exercising the discretion conferred by this Rule, the lawyer may consider such factors as the nature of the lawyer's relationship with the client and with those who might be injured by the client, the lawyer's own involvement in the transaction and factors that may extenuate the conduct in question. A lawyer's decision not to disclose as permitted by paragraph (b) does not violate this Rule. Disclosure may be required, however, by other Rules. Some Rules require disclosure only if such disclosure would be permitted by paragraph (b). See Rules 1.2(d), 4.1(b), 8.1 and 8.3. Rule 3.3, on the other hand,

requires disclosure in some circumstances regardless of whether such disclosure is permitted by this Rule. See Rule 3.3(c).

Acting Competently to Preserve Confidentiality

[18] Paragraph (c) requires a lawyer to act competently to safeguard information relating to the representation of a client against unauthorized access by third parties and against inadvertent or unauthorized disclosure by the lawyer or other persons who are participating in the representation of the client or who are subject to the lawyer's supervision. See Rules 1.1, 5.1 and 5.3. The unauthorized access to, or the inadvertent or unauthorized disclosure of, information relating to the representation of a client does not constitute a violation of paragraph (c) if the lawyer has made reasonable efforts to prevent the access or disclosure. Factors to be considered in determining the reasonableness of the lawyer's efforts include, but are not limited to, the sensitivity of the information, the likelihood of disclosure if additional safeguards are not employed, the cost of employing additional safeguards, the difficulty of implementing the safeguards, and the extent to which the safeguards adversely affect the lawyer's ability to represent clients (e.g., by making a device or important piece of software excessively difficult to use). A client may require the lawyer to implement special security measures not required by this Rule or may give informed consent to forgo security measures that would otherwise be required by this Rule. Whether a lawyer may be required to take additional steps to safeguard a client's information in order to comply with other law, such as state and federal laws that govern data privacy or that impose notification requirements upon the loss of, or unauthorized access to, electronic information, is beyond the scope of these Rules. For a lawyer's duties when sharing information with nonlawyers outside the lawyer's own firm, see Rule 5.3, Comments [3]-[4].

[19] When transmitting a communication that includes information relating to the representation of a client, the lawyer must take reasonable precautions to prevent the information from coming into the hands of unintended recipients. This duty, however, does not require that the lawyer use special security measures if the method of communication affords a reasonable expectation of privacy. Special circumstances, however, may warrant special precautions. Factors to be considered in determining the reasonableness of the lawyer's expectation of confidentiality include the sensitivity of the information and the extent to which the privacy of the communication is protected by law or by a confidentiality agreement. A client may require the lawyer to implement special security measures

not required by this Rule or may give informed consent to the use of a means of communication that would otherwise be prohibited by this Rule. Whether a lawyer may be required to take additional steps in order to comply with other law, such as state and federal laws that govern data privacy, is beyond the scope of these Rules.

Former Client

[20] The duty of confidentiality continues after the client-lawyer relationship has terminated. See Rule 1.9(c)(2). See Rule 1.9(c)(1) for the prohibition against using such information to the disadvantage of the former client.

Definitional Cross-References

"Firm" *See* Rule 1.0(c)
"Fraud" *See* Rule 1.0(d)
"Informed consent" *See* Rule 1.0(e)
"Reasonable" and "Reasonably" *See* Rule 1.0(h)
"Reasonably believes" *See* Rule 1.0(i)
"Substantial" *See* Rule 1.0(l)

RULE 1.7: CONFLICT OF INTEREST: CURRENT CLIENTS

(a) Except as provided in paragraph (b), a lawyer shall not represent a client if the representation involves a concurrent conflict of interest. A concurrent conflict of interest exists if:

(1) the representation of one client will be directly adverse to another client; or

(2) there is a significant risk that the representation of one or more clients will be materially limited by the lawyer's responsibilities to another client, a former client or a third person or by a personal interest of the lawyer.

(b) Notwithstanding the existence of a concurrent conflict of interest under paragraph (a), a lawyer may represent a client if:

(1) the lawyer reasonably believes that the lawyer will be able to provide competent and diligent representation to each affected client;

(2) the representation is not prohibited by law;

(3) the representation does not involve the assertion of a claim by one client against another client represented by

the lawyer in the same litigation or other proceeding before a tribunal; and

> (4) each affected client gives informed consent, confirmed in writing.

Comment

General Principles

[1] Loyalty and independent judgment are essential elements in the lawyer's relationship to a client. Concurrent conflicts of interest can arise from the lawyer's responsibilities to another client, a former client or a third person or from the lawyer's own interests. For specific Rules regarding certain concurrent conflicts of interest, see Rule 1.8. For former client conflicts of interest, see Rule 1.9. For conflicts of interest involving prospective clients, see Rule 1.18. For definitions of "informed consent" and "confirmed in writing," see Rule 1.0(e) and (b).

[2] Resolution of a conflict of interest problem under this Rule requires the lawyer to: 1) clearly identify the client or clients; 2) determine whether a conflict of interest exists; 3) decide whether the representation may be undertaken despite the existence of a conflict, i.e., whether the conflict is consentable; and 4) if so, consult with the clients affected under paragraph (a) and obtain their informed consent, confirmed in writing. The clients affected under paragraph (a) include both of the clients referred to in paragraph (a)(1) and the one or more clients whose representation might be materially limited under paragraph (a)(2).

[3] A conflict of interest may exist before representation is undertaken, in which event the representation must be declined, unless the lawyer obtains the informed consent of each client under the conditions of paragraph (b). To determine whether a conflict of interest exists, a lawyer should adopt reasonable procedures, appropriate for the size and type of firm and practice, to determine in both litigation and non-litigation matters the persons and issues involved. See also Comment to Rule 5.1. Ignorance caused by a failure to institute such procedures will not excuse a lawyer's violation of this Rule. As to whether a client-lawyer relationship exists or, having once been established, is continuing, see Comment to Rule 1.3 and Scope.

[4] If a conflict arises after representation has been undertaken, the lawyer ordinarily must withdraw from the representation, unless the lawyer has obtained the informed consent of the client under the conditions of paragraph (b). See Rule 1.16. Where more than one client is in-

volved, whether the lawyer may continue to represent any of the clients is determined both by the lawyer's ability to comply with duties owed to the former client and by the lawyer's ability to represent adequately the remaining client or clients, given the lawyer's duties to the former client. See Rule 1.9. See also Comments [5] and [29].

[5] Unforeseeable developments, such as changes in corporate and other organizational affiliations or the addition or realignment of parties in litigation, might create conflicts in the midst of a representation, as when a company sued by the lawyer on behalf of one client is bought by another client represented by the lawyer in an unrelated matter. Depending on the circumstances, the lawyer may have the option to withdraw from one of the representations in order to avoid the conflict. The lawyer must seek court approval where necessary and take steps to minimize harm to the clients. See Rule 1.16. The lawyer must continue to protect the confidences of the client from whose representation the lawyer has withdrawn. See Rule 1.9(c).

Identifying Conflicts of Interest: Directly Adverse

[6] Loyalty to a current client prohibits undertaking representation directly adverse to that client without that client's informed consent. Thus, absent consent, a lawyer may not act as an advocate in one matter against a person the lawyer represents in some other matter, even when the matters are wholly unrelated. The client as to whom the representation is directly adverse is likely to feel betrayed, and the resulting damage to the client-lawyer relationship is likely to impair the lawyer's ability to represent the client effectively. In addition, the client on whose behalf the adverse representation is undertaken reasonably may fear that the lawyer will pursue that client's case less effectively out of deference to the other client, i.e., that the representation may be materially limited by the lawyer's interest in retaining the current client. Similarly, a directly adverse conflict may arise when a lawyer is required to cross-examine a client who appears as a witness in a lawsuit involving another client, as when the testimony will be damaging to the client who is represented in the lawsuit. On the other hand, simultaneous representation in unrelated matters of clients whose interests are only economically adverse, such as representation of competing economic enterprises in unrelated litigation, does not ordinarily constitute a conflict of interest and thus may not require consent of the respective clients.

[7] Directly adverse conflicts can also arise in transactional matters. For example, if a lawyer is asked to represent the seller of a business in negotiations with a buyer represented by the lawyer, not in the same transaction but in another, unrelated matter, the lawyer could not undertake the representation without the informed consent of each client.

Identifying Conflicts of Interest: Material Limitation

[8] Even where there is no direct adverseness, a conflict of interest exists if there is a significant risk that a lawyer's ability to consider, recommend or carry out an appropriate course of action for the client will be materially limited as a result of the lawyer's other responsibilities or interests. For example, a lawyer asked to represent several individuals seeking to form a joint venture is likely to be materially limited in the lawyer's ability to recommend or advocate all possible positions that each might take because of the lawyer's duty of loyalty to the others. The conflict in effect forecloses alternatives that would otherwise be available to the client. The mere possibility of subsequent harm does not itself require disclosure and consent. The critical questions are the likelihood that a difference in interests will eventuate and, if it does, whether it will materially interfere with the lawyer's independent professional judgment in considering alternatives or foreclose courses of action that reasonably should be pursued on behalf of the client.

Lawyer's Responsibilities to Former Clients and Other Third Persons

[9] In addition to conflicts with other current clients, a lawyer's duties of loyalty and independence may be materially limited by responsibilities to former clients under Rule 1.9 or by the lawyer's responsibilities to other persons, such as fiduciary duties arising from a lawyer's service as a trustee, executor or corporate director.

Personal Interest Conflicts

[10] The lawyer's own interests should not be permitted to have an adverse effect on representation of a client. For example, if the probity of a lawyer's own conduct in a transaction is in serious question, it may be difficult or impossible for the lawyer to give a client detached advice. Similarly, when a lawyer has discussions concerning possible employment with an opponent of the lawyer's client, or with a law firm repre-

senting the opponent, such discussions could materially limit the lawyer's representation of the client. In addition, a lawyer may not allow related business interests to affect representation, for example, by referring clients to an enterprise in which the lawyer has an undisclosed financial interest. See Rule 1.8 for specific Rules pertaining to a number of personal interest conflicts, including business transactions with clients. See also Rule 1.10 (personal interest conflicts under Rule 1.7 ordinarily are not imputed to other lawyers in a law firm).

[11] When lawyers representing different clients in the same matter or in substantially related matters are closely related by blood or marriage, there may be a significant risk that client confidences will be revealed and that the lawyer's family relationship will interfere with both loyalty and independent professional judgment. As a result, each client is entitled to know of the existence and implications of the relationship between the lawyers before the lawyer agrees to undertake the representation. Thus, a lawyer related to another lawyer, e.g., as parent, child, sibling or spouse, ordinarily may not represent a client in a matter where that lawyer is representing another party, unless each client gives informed consent. The disqualification arising from a close family relationship is personal and ordinarily is not imputed to members of firms with whom the lawyers are associated. See Rule 1.10.

[12] A lawyer is prohibited from engaging in sexual relationships with a client unless the sexual relationship predates the formation of the client-lawyer relationship. See Rule 1.8(j).

Interest of Person Paying for a Lawyer's Service

[13] A lawyer may be paid from a source other than the client, including a co-client, if the client is informed of that fact and consents and the arrangement does not compromise the lawyer's duty of loyalty or independent judgment to the client. See Rule 1.8(f). If acceptance of the payment from any other source presents a significant risk that the lawyer's representation of the client will be materially limited by the lawyer's own interest in accommodating the person paying the lawyer's fee or by the lawyer's responsibilities to a payer who is also a co-client, then the lawyer must comply with the requirements of paragraph (b) before accepting the representation, including determining whether the conflict is consentable and, if so, that the client has adequate information about the material risks of the representation.

Prohibited Representations

[14] Ordinarily, clients may consent to representation notwithstanding a conflict. However, as indicated in paragraph (b), some conflicts are nonconsentable, meaning that the lawyer involved cannot properly ask for such agreement or provide representation on the basis of the client's consent. When the lawyer is representing more than one client, the question of consentability must be resolved as to each client.

[15] Consentability is typically determined by considering whether the interests of the clients will be adequately protected if the clients are permitted to give their informed consent to representation burdened by a conflict of interest. Thus, under paragraph (b)(1), representation is prohibited if in the circumstances the lawyer cannot reasonably conclude that the lawyer will be able to provide competent and diligent representation. See Rule 1.1 (competence) and Rule 1.3 (diligence).

[16] Paragraph (b)(2) describes conflicts that are nonconsentable because the representation is prohibited by applicable law. For example, in some states substantive law provides that the same lawyer may not represent more than one defendant in a capital case, even with the consent of the clients, and under federal criminal statutes certain representations by a former government lawyer are prohibited, despite the informed consent of the former client. In addition, decisional law in some states limits the ability of a governmental client, such as a municipality, to consent to a conflict of interest.

[17] Paragraph (b)(3) describes conflicts that are nonconsentable because of the institutional interest in vigorous development of each client's position when the clients are aligned directly against each other in the same litigation or other proceeding before a tribunal. Whether clients are aligned directly against each other within the meaning of this paragraph requires examination of the context of the proceeding. Although this paragraph does not preclude a lawyer's multiple representation of adverse parties to a mediation (because mediation is not a proceeding before a "tribunal" under Rule 1.0(m)), such representation may be precluded by paragraph (b)(1).

Informed Consent

[18] Informed consent requires that each affected client be aware of the relevant circumstances and of the material and reasonably foreseeable ways that the conflict could have adverse effects on the interests of that client. See Rule 1.0(e) (informed consent). The information required

depends on the nature of the conflict and the nature of the risks involved. When representation of multiple clients in a single matter is undertaken, the information must include the implications of the common representation, including possible effects on loyalty, confidentiality and the attorney-client privilege and the advantages and risks involved. See Comments [30] and [31] (effect of common representation on confidentiality).

[19] Under some circumstances it may be impossible to make the disclosure necessary to obtain consent. For example, when the lawyer represents different clients in related matters and one of the clients refuses to consent to the disclosure necessary to permit the other client to make an informed decision, the lawyer cannot properly ask the latter to consent. In some cases the alternative to common representation can be that each party may have to obtain separate representation with the possibility of incurring additional costs. These costs, along with the benefits of securing separate representation, are factors that may be considered by the affected client in determining whether common representation is in the client's interests.

Consent Confirmed in Writing

[20] Paragraph (b) requires the lawyer to obtain the informed consent of the client, confirmed in writing. Such a writing may consist of a document executed by the client or one that the lawyer promptly records and transmits to the client following an oral consent. See Rule 1.0(b). See also Rule 1.0(n) (writing includes electronic transmission). If it is not feasible to obtain or transmit the writing at the time the client gives informed consent, then the lawyer must obtain or transmit it within a reasonable time thereafter. See Rule 1.0(b). The requirement of a writing does not supplant the need in most cases for the lawyer to talk with the client, to explain the risks and advantages, if any, of representation burdened with a conflict of interest, as well as reasonably available alternatives, and to afford the client a reasonable opportunity to consider the risks and alternatives and to raise questions and concerns. Rather, the writing is required in order to impress upon clients the seriousness of the decision the client is being asked to make and to avoid disputes or ambiguities that might later occur in the absence of a writing.

Revoking Consent

[21] A client who has given consent to a conflict may revoke the consent and, like any other client, may terminate the lawyer's representation

at any time. Whether revoking consent to the client's own representation precludes the lawyer from continuing to represent other clients depends on the circumstances, including the nature of the conflict, whether the client revoked consent because of a material change in circumstances, the reasonable expectations of the other clients and whether material detriment to the other clients or the lawyer would result.

Consent to Future Conflict

[22] Whether a lawyer may properly request a client to waive conflicts that might arise in the future is subject to the test of paragraph (b). The effectiveness of such waivers is generally determined by the extent to which the client reasonably understands the material risks that the waiver entails. The more comprehensive the explanation of the types of future representations that might arise and the actual and reasonably foreseeable adverse consequences of those representations, the greater the likelihood that the client will have the requisite understanding. Thus, if the client agrees to consent to a particular type of conflict with which the client is already familiar, then the consent ordinarily will be effective with regard to that type of conflict. If the consent is general and open-ended, then the consent ordinarily will be ineffective, because it is not reasonably likely that the client will have understood the material risks involved. On the other hand, if the client is an experienced user of the legal services involved and is reasonably informed regarding the risk that a conflict may arise, such consent is more likely to be effective, particularly if, e.g., the client is independently represented by other counsel in giving consent and the consent is limited to future conflicts unrelated to the subject of the representation. In any case, advance consent cannot be effective if the circumstances that materialize in the future are such as would make the conflict nonconsentable under paragraph (b).

Conflicts in Litigation

[23] Paragraph (b)(3) prohibits representation of opposing parties in the same litigation, regardless of the clients' consent. On the other hand, simultaneous representation of parties whose interests in litigation may conflict, such as coplaintiffs or codefendants, is governed by paragraph (a)(2). A conflict may exist by reason of substantial discrepancy in the parties' testimony, incompatibility in positions in relation to an opposing party or the fact that there are substantially different possibilities of settlement of the claims or liabilities in question. Such conflicts can arise in

criminal cases as well as civil. The potential for conflict of interest in representing multiple defendants in a criminal case is so grave that ordinarily a lawyer should decline to represent more than one codefendant. On the other hand, common representation of persons having similar interests in civil litigation is proper if the requirements of paragraph (b) are met.

[24] Ordinarily a lawyer may take inconsistent legal positions in different tribunals at different times on behalf of different clients. The mere fact that advocating a legal position on behalf of one client might create precedent adverse to the interests of a client represented by the lawyer in an unrelated matter does not create a conflict of interest. A conflict of interest exists, however, if there is a significant risk that a lawyer's action on behalf of one client will materially limit the lawyer's effectiveness in representing another client in a different case; for example, when a decision favoring one client will create a precedent likely to seriously weaken the position taken on behalf of the other client. Factors relevant in determining whether the clients need to be advised of the risk include: where the cases are pending, whether the issue is substantive or procedural, the temporal relationship between the matters, the significance of the issue to the immediate and long-term interests of the clients involved and the clients' reasonable expectations in retaining the lawyer. If there is significant risk of material limitation, then absent informed consent of the affected clients, the lawyer must refuse one of the representations or withdraw from one or both matters.

[25] When a lawyer represents or seeks to represent a class of plaintiffs or defendants in a class-action lawsuit, unnamed members of the class are ordinarily not considered to be clients of the lawyer for purposes of applying paragraph (a)(1) of this Rule. Thus, the lawyer does not typically need to get the consent of such a person before representing a client suing the person in an unrelated matter. Similarly, a lawyer seeking to represent an opponent in a class action does not typically need the consent of an unnamed member of the class whom the lawyer represents in an unrelated matter.

Nonlitigation Conflicts

[26] Conflicts of interest under paragraphs (a)(1) and (a)(2) arise in contexts other than litigation. For a discussion of directly adverse conflicts in transactional matters, see Comment [7]. Relevant factors in determining whether there is significant potential for material limitation include the duration and intimacy of the lawyer's relationship with the

client or clients involved, the functions being performed by the lawyer, the likelihood that disagreements will arise and the likely prejudice to the client from the conflict. The question is often one of proximity and degree. See Comment [8].

[27] For example, conflict questions may arise in estate planning and estate administration. A lawyer may be called upon to prepare wills for several family members, such as husband and wife, and, depending upon the circumstances, a conflict of interest may be present. In estate administration the identity of the client may be unclear under the law of a particular jurisdiction. Under one view, the client is the fiduciary; under another view the client is the estate or trust, including its beneficiaries. In order to comply with conflict of interest rules, the lawyer should make clear the lawyer's relationship to the parties involved.

[28] Whether a conflict is consentable depends on the circumstances. For example, a lawyer may not represent multiple parties to a negotiation whose interests are fundamentally antagonistic to each other, but common representation is permissible where the clients are generally aligned in interest even though there is some difference in interest among them. Thus, a lawyer may seek to establish or adjust a relationship between clients on an amicable and mutually advantageous basis; for example, in helping to organize a business in which two or more clients are entrepreneurs, working out the financial reorganization of an enterprise in which two or more clients have an interest or arranging a property distribution in settlement of an estate. The lawyer seeks to resolve potentially adverse interests by developing the parties' mutual interests. Otherwise, each party might have to obtain separate representation, with the possibility of incurring additional cost, complication or even litigation. Given these and other relevant factors, the clients may prefer that the lawyer act for all of them.

Special Considerations in Common Representation

[29] In considering whether to represent multiple clients in the same matter, a lawyer should be mindful that if the common representation fails because the potentially adverse interests cannot be reconciled, the result can be additional cost, embarrassment and recrimination. Ordinarily, the lawyer will be forced to withdraw from representing all of the clients if the common representation fails. In some situations, the risk of failure is so great that multiple representation is plainly impossible. For example, a lawyer cannot undertake common representation of clients where

contentious litigation or negotiations between them are imminent or contemplated. Moreover, because the lawyer is required to be impartial between commonly represented clients, representation of multiple clients is improper when it is unlikely that impartiality can be maintained. Generally, if the relationship between the parties has already assumed antagonism, the possibility that the clients' interests can be adequately served by common representation is not very good. Other relevant factors are whether the lawyer subsequently will represent both parties on a continuing basis and whether the situation involves creating or terminating a relationship between the parties.

[30] A particularly important factor in determining the appropriateness of common representation is the effect on client-lawyer confidentiality and the attorney-client privilege. With regard to the attorney-client privilege, the prevailing rule is that, as between commonly represented clients, the privilege does not attach. Hence, it must be assumed that if litigation eventuates between the clients, the privilege will not protect any such communications, and the clients should be so advised.

[31] As to the duty of confidentiality, continued common representation will almost certainly be inadequate if one client asks the lawyer not to disclose to the other client information relevant to the common representation. This is so because the lawyer has an equal duty of loyalty to each client, and each client has the right to be informed of anything bearing on the representation that might affect that client's interests and the right to expect that the lawyer will use that information to that client's benefit. See Rule 1.4. The lawyer should, at the outset of the common representation and as part of the process of obtaining each client's informed consent, advise each client that information will be shared and that the lawyer will have to withdraw if one client decides that some matter material to the representation should be kept from the other. In limited circumstances, it may be appropriate for the lawyer to proceed with the representation when the clients have agreed, after being properly informed, that the lawyer will keep certain information confidential. For example, the lawyer may reasonably conclude that failure to disclose one client's trade secrets to another client will not adversely affect representation involving a joint venture between the clients and agree to keep that information confidential with the informed consent of both clients.

[32] When seeking to establish or adjust a relationship between clients, the lawyer should make clear that the lawyer's role is not that of partisanship normally expected in other circumstances and, thus, that

the clients may be required to assume greater responsibility for decisions than when each client is separately represented. Any limitations on the scope of the representation made necessary as a result of the common representation should be fully explained to the clients at the outset of the representation. See Rule 1.2(c).

[33] Subject to the above limitations, each client in the common representation has the right to loyal and diligent representation and the protection of Rule 1.9 concerning the obligations to a former client. The client also has the right to discharge the lawyer as stated in Rule 1.16.

Organizational Clients

[34] A lawyer who represents a corporation or other organization does not, by virtue of that representation, necessarily represent any constituent or affiliated organization, such as a parent or subsidiary. See Rule 1.13(a). Thus, the lawyer for an organization is not barred from accepting representation adverse to an affiliate in an unrelated matter, unless the circumstances are such that the affiliate should also be considered a client of the lawyer, there is an understanding between the lawyer and the organizational client that the lawyer will avoid representation adverse to the client's affiliates, or the lawyer's obligations to either the organizational client or the new client are likely to limit materially the lawyer's representation of the other client.

[35] A lawyer for a corporation or other organization who is also a member of its board of directors should determine whether the responsibilities of the two roles may conflict. The lawyer may be called on to advise the corporation in matters involving actions of the directors. Consideration should be given to the frequency with which such situations may arise, the potential intensity of the conflict, the effect of the lawyer's resignation from the board and the possibility of the corporation's obtaining legal advice from another lawyer in such situations. If there is material risk that the dual role will compromise the lawyer's independence of professional judgment, the lawyer should not serve as a director or should cease to act as the corporation's lawyer when conflicts of interest arise. The lawyer should advise the other members of the board that in some circumstances matters discussed at board meetings while the lawyer is present in the capacity of director might not be protected by the attorney-client privilege and that conflict of interest considerations might require the lawyer's recusal as a director or might require the lawyer and the lawyer's firm to decline representation of the corporation in a matter.

Definitional Cross-References

"Confirmed in writing" *See* Rule 1.0(b)
"Informed consent" *See* Rule 1.0(e)
"Reasonably believes" *See* Rule 1.0(i)
"Tribunal" *See* Rule 1.0(m)

RULE 1.8: CONFLICT OF INTEREST: CURRENT CLIENTS: SPECIFIC RULES

(a) A lawyer shall not enter into a business transaction with a client or knowingly acquire an ownership, possessory, security or other pecuniary interest adverse to a client unless:

(1) the transaction and terms on which the lawyer acquires the interest are fair and reasonable to the client and are fully disclosed and transmitted in writing in a manner that can be reasonably understood by the client;

(2) the client is advised in writing of the desirability of seeking and is given a reasonable opportunity to seek the advice of independent legal counsel on the transaction; and

(3) the client gives informed consent, in a writing signed by the client, to the essential terms of the transaction and the lawyer's role in the transaction, including whether the lawyer is representing the client in the transaction.

(b) A lawyer shall not use information relating to representation of a client to the disadvantage of the client unless the client gives informed consent, except as permitted or required by these Rules.

(c) A lawyer shall not solicit any substantial gift from a client, including a testamentary gift, or prepare on behalf of a client an instrument giving the lawyer or a person related to the lawyer any substantial gift unless the lawyer or other recipient of the gift is related to the client. For purposes of this paragraph, related persons include a spouse, child, grandchild, parent, grandparent or other relative or individual with whom the lawyer or the client maintains a close, familial relationship.

(d) Prior to the conclusion of representation of a client, a lawyer shall not make or negotiate an agreement giving the lawyer literary or media rights to a portrayal or account based in substantial part on information relating to the representation.

(e) A lawyer shall not provide financial assistance to a client in connection with pending or contemplated litigation, except that:

(1) a lawyer may advance court costs and expenses of litigation, the repayment of which may be contingent on the outcome of the matter; and

(2) a lawyer representing an indigent client may pay court costs and expenses of litigation on behalf of the client.

(f) A lawyer shall not accept compensation for representing a client from one other than the client unless:

(1) the client gives informed consent;

(2) there is no interference with the lawyer's independence of professional judgment or with the client-lawyer relationship; and

(3) information relating to representation of a client is protected as required by Rule 1.6.

(g) A lawyer who represents two or more clients shall not participate in making an aggregate settlement of the claims of or against the clients, or in a criminal case an aggregated agreement as to guilty or nolo contendere pleas, unless each client gives informed consent, in a writing signed by the client. The lawyer's disclosure shall include the existence and nature of all the claims or pleas involved and of the participation of each person in the settlement.

(h) A lawyer shall not:

(1) make an agreement prospectively limiting the lawyer's liability to a client for malpractice unless the client is independently represented in making the agreement; or

(2) settle a claim or potential claim for such liability with an unrepresented client or former client unless that person is advised in writing of the desirability of seeking and is given a reasonable opportunity to seek the advice of independent legal counsel in connection therewith.

(i) A lawyer shall not acquire a proprietary interest in the cause of action or subject matter of litigation the lawyer is conducting for a client, except that the lawyer may:

(1) acquire a lien authorized by law to secure the lawyer's fee or expenses; and

(2) contract with a client for a reasonable contingent fee in a civil case.

(j) A lawyer shall not have sexual relations with a client unless a consensual sexual relationship existed between them when the client-lawyer relationship commenced.

(k) While lawyers are associated in a firm, a prohibition in the foregoing paragraphs (a) through (i) that applies to any one of them shall apply to all of them.

Comment
Business Transactions between Client and Lawyer

[1] A lawyer's legal skill and training, together with the relationship of trust and confidence between lawyer and client, create the possibility of overreaching when the lawyer participates in a business, property or financial transaction with a client, for example, a loan or sales transaction or a lawyer investment on behalf of a client. The requirements of paragraph (a) must be met even when the transaction is not closely related to the subject matter of the representation, as when a lawyer drafting a will for a client learns that the client needs money for unrelated expenses and offers to make a loan to the client. The Rule applies to lawyers engaged in the sale of goods or services related to the practice of law, for example, the sale of title insurance or investment services to existing clients of the lawyer's legal practice. See Rule 5.7. It also applies to lawyers purchasing property from estates they represent. It does not apply to ordinary fee arrangements between client and lawyer, which are governed by Rule 1.5, although its requirements must be met when the lawyer accepts an interest in the client's business or other nonmonetary property as payment of all or part of a fee. In addition, the Rule does not apply to standard commercial transactions between the lawyer and the client for products or services that the client generally markets to others, for example, banking or brokerage services, medical services, products manufactured or distributed by the client, and utilities' services. In such transactions, the lawyer has no advantage in dealing with the client, and the restrictions in paragraph (a) are unnecessary and impracticable.

[2] Paragraph (a)(1) requires that the transaction itself be fair to the client and that its essential terms be communicated to the client, in writing, in a manner that can be reasonably understood. Paragraph (a)(2) requires that the client also be advised, in writing, of the desirability of seeking the advice of independent legal counsel. It also requires that the client be given a reasonable opportunity to obtain such advice. Paragraph (a)(3) requires that the lawyer obtain the client's informed consent, in a

writing signed by the client, both to the essential terms of the transaction and to the lawyer's role. When necessary, the lawyer should discuss both the material risks of the proposed transaction, including any risk presented by the lawyer's involvement, and the existence of reasonably available alternatives and should explain why the advice of independent legal counsel is desirable. See Rule 1.0(e) (definition of informed consent).

[3] The risk to a client is greatest when the client expects the lawyer to represent the client in the transaction itself or when the lawyer's financial interest otherwise poses a significant risk that the lawyer's representation of the client will be materially limited by the lawyer's financial interest in the transaction. Here the lawyer's role requires that the lawyer must comply, not only with the requirements of paragraph (a), but also with the requirements of Rule 1.7. Under that Rule, the lawyer must disclose the risks associated with the lawyer's dual role as both legal adviser and participant in the transaction, such as the risk that the lawyer will structure the transaction or give legal advice in a way that favors the lawyer's interests at the expense of the client. Moreover, the lawyer must obtain the client's informed consent. In some cases, the lawyer's interest may be such that Rule 1.7 will preclude the lawyer from seeking the client's consent to the transaction.

[4] If the client is independently represented in the transaction, paragraph (a)(2) of this Rule is inapplicable, and the paragraph (a)(1) requirement for full disclosure is satisfied either by a written disclosure by the lawyer involved in the transaction or by the client's independent counsel. The fact that the client was independently represented in the transaction is relevant in determining whether the agreement was fair and reasonable to the client as paragraph (a)(1) further requires.

Use of Information Related to Representation

[5] Use of information relating to the representation to the disadvantage of the client violates the lawyer's duty of loyalty. Paragraph (b) applies when the information is used to benefit either the lawyer or a third person, such as another client or business associate of the lawyer. For example, if a lawyer learns that a client intends to purchase and develop several parcels of land, the lawyer may not use that information to purchase one of the parcels in competition with the client or to recommend that another client make such a purchase. The Rule does not prohibit uses that do not disadvantage the client. For example, a lawyer who learns a government agency's interpretation of trade legislation during the repre-

sentation of one client may properly use that information to benefit other clients. Paragraph (b) prohibits disadvantageous use of client information unless the client gives informed consent, except as permitted or required by these Rules. See Rules 1.2(d), 1.6, 1.9(c), 3.3, 4.1(b), 8.1 and 8.3.

Gifts to Lawyers

[6] A lawyer may accept a gift from a client, if the transaction meets general standards of fairness. For example, a simple gift such as a present given at a holiday or as a token of appreciation is permitted. If a client offers the lawyer a more substantial gift, paragraph (c) does not prohibit the lawyer from accepting it, although such a gift may be voidable by the client under the doctrine of undue influence, which treats client gifts as presumptively fraudulent. In any event, due to concerns about overreaching and imposition on clients, a lawyer may not suggest that a substantial gift be made to the lawyer or for the lawyer's benefit, except where the lawyer is related to the client as set forth in paragraph (c).

[7] If effectuation of a substantial gift requires preparing a legal instrument such as a will or conveyance, the client should have the detached advice that another lawyer can provide. The sole exception to this Rule is where the client is a relative of the donee.

[8] This Rule does not prohibit a lawyer from seeking to have the lawyer or a partner or associate of the lawyer named as executor of the client's estate or to another potentially lucrative fiduciary position. Nevertheless, such appointments will be subject to the general conflict of interest provision in Rule 1.7 when there is a significant risk that the lawyer's interest in obtaining the appointment will materially limit the lawyer's independent professional judgment in advising the client concerning the choice of an executor or other fiduciary. In obtaining the client's informed consent to the conflict, the lawyer should advise the client concerning the nature and extent of the lawyer's financial interest in the appointment, as well as the availability of alternative candidates for the position.

Literary Rights

[9] An agreement by which a lawyer acquires literary or media rights concerning the conduct of the representation creates a conflict between the interests of the client and the personal interests of the lawyer. Measures suitable in the representation of the client may detract from the publication value of an account of the representation. Paragraph (d) does

not prohibit a lawyer representing a client in a transaction concerning literary property from agreeing that the lawyer's fee shall consist of a share in ownership in the property, if the arrangement conforms to Rule 1.5 and paragraphs (a) and (i).

Financial Assistance

[10] Lawyers may not subsidize lawsuits or administrative proceedings brought on behalf of their clients, including making or guaranteeing loans to their clients for living expenses, because to do so would encourage clients to pursue lawsuits that might not otherwise be brought and because such assistance gives lawyers too great a financial stake in the litigation. These dangers do not warrant a prohibition on a lawyer lending a client court costs and litigation expenses, including the expenses of medical examination and the costs of obtaining and presenting evidence, because these advances are virtually indistinguishable from contingent fees and help ensure access to the courts. Similarly, an exception allowing lawyers representing indigent clients to pay court costs and litigation expenses regardless of whether these funds will be repaid is warranted.

Person Paying for a Lawyer's Services

[11] Lawyers are frequently asked to represent a client under circumstances in which a third person will compensate the lawyer, in whole or in part. The third person might be a relative or friend, an indemnitor (such as a liability insurance company) or a co-client (such as a corporation sued along with one or more of its employees). Because third-party payers frequently have interests that differ from those of the client, including interests in minimizing the amount spent on the representation and in learning how the representation is progressing, lawyers are prohibited from accepting or continuing such representations unless the lawyer determines that there will be no interference with the lawyer's independent professional judgment and there is informed consent from the client. See also Rule 5.4(c) (prohibiting interference with a lawyer's professional judgment by one who recommends, employs or pays the lawyer to render legal services for another).

[12] Sometimes, it will be sufficient for the lawyer to obtain the client's informed consent regarding the fact of the payment and the identity of the third-party payer. If, however, the fee arrangement creates a conflict of interest for the lawyer, then the lawyer must comply with Rule 1.7. The lawyer must also conform to the requirements of Rule 1.6 concern-

ing confidentiality. Under Rule 1.7(a), a conflict of interest exists if there is significant risk that the lawyer's representation of the client will be materially limited by the lawyer's own interest in the fee arrangement or by the lawyer's responsibilities to the third-party payer (for example, when the third-party payer is a co-client). Under Rule 1.7(b), the lawyer may accept or continue the representation with the informed consent of each affected client, unless the conflict is nonconsentable under that paragraph. Under Rule 1.7(b), the informed consent must be confirmed in writing.

Aggregate Settlements

[13] Differences in willingness to make or accept an offer of settlement are among the risks of common representation of multiple clients by a single lawyer. Under Rule 1.7, this is one of the risks that should be discussed before undertaking the representation, as part of the process of obtaining the clients' informed consent. In addition, Rule 1.2(a) protects each client's right to have the final say in deciding whether to accept or reject an offer of settlement and in deciding whether to enter a guilty or nolo contendere plea in a criminal case. The rule stated in this paragraph is a corollary of both these Rules and provides that, before any settlement offer or plea bargain is made or accepted on behalf of multiple clients, the lawyer must inform each of them about all the material terms of the settlement, including what the other clients will receive or pay if the settlement or plea offer is accepted. See also Rule 1.0(e) (definition of informed consent). Lawyers representing a class of plaintiffs or defendants, or those proceeding derivatively, may not have a full client-lawyer relationship with each member of the class; nevertheless, such lawyers must comply with applicable rules regulating notification of class members and other procedural requirements designed to ensure adequate protection of the entire class.

Limiting Liability and Settling Malpractice Claims

[14] Agreements prospectively limiting a lawyer's liability for malpractice are prohibited unless the client is independently represented in making the agreement because they are likely to undermine competent and diligent representation. Also, many clients are unable to evaluate the desirability of making such an agreement before a dispute has arisen, particularly if they are then represented by the lawyer seeking the agreement. This paragraph does not, however, prohibit a lawyer from entering into an agreement with the client to arbitrate legal malpractice claims,

provided such agreements are enforceable and the client is fully informed of the scope and effect of the agreement. Nor does this paragraph limit the ability of lawyers to practice in the form of a limited-liability entity, where permitted by law, provided that each lawyer remains personally liable to the client for his or her own conduct and the firm complies with any conditions required by law, such as provisions requiring client notification or maintenance of adequate liability insurance. Nor does it prohibit an agreement in accordance with Rule 1.2 that defines the scope of the representation, although a definition of scope that makes the obligations of representation illusory will amount to an attempt to limit liability.

[15] Agreements settling a claim or a potential claim for malpractice are not prohibited by this Rule. Nevertheless, in view of the danger that a lawyer will take unfair advantage of an unrepresented client or former client, the lawyer must first advise such a person in writing of the appropriateness of independent representation in connection with such a settlement. In addition, the lawyer must give the client or former client a reasonable opportunity to find and consult independent counsel.

Acquiring Proprietary Interest in Litigation

[16] Paragraph (i) states the traditional general rule that lawyers are prohibited from acquiring a proprietary interest in litigation. Like paragraph (e), the general rule has its basis in common law champerty and maintenance and is designed to avoid giving the lawyer too great an interest in the representation. In addition, when the lawyer acquires an ownership interest in the subject of the representation, it will be more difficult for a client to discharge the lawyer if the client so desires. The Rule is subject to specific exceptions developed in decisional law and continued in these Rules. The exception for certain advances of the costs of litigation is set forth in paragraph (e). In addition, paragraph (i) sets forth exceptions for liens authorized by law to secure the lawyer's fees or expenses and contracts for reasonable contingent fees. The law of each jurisdiction determines which liens are authorized by law. These may include liens granted by statute, liens originating in common law and liens acquired by contract with the client. When a lawyer acquires by contract a security interest in property other than that recovered through the lawyer's efforts in the litigation, such an acquisition is a business or financial transaction with a client and is governed by the requirements of paragraph (a). Contracts for contingent fees in civil cases are governed by Rule 1.5.

Client-Lawyer Sexual Relationships

[17] The relationship between lawyer and client is a fiduciary one in which the lawyer occupies the highest position of trust and confidence. The relationship is almost always unequal; thus, a sexual relationship between lawyer and client can involve unfair exploitation of the lawyer's fiduciary role, in violation of the lawyer's basic ethical obligation not to use the trust of the client to the client's disadvantage. In addition, such a relationship presents a significant danger that, because of the lawyer's emotional involvement, the lawyer will be unable to represent the client without impairment of the exercise of independent professional judgment. Moreover, a blurred line between the professional and personal relationships may make it difficult to predict to what extent client confidences will be protected by the attorney-client evidentiary privilege, since client confidences are protected by privilege only when they are imparted in the context of the client-lawyer relationship. Because of the significant danger of harm to client interests and because the client's own emotional involvement renders it unlikely that the client could give adequate informed consent, this Rule prohibits the lawyer from having sexual relations with a client regardless of whether the relationship is consensual and regardless of the absence of prejudice to the client.

[18] Sexual relationships that predate the client-lawyer relationship are not prohibited. Issues relating to the exploitation of the fiduciary relationship and client dependency are diminished when the sexual relationship existed prior to the commencement of the client-lawyer relationship. However, before proceeding with the representation in these circumstances, the lawyer should consider whether the lawyer's ability to represent the client will be materially limited by the relationship. See Rule 1.7(a)(2).

[19] When the client is an organization, paragraph (j) of this Rule prohibits a lawyer for the organization (whether inside counsel or outside counsel) from having a sexual relationship with a constituent of the organization who supervises, directs or regularly consults with that lawyer concerning the organization's legal matters.

Imputation of Prohibitions

[20] Under paragraph (k), a prohibition on conduct by an individual lawyer in paragraphs (a) through (i) also applies to all lawyers associated in a firm with the personally prohibited lawyer. For example, one lawyer in a firm may not enter into a business transaction with a client of

another member of the firm without complying with paragraph (a), even if the first lawyer is not personally involved in the representation of the client. The prohibition set forth in paragraph (j) is personal and is not applied to associated lawyers.

Definitional Cross-References

"Firm" *See* Rule 1.0(c)
"Informed consent" *See* Rule 1.0(e)
"Knowingly" *See* Rule 1.0(f)
"Substantial" *See* Rule 1.0(l)
"Writing" and "Signed" *See* Rule 1.0(n)

RULE 1.9: DUTIES TO FORMER CLIENTS

(a) A lawyer who has formerly represented a client in a matter shall not thereafter represent another person in the same or a substantially related matter in which that person's interests are materially adverse to the interests of the former client unless the former client gives informed consent, confirmed in writing.

(b) A lawyer shall not knowingly represent a person in the same or a substantially related matter in which a firm with which the lawyer formerly was associated had previously represented a client

(1) whose interests are materially adverse to that person; and

(2) about whom the lawyer had acquired information protected by Rules 1.6 and 1.9(c) that is material to the matter; unless the former client gives informed consent, confirmed in writing.

(c) A lawyer who has formerly represented a client in a matter or whose present or former firm has formerly represented a client in a matter shall not thereafter:

(1) use information relating to the representation to the disadvantage of the former client except as these Rules would permit or require with respect to a client, or when the information has become generally known; or

(2) reveal information relating to the representation except as these Rules would permit or require with respect to a client.

Comment

[1] After termination of a client-lawyer relationship, a lawyer has certain continuing duties with respect to confidentiality and conflicts of interest and thus may not represent another client except in conformity with this Rule. Under this Rule, for example, a lawyer could not properly seek to rescind on behalf of a new client a contract drafted on behalf of the former client. So also a lawyer who has prosecuted an accused person could not properly represent the accused in a subsequent civil action against the government concerning the same transaction. Nor could a lawyer who has represented multiple clients in a matter represent one of the clients against the others in the same or a substantially related matter after a dispute arose among the clients in that matter, unless all affected clients give informed consent. See Comment [9]. Current and former government lawyers must comply with this Rule to the extent required by Rule 1.11.

[2] The scope of a "matter" for purposes of this Rule depends on the facts of a particular situation or transaction. The lawyer's involvement in a matter can also be a question of degree. When a lawyer has been directly involved in a specific transaction, subsequent representation of other clients with materially adverse interests in that transaction clearly is prohibited. On the other hand, a lawyer who recurrently handled a type of problem for a former client is not precluded from later representing another client in a factually distinct problem of that type even though the subsequent representation involves a position adverse to the prior client. Similar considerations can apply to the reassignment of military lawyers between defense and prosecution functions within the same military jurisdictions. The underlying question is whether the lawyer was so involved in the matter that the subsequent representation can be justly regarded as a changing of sides in the matter in question.

[3] Matters are "substantially related" for purposes of this Rule if they involve the same transaction or legal dispute or if there otherwise is a substantial risk that confidential factual information as would normally have been obtained in the prior representation would materially advance the client's position in the subsequent matter. For example, a lawyer who has represented a businessperson and learned extensive private financial information about that person may not then represent that person's spouse in seeking a divorce. Similarly, a lawyer who has previously represented a client in securing environmental permits to build a shopping

center would be precluded from representing neighbors seeking to oppose rezoning of the property on the basis of environmental considerations; however, the lawyer would not be precluded, on the grounds of substantial relationship, from defending a tenant of the completed shopping center in resisting eviction for nonpayment of rent. Information that has been disclosed to the public or to other parties adverse to the former client ordinarily will not be disqualifying. Information acquired in a prior representation may have been rendered obsolete by the passage of time, a circumstance that may be relevant in determining whether two representations are substantially related. In the case of an organizational client, general knowledge of the client's policies and practices ordinarily will not preclude a subsequent representation; on the other hand, knowledge of specific facts gained in a prior representation that are relevant to the matter in question ordinarily will preclude such a representation. A former client is not required to reveal the confidential information learned by the lawyer in order to establish a substantial risk that the lawyer has confidential information to use in the subsequent matter. A conclusion about the possession of such information may be based on the nature of the services the lawyer provided the former client and information that would in ordinary practice be learned by a lawyer providing such services.

Lawyers Moving Between Firms

[4] When lawyers have been associated within a firm but then end their association, the question of whether a lawyer should undertake representation is more complicated. There are several competing considerations. First, the client previously represented by the former firm must be reasonably assured that the principle of loyalty to the client is not compromised. Second, the rule should not be so broadly cast as to preclude other persons from having reasonable choice of legal counsel. Third, the rule should not unreasonably hamper lawyers from forming new associations and taking on new clients after having left a previous association. In this connection, it should be recognized that today many lawyers practice in firms, that many lawyers to some degree limit their practice to one field or another, and that many move from one association to another several times in their careers. If the concept of imputation were applied with unqualified rigor, the result would be radical curtailment of the opportunity of lawyers to move from one practice setting to another and of the opportunity of clients to change counsel.

[5] Paragraph (b) operates to disqualify the lawyer only when the lawyer involved has actual knowledge of information protected by Rules 1.6 and 1.9(c). Thus, if a lawyer while with one firm acquired no knowledge or information relating to a particular client of the firm, and that lawyer later joined another firm, neither the lawyer individually nor the second firm is disqualified from representing another client in the same or a related matter even though the interests of the two clients conflict. See Rule 1.10(b) for the restrictions on a firm once a lawyer has terminated association with the firm.

[6] Application of paragraph (b) depends on a situation's particular facts, aided by inferences, deductions or working presumptions that reasonably may be made about the way in which lawyers work together. A lawyer may have general access to files of all clients of a law firm and may regularly participate in discussions of their affairs; it should be inferred that such a lawyer in fact is privy to all information about all the firm's clients. In contrast, another lawyer may have access to the files of only a limited number of clients and participate in discussions of the affairs of no other clients; in the absence of information to the contrary, it should be inferred that such a lawyer in fact is privy to information about the clients actually served but not those of other clients. In such an inquiry, the burden of proof should rest upon the firm whose disqualification is sought.

[7] Independent of the question of disqualification of a firm, a lawyer changing professional association has a continuing duty to preserve confidentiality of information about a client formerly represented. See Rules 1.6 and 1.9(c).

[8] Paragraph (c) provides that information acquired by the lawyer in the course of representing a client may not subsequently be used or revealed by the lawyer to the disadvantage of the client. However, the fact that a lawyer has once served a client does not preclude the lawyer from using generally known information about that client when later representing another client.

[9] The provisions of this Rule are for the protection of former clients and can be waived if the client gives informed consent, which consent must be confirmed in writing under paragraphs (a) and (b). See Rule 1.0(e). With regard to the effectiveness of an advance waiver, see Comment [22] to Rule 1.7. With regard to disqualification of a firm with which a lawyer is or was formerly associated, see Rule 1.10.

Definitional Cross-References

"Confirmed in writing" *See* Rule 1.0(b)
"Firm" *See* Rule 1.0(c)
"Informed consent" *See* Rule 1.0(e)
"Knowingly" and "Known" *See* Rule 1.0(f)
"Writing" *See* Rule 1.0(n)

RULE 1.10: IMPUTATION OF CONFLICTS OF INTEREST: GENERAL RULE

(a) While lawyers are associated in a firm, none of them shall knowingly represent a client when any one of them practicing alone would be prohibited from doing so by Rules 1.7 or 1.9, unless

(1) the prohibition is based on a personal interest of the disqualified lawyer and does not present a significant risk of materially limiting the representation of the client by the remaining lawyers in the firm; or

(2) the prohibition is based upon Rule 1.9(a) or (b), and arises out of the disqualified lawyer's association with a prior firm, and

(i) the disqualified lawyer is timely screened from any participation in the matter and is apportioned no part of the fee therefrom;

(ii) written notice is promptly given to any affected former client to enable the former client to ascertain compliance with the provisions of this Rule, which shall include a description of the screening procedures employed; a statement of the firm's and of the screened lawyer's compliance with these Rules; a statement that review may be available before a tribunal; and an agreement by the firm to respond promptly to any written inquiries or objections by the former client about the screening procedures; and

(iii) certifications of compliance with these Rules and with the screening procedures are provided to the former client by the screened lawyer and by a partner of the firm, at reasonable intervals upon the former client's written request and upon termination of the screening procedures.

(b) When a lawyer has terminated an association with a firm, the firm is not prohibited from thereafter representing a person with interests materially adverse to those of a client represented by the formerly associated lawyer and not currently represented by the firm, unless:

(1) the matter is the same or substantially related to that in which the formerly associated lawyer represented the client; and

(2) any lawyer remaining in the firm has information protected by Rules 1.6 and 1.9(c) that is material to the matter.

(c) A disqualification prescribed by this Rule may be waived by the affected client under the conditions stated in Rule 1.7.

(d) The disqualification of lawyers associated in a firm with former or current government lawyers is governed by Rule 1.11.

Comment
Definition of "Firm"

[1] For purposes of the Rules of Professional Conduct, the term "firm" denotes lawyers in a law partnership, professional corporation, sole proprietorship or other association authorized to practice law; or lawyers employed in a legal services organization or the legal department of a corporation or other organization. See Rule 1.0(c). Whether two or more lawyers constitute a firm within this definition can depend on the specific facts. See Rule 1.0, Comments [2]–[4].

Principles of Imputed Disqualification

[2] The rule of imputed disqualification stated in paragraph (a) gives effect to the principle of loyalty to the client as it applies to lawyers who practice in a law firm. Such situations can be considered from the premise that a firm of lawyers is essentially one lawyer for purposes of the rules governing loyalty to the client, or from the premise that each lawyer is vicariously bound by the obligation of loyalty owed by each lawyer with whom the lawyer is associated. Paragraph (a)(1) operates only among the lawyers currently associated in a firm. When a lawyer moves from one firm to another, the situation is governed by Rules 1.9(b) and 1.10(a)(2) and 1.10(b).

[3] The rule in paragraph (a) does not prohibit representation where neither questions of client loyalty nor protection of confidential information are presented. Where one lawyer in a firm could not effectively represent a given client because of strong political beliefs, for example, but that lawyer will do no work on the case and the personal beliefs of the lawyer will not materially limit the representation by others in the firm,

the firm should not be disqualified. On the other hand, if an opposing party in a case were owned by a lawyer in the law firm, and others in the firm would be materially limited in pursuing the matter because of loyalty to that lawyer, the personal disqualification of the lawyer would be imputed to all others in the firm.

[4] The rule in paragraph (a) also does not prohibit representation by others in the law firm where the person prohibited from involvement in a matter is a nonlawyer, such as a paralegal or legal secretary. Nor does paragraph (a) prohibit representation if the lawyer is prohibited from acting because of events before the person became a lawyer, for example, work that the person did while a law student. Such persons, however, ordinarily must be screened from any personal participation in the matter to avoid communication to others in the firm of confidential information that both the nonlawyers and the firm have a legal duty to protect. See Rules 1.0(k) and 5.3.

[5] Rule 1.10(b) operates to permit a law firm, under certain circumstances, to represent a person with interests directly adverse to those of a client represented by a lawyer who formerly was associated with the firm. The Rule applies regardless of when the formerly associated lawyer represented the client. However, the law firm may not represent a person with interests adverse to those of a present client of the firm, which would violate Rule 1.7. Moreover, the firm may not represent the person where the matter is the same or substantially related to that in which the formerly associated lawyer represented the client and any other lawyer currently in the firm has material information protected by Rules 1.6 and 1.9(c).

[6] Rule 1.10(c) removes imputation with the informed consent of the affected client or former client under the conditions stated in Rule 1.7. The conditions stated in Rule 1.7 require the lawyer to determine that the representation is not prohibited by Rule 1.7(b) and that each affected client or former client has given informed consent to the representation, confirmed in writing. In some cases, the risk may be so severe that the conflict may not be cured by client consent. For a discussion of the effectiveness of client waivers of conflicts that might arise in the future, see Rule 1.7, Comment [22]. For a definition of informed consent, see Rule 1.0(e).

[7] Rule 1.10(a)(2) similarly removes the imputation otherwise required by Rule 1.10(a), but unlike section (c), it does so without requiring that there be informed consent by the former client. Instead, it requires that the procedures laid out in sections (a)(2)(i)-(iii) be followed. A description of effective screening mechanisms appears in Rule 1.0(k). Law-

yers should be aware, however, that, even where screening mechanisms have been adopted, tribunals may consider additional factors in ruling upon motions to disqualify a lawyer from pending litigation.

[8] Paragraph (a)(2)(i) does not prohibit the screened lawyer from receiving a salary or partnership share established by prior independent agreement, but that lawyer may not receive compensation directly related to the matter in which the lawyer is disqualified.

[9] The notice required by paragraph (a)(2)(ii) generally should include a description of the screened lawyer's prior representation and be given as soon as practicable after the need for screening becomes apparent. It also should include a statement by the screened lawyer and the firm that the client's material confidential information has not been disclosed or used in violation of the Rules. The notice is intended to enable the former client to evaluate and comment upon the effectiveness of the screening procedures.

[10] The certifications required by paragraph (a)(2)(iii) give the former client assurance that the client's material confidential information has not been disclosed or used inappropriately, either prior to timely implementation of a screen or thereafter. If compliance cannot be certified, the certificate must describe the failure to comply.

[11] Where a lawyer has joined a private firm after having represented the government, imputation is governed by Rule 1.11(b) and (c), not this Rule. Under Rule 1.11(d), where a lawyer represents the government after having served clients in private practice, nongovernmental employment or in another government agency, former-client conflicts are not imputed to government lawyers associated with the individually disqualified lawyer.

[12] Where a lawyer is prohibited from engaging in certain transactions under Rule 1.8, paragraph (k) of that Rule, and not this Rule, determines whether that prohibition also applies to other lawyers associated in a firm with the personally prohibited lawyer.

Definitional Cross-References

"Firm" *See* Rule 1.0(c)
"Knowingly" *See* Rule 1.0(f)
"Partner" *See* Rule 1.0(g)
"Screened" *See* Rule 1.0(k)
"Tribunal" *See* Rule 1.0(m)
"Written" *See* Rule 1.0(n)

RULE 1.11: SPECIAL CONFLICTS OF INTEREST FOR FORMER AND CURRENT GOVERNMENT OFFICERS AND EMPLOYEES

(a) Except as law may otherwise expressly permit, a lawyer who has formerly served as a public officer or employee of the government:

(1) is subject to Rule 1.9(c); and

(2) shall not otherwise represent a client in connection with a matter in which the lawyer participated personally and substantially as a public officer or employee, unless the appropriate government agency gives its informed consent, confirmed in writing, to the representation.

(b) When a lawyer is disqualified from representation under paragraph (a), no lawyer in a firm with which that lawyer is associated may knowingly undertake or continue representation in such a matter unless:

(1) the disqualified lawyer is timely screened from any participation in the matter and is apportioned no part of the fee therefrom; and

(2) written notice is promptly given to the appropriate government agency to enable it to ascertain compliance with the provisions of this Rule.

(c) Except as law may otherwise expressly permit, a lawyer having information that the lawyer knows is confidential government information about a person acquired when the lawyer was a public officer or employee, may not represent a private client whose interests are adverse to that person in a matter in which the information could be used to the material disadvantage of that person. As used in this Rule, the term "confidential government information" means information that has been obtained under governmental authority and which, at the time this Rule is applied, the government is prohibited by law from disclosing to the public or has a legal privilege not to disclose and which is not otherwise available to the public. A firm with which that lawyer is associated may undertake or continue representation in the matter only if the disqualified lawyer is timely screened from any participation in the matter and is apportioned no part of the fee therefrom.

(d) Except as law may otherwise expressly permit, a lawyer currently serving as a public officer or employee:

(1) is subject to Rules 1.7 and 1.9; and

(2) shall not:

(i) participate in a matter in which the lawyer participated personally and substantially while in private practice or nongovernmental employment, unless the appropriate government agency gives its informed consent, confirmed in writing; or

(ii) negotiate for private employment with any person who is involved as a party or as lawyer for a party in a matter in which the lawyer is participating personally and substantially, except that a lawyer serving as a law clerk to a judge, other adjudicative officer or arbitrator may negotiate for private employment as permitted by Rule 1.12(b) and subject to the conditions stated in Rule 1.12(b).

(e) As used in this Rule, the term "matter" includes:

(1) any judicial or other proceeding, application, request for a ruling or other determination, contract, claim, controversy, investigation, charge, accusation, arrest or other particular matter involving a specific party or parties, and

(2) any other matter covered by the conflict of interest rules of the appropriate government agency.

Comment

[1] A lawyer who has served or is currently serving as a public officer or employee is personally subject to the Rules of Professional Conduct, including the prohibition against concurrent conflicts of interest stated in Rule 1.7. In addition, such a lawyer may be subject to statutes and government regulations regarding conflict of interest. Such statutes and regulations may circumscribe the extent to which the government agency may give consent under this Rule. See Rule 1.0(e) for the definition of informed consent.

[2] Paragraphs (a)(1), (a)(2) and (d)(1) restate the obligations of an individual lawyer who has served or is currently serving as an officer or employee of the government toward a former government or private client. Rule 1.10 is not applicable to the conflicts of interest addressed by this Rule. Rather, paragraph (b) sets forth a special imputation rule for former government lawyers that provides for screening and notice. Because of the special problems raised by imputation within a government

agency, paragraph (d) does not impute the conflicts of a lawyer currently serving as an officer or employee of the government to other associated government officers or employees, although ordinarily it will be prudent to screen such lawyers.

[3] Paragraphs (a)(2) and (d)(2) apply regardless of whether a lawyer is adverse to a former client and are thus designed not only to protect the former client, but also to prevent a lawyer from exploiting public office for the advantage of another client. For example, a lawyer who has pursued a claim on behalf of the government may not pursue the same claim on behalf of a later private client after the lawyer has left government service, except when authorized to do so by the government agency under paragraph (a). Similarly, a lawyer who has pursued a claim on behalf of a private client may not pursue the claim on behalf of the government, except when authorized to do so by paragraph (d). As with paragraphs (a)(1) and (d)(1), Rule 1.10 is not applicable to the conflicts of interest addressed by these paragraphs.

[4] This Rule represents a balancing of interests. On the one hand, where the successive clients are a government agency and another client, public or private, the risk exists that power or discretion vested in that agency might be used for the special benefit of the other client. A lawyer should not be in a position where benefit to the other client might affect performance of the lawyer's professional functions on behalf of the government. Also, unfair advantage could accrue to the other client by reason of access to confidential government information about the client's adversary obtainable only through the lawyer's government service. On the other hand, the rules governing lawyers presently or formerly employed by a government agency should not be so restrictive as to inhibit transfer of employment to and from the government. The government has a legitimate need to attract qualified lawyers as well as to maintain high ethical standards. Thus a former government lawyer is disqualified only from particular matters in which the lawyer participated personally and substantially. The provisions for screening and waiver in paragraph (b) are necessary to prevent the disqualification rule from imposing too severe a deterrent against entering public service. The limitation of disqualification in paragraphs (a)(2) and (d)(2) to matters involving a specific party or parties, rather than extending disqualification to all substantive issues on which the lawyer worked, serves a similar function.

[5] When a lawyer has been employed by one government agency and then moves to a second government agency, it may be appropriate

to treat that second agency as another client for purposes of this Rule, as when a lawyer is employed by a city and subsequently is employed by a federal agency. However, because the conflict of interest is governed by paragraph (d), the latter agency is not required to screen the lawyer as paragraph (b) requires a law firm to do. The question of whether two government agencies should be regarded as the same or different clients for conflict of interest purposes is beyond the scope of these Rules. See Rule 1.13 Comment [9].

[6] Paragraphs (b) and (c) contemplate a screening arrangement. See Rule 1.0(k) (requirements for screening procedures). These paragraphs do not prohibit a lawyer from receiving a salary or partnership share established by prior independent agreement, but that lawyer may not receive compensation directly relating the lawyer's compensation to the fee in the matter in which the lawyer is disqualified.

[7] Notice, including a description of the screened lawyer's prior representation and of the screening procedures employed, generally should be given as soon as practicable after the need for screening becomes apparent.

[8] Paragraph (c) operates only when the lawyer in question has knowledge of the information, which means actual knowledge; it does not operate with respect to information that merely could be imputed to the lawyer.

[9] Paragraphs (a) and (d) do not prohibit a lawyer from jointly representing a private party and a government agency when doing so is permitted by Rule 1.7 and is not otherwise prohibited by law.

[10] For purposes of paragraph (e) of this Rule, a "matter" may continue in another form. In determining whether two particular matters are the same, the lawyer should consider the extent to which the matters involve the same basic facts, the same or related parties, and the time elapsed.

Definitional Cross-References

"Confirmed in writing" *See* Rule 1.0(b)
"Firm" *See* Rule 1.0(c)
"Informed consent" *See* Rule 1.0(e)
"Knowingly" and "Knows" *See* Rule 1.0(f)
"Screened" *See* Rule 1.0(k)
"Written" *See* Rule 1.0(n)

RULE 1.12: FORMER JUDGE, ARBITRATOR, MEDIATOR OR OTHER THIRD-PARTY NEUTRAL

(a) Except as stated in paragraph (d), a lawyer shall not represent anyone in connection with a matter in which the lawyer participated personally and substantially as a judge or other adjudicative officer or law clerk to such a person or as an arbitrator, mediator or other third-party neutral, unless all parties to the proceeding give informed consent, confirmed in writing.

(b) A lawyer shall not negotiate for employment with any person who is involved as a party or as lawyer for a party in a matter in which the lawyer is participating personally and substantially as a judge or other adjudicative officer or as an arbitrator, mediator or other third-party neutral. A lawyer serving as a law clerk to a judge or other adjudicative officer may negotiate for employment with a party or lawyer involved in a matter in which the clerk is participating personally and substantially, but only after the lawyer has notified the judge or other adjudicative officer.

(c) If a lawyer is disqualified by paragraph (a), no lawyer in a firm with which that lawyer is associated may knowingly undertake or continue representation in the matter unless:

(1) the disqualified lawyer is timely screened from any participation in the matter and is apportioned no part of the fee therefrom; and

(2) written notice is promptly given to the parties and any appropriate tribunal to enable them to ascertain compliance with the provisions of this Rule.

(d) An arbitrator selected as a partisan of a party in a multimember arbitration panel is not prohibited from subsequently representing that party.

Comment

[1] This Rule generally parallels Rule 1.11. The term "personally and substantially" signifies that a judge who was a member of a multimember court, and thereafter left judicial office to practice law, is not prohibited from representing a client in a matter pending in the court, but in which the former judge did not participate. So also the fact that a former

judge exercised administrative responsibility in a court does not prevent the former judge from acting as a lawyer in a matter where the judge had previously exercised remote or incidental administrative responsibility that did not affect the merits. Compare the Comment to Rule 1.11. The term "adjudicative officer" includes such officials as judges pro tempore, referees, special masters, hearing officers and other parajudicial officers, and also lawyers who serve as part-time judges. Paragraphs C(2), D(2) and E(2) of the Application Section of the Model Code of Judicial Conduct provide that a part-time judge, judge pro tempore or retired judge recalled to active service, shall not "act as a lawyer in a proceeding in which the judge has served as a judge or in any other proceeding related thereto." Although phrased differently from this Rule, those Rules correspond in meaning.

[2] Like former judges, lawyers who have served as arbitrators, mediators or other third-party neutrals may be asked to represent a client in a matter in which the lawyer participated personally and substantially. This Rule forbids such representation unless all of the parties to the proceedings give their informed consent, confirmed in writing. See Rule 1.0(e) and (b). Other law or codes of ethics governing third-party neutrals may impose more stringent standards of personal or imputed disqualification. See Rule 2.4.

[3] Although lawyers who serve as third-party neutrals do not have information concerning the parties that is protected under Rule 1.6, they typically owe the parties an obligation of confidentiality under law or codes of ethics governing third-party neutrals. Thus, paragraph (c) provides that conflicts of the personally disqualified lawyer will be imputed to other lawyers in a law firm unless the conditions of this paragraph are met.

[4] Requirements for screening procedures are stated in Rule 1.0(k). Paragraph (c)(1) does not prohibit the screened lawyer from receiving a salary or partnership share established by prior independent agreement, but that lawyer may not receive compensation directly related to the matter in which the lawyer is disqualified.

[5] Notice, including a description of the screened lawyer's prior representation and of the screening procedures employed, generally should be given as soon as practicable after the need for screening becomes apparent.

Definitional Cross-References

"Confirmed in writing" *See* Rule 1.0(b)
"Firm" *See* Rule 1.0(c)
"Informed consent" *See* Rule 1.0(e)
"Knowingly" *See* Rule 1.0(f)
"Screened" *See* Rule 1.0(k)
"Tribunal" *See* Rule 1.0(m)
"Writing" and "Written" *See* Rule 1.0(n)

RULE 1.13: ORGANIZATION AS CLIENT

(a) A lawyer employed or retained by an organization represents the organization acting through its duly authorized constituents.

(b) If a lawyer for an organization knows that an officer, employee or other person associated with the organization is engaged in action, intends to act or refuses to act in a matter related to the representation that is a violation of a legal obligation to the organization, or a violation of law that reasonably might be imputed to the organization, and that is likely to result in substantial injury to the organization, then the lawyer shall proceed as is reasonably necessary in the best interest of the organization. Unless the lawyer reasonably believes that it is not necessary in the best interest of the organization to do so, the lawyer shall refer the matter to higher authority in the organization, including, if warranted by the circumstances, to the highest authority that can act on behalf of the organization as determined by applicable law.

(c) Except as provided in paragraph (d), if

(1) despite the lawyer's efforts in accordance with paragraph (b) the highest authority that can act on behalf of the organization insists upon or fails to address in a timely and appropriate manner an action or a refusal to act, that is clearly a violation of law; and

(2) the lawyer reasonably believes that the violation is reasonably certain to result in substantial injury to the organization,

then the lawyer may reveal information relating to the representation whether or not Rule 1.6 permits such disclosure, but only if and to the extent the lawyer reasonably believes necessary to prevent substantial injury to the organization.

(d) Paragraph (c) shall not apply with respect to information relating to a lawyer's representation of an organization to investigate an alleged violation of law, or to defend the organization or an officer, employee or other constituent associated with the organization against a claim arising out of an alleged violation of law.

(e) A lawyer who reasonably believes that he or she has been discharged because of the lawyer's actions taken pursuant to paragraphs (b) or (c), or who withdraws under circumstances that require or permit the lawyer to take action under either of those paragraphs, shall proceed as the lawyer reasonably believes necessary to assure that the organization's highest authority is informed of the lawyer's discharge or withdrawal.

(f) In dealing with an organization's directors, officers, employees, members, shareholders or other constituents, a lawyer shall explain the identity of the client when the lawyer knows or reasonably should know that the organization's interests are adverse to those of the constituents with whom the lawyer is dealing.

(g) A lawyer representing an organization may also represent any of its directors, officers, employees, members, shareholders or other constituents, subject to the provisions of Rule 1.7. If the organization's consent to the dual representation is required by Rule 1.7, the consent shall be given by an appropriate official of the organization other than the individual who is to be represented, or by the shareholders.

Comment
The Entity as the Client

[1] An organizational client is a legal entity, but it cannot act except through its officers, directors, employees, shareholders and other constituents. Officers, directors, employees and shareholders are the constituents of the corporate organizational client. The duties defined in this Comment apply equally to unincorporated associations. "Other constituents" as used in this Comment means the positions equivalent to officers, directors, employees and shareholders held by persons acting for organizational clients that are not corporations.

[2] When one of the constituents of an organizational client communicates with the organization's lawyer in that person's organizational

capacity, the communication is protected by Rule 1.6. Thus, by way of example, if an organizational client requests its lawyer to investigate allegations of wrongdoing, interviews made in the course of that investigation between the lawyer and the client's employees or other constituents are covered by Rule 1.6. This does not mean, however, that constituents of an organizational client are the clients of the lawyer. The lawyer may not disclose to such constituents information relating to the representation except for disclosures explicitly or impliedly authorized by the organizational client in order to carry out the representation or as otherwise permitted by Rule 1.6.

[3] When constituents of the organization make decisions for it, the decisions ordinarily must be accepted by the lawyer even if their utility or prudence is doubtful. Decisions concerning policy and operations, including ones entailing serious risk, are not as such in the lawyer's province. Paragraph (b) makes clear, however, that when the lawyer knows that the organization is likely to be substantially injured by action of an officer or other constituent that violates a legal obligation to the organization or is in violation of law that might be imputed to the organization, the lawyer must proceed as is reasonably necessary in the best interest of the organization. As defined in Rule 1.0(f), knowledge can be inferred from circumstances, and a lawyer cannot ignore the obvious.

[4] In determining how to proceed under paragraph (b), the lawyer should give due consideration to the seriousness of the violation and its consequences, the responsibility in the organization and the apparent motivation of the person involved, the policies of the organization concerning such matters, and any other relevant considerations. Ordinarily, referral to a higher authority would be necessary. In some circumstances, however, it may be appropriate for the lawyer to ask the constituent to reconsider the matter; for example, if the circumstances involve a constituent's innocent misunderstanding of law and subsequent acceptance of the lawyer's advice, the lawyer may reasonably conclude that the best interest of the organization does not require that the matter be referred to higher authority. If a constituent persists in conduct contrary to the lawyer's advice, it will be necessary for the lawyer to take steps to have the matter reviewed by a higher authority in the organization. If the matter is of sufficient seriousness and importance or urgency to the organization, referral to higher authority in the organization may be necessary even if the lawyer has not communicated with the constituent. Any measures taken should, to the extent practicable, minimize the risk of revealing

information relating to the representation to persons outside the organization. Even in circumstances where a lawyer is not obligated by Rule 1.13 to proceed, a lawyer may bring to the attention of an organizational client, including its highest authority, matters that the lawyer reasonably believes to be of sufficient importance to warrant doing so in the best interest of the organization.

[5] Paragraph (b) also makes clear that when it is reasonably necessary to enable the organization to address the matter in a timely and appropriate manner, the lawyer must refer the matter to higher authority, including, if warranted by the circumstances, the highest authority that can act on behalf of the organization under applicable law. The organization's highest authority to whom a matter may be referred ordinarily will be the board of directors or similar governing body. However, applicable law may prescribe that under certain conditions the highest authority reposes elsewhere, for example, in the independent directors of a corporation.

Relation to Other Rules

[6] The authority and responsibility provided in this Rule are concurrent with the authority and responsibility provided in other Rules. In particular, this Rule does not limit or expand the lawyer's responsibility under Rules 1.8, 1.16, 3.3 or 4.1. Paragraph (c) of this Rule supplements Rule 1.6(b) by providing an additional basis upon which the lawyer may reveal information relating to the representation, but does not modify, restrict, or limit the provisions of Rule 1.6(b)(1) – (6). Under paragraph (c) the lawyer may reveal such information only when the organization's highest authority insists upon or fails to address threatened or ongoing action that is clearly a violation of law, and then only to the extent the lawyer reasonably believes necessary to prevent reasonably certain substantial injury to the organization. It is not necessary that the lawyer's services be used in furtherance of the violation, but it is required that the matter be related to the lawyer's representation of the organization. If the lawyer's services are being used by an organization to further a crime or fraud by the organization, Rules 1.6(b)(2) and 1.6(b)(3) may permit the lawyer to disclose confidential information. In such circumstances Rule 1.2(d) may also be applicable, in which event, withdrawal from the representation under Rule 1.16(a)(1) may be required.

[7] Paragraph (d) makes clear that the authority of a lawyer to disclose information relating to a representation in circumstances described

in paragraph (c) does not apply with respect to information relating to a lawyer's engagement by an organization to investigate an alleged violation of law or to defend the organization or an officer, employee or other person associated with the organization against a claim arising out of an alleged violation of law. This is necessary in order to enable organizational clients to enjoy the full benefits of legal counsel in conducting an investigation or defending against a claim.

[8] A lawyer who reasonably believes that he or she has been discharged because of the lawyer's actions taken pursuant to paragraph (b) or (c), or who withdraws in circumstances that require or permit the lawyer to take action under either of these paragraphs, must proceed as the lawyer reasonably believes necessary to assure that the organization's highest authority is informed of the lawyer's discharge or withdrawal.

Government Agency

[9] The duty defined in this Rule applies to governmental organizations. Defining precisely the identity of the client and prescribing the resulting obligations of such lawyers may be more difficult in the government context and is a matter beyond the scope of these Rules. See Scope [18]. Although in some circumstances the client may be a specific agency, it may also be a branch of government, such as the executive branch, or the government as a whole. For example, if the action or failure to act involves the head of a bureau, either the department of which the bureau is a part or the relevant branch of government may be the client for purposes of this Rule. Moreover, in a matter involving the conduct of government officials, a government lawyer may have authority under applicable law to question such conduct more extensively than that of a lawyer for a private organization in similar circumstances. Thus, when the client is a governmental organization, a different balance may be appropriate between maintaining confidentiality and assuring that the wrongful act is prevented or rectified, for public business is involved. In addition, duties of lawyers employed by the government or lawyers in military service may be defined by statutes and regulation. This Rule does not limit that authority. See Scope.

Clarifying the Lawyer's Role

[10] There are times when the organization's interest may be or become adverse to those of one or more of its constituents. In such circumstances the lawyer should advise any constituent, whose interest the law-

yer finds adverse to that of the organization of the conflict or potential conflict of interest, that the lawyer cannot represent such constituent, and that such person may wish to obtain independent representation. Care must be taken to assure that the individual understands that, when there is such adversity of interest, the lawyer for the organization cannot provide legal representation for that constituent individual, and that discussions between the lawyer for the organization and the individual may not be privileged.

[11] Whether such a warning should be given by the lawyer for the organization to any constituent individual may turn on the facts of each case.

Dual Representation

[12] Paragraph (g) recognizes that a lawyer for an organization may also represent a principal officer or major shareholder.

Derivative Actions

[13] Under generally prevailing law, the shareholders or members of a corporation may bring suit to compel the directors to perform their legal obligations in the supervision of the organization. Members of unincorporated associations have essentially the same right. Such an action may be brought nominally by the organization, but usually is, in fact, a legal controversy over management of the organization.

[14] The question can arise whether counsel for the organization may defend such an action. The proposition that the organization is the lawyer's client does not alone resolve the issue. Most derivative actions are a normal incident of an organization's affairs, to be defended by the organization's lawyer like any other suit. However, if the claim involves serious charges of wrongdoing by those in control of the organization, a conflict may arise between the lawyer's duty to the organization and the lawyer's relationship with the board. In those circumstances, Rule 1.7 governs who should represent the directors and the organization.

Definitional Cross-References

"Knows" *See* Rule 1.0(f)
"Reasonably" *See* Rule 1.0(h)
"Reasonably believes" *See* Rule 1.0(i)
"Reasonably should know" *See* Rule 1.0(j)
"Substantial" *See* Rule 1.0(l)

RULE 1.14: CLIENT WITH DIMINISHED CAPACITY

(a) When a client's capacity to make adequately considered decisions in connection with a representation is diminished, whether because of minority, mental impairment or for some other reason, the lawyer shall, as far as reasonably possible, maintain a normal client-lawyer relationship with the client.

(b) When the lawyer reasonably believes that the client has diminished capacity, is at risk of substantial physical, financial or other harm unless action is taken and cannot adequately act in the client's own interest, the lawyer may take reasonably necessary protective action, including consulting with individuals or entities that have the ability to take action to protect the client and, in appropriate cases, seeking the appointment of a guardian ad litem, conservator or guardian.

(c) Information relating to the representation of a client with diminished capacity is protected by Rule 1.6. When taking protective action pursuant to paragraph (b), the lawyer is impliedly authorized under Rule 1.6(a) to reveal information about the client, but only to the extent reasonably necessary to protect the client's interests.

Comment

[1] The normal client-lawyer relationship is based on the assumption that the client, when properly advised and assisted, is capable of making decisions about important matters. When the client is a minor or suffers from a diminished mental capacity, however, maintaining the ordinary client-lawyer relationship may not be possible in all respects. In particular, a severely incapacitated person may have no power to make legally binding decisions. Nevertheless, a client with diminished capacity often has the ability to understand, deliberate upon, and reach conclusions about matters affecting the client's own well-being. For example, children as young as five or six years of age, and certainly those of ten or twelve, are regarded as having opinions that are entitled to weight in legal proceedings concerning their custody. So also, it is recognized that some persons of advanced age can be quite capable of handling routine financial matters while needing special legal protection concerning major transactions.

[2] The fact that a client suffers a disability does not diminish the

lawyer's obligation to treat the client with attention and respect. Even if the person has a legal representative, the lawyer should as far as possible accord the represented person the status of client, particularly in maintaining communication.

[3] The client may wish to have family members or other persons participate in discussions with the lawyer. When necessary to assist in the representation, the presence of such persons generally does not affect the applicability of the attorney-client evidentiary privilege. Nevertheless, the lawyer must keep the client's interests foremost and, except for protective action authorized under paragraph (b), must look to the client, and not family members, to make decisions on the client's behalf.

[4] If a legal representative has already been appointed for the client, the lawyer should ordinarily look to the representative for decisions on behalf of the client. In matters involving a minor, whether the lawyer should look to the parents as natural guardians may depend on the type of proceeding or matter in which the lawyer is representing the minor. If the lawyer represents the guardian as distinct from the ward, and is aware that the guardian is acting adversely to the ward's interest, the lawyer may have an obligation to prevent or rectify the guardian's misconduct. See Rule 1.2(d).

Taking Protective Action

[5] If a lawyer reasonably believes that a client is at risk of substantial physical, financial or other harm unless action is taken, and that a normal client-lawyer relationship cannot be maintained as provided in paragraph (a) because the client lacks sufficient capacity to communicate or to make adequately considered decisions in connection with the representation, then paragraph (b) permits the lawyer to take protective measures deemed necessary. Such measures could include: consulting with family members, using a reconsideration period to permit clarification or improvement of circumstances, using voluntary surrogate decisionmaking tools such as durable powers of attorney or consulting with support groups, professional services, adult-protective agencies or other individuals or entities that have the ability to protect the client. In taking any protective action, the lawyer should be guided by such factors as the wishes and values of the client to the extent known, the client's best interests and the goals of intruding into the client's decisionmaking autonomy to the least extent feasible, maximizing client capacities and respecting the client's family and social connections.

[6] In determining the extent of the client's diminished capacity, the lawyer should consider and balance such factors as: the client's ability to articulate reasoning leading to a decision, variability of state of mind and ability to appreciate consequences of a decision; the substantive fairness of a decision; and the consistency of a decision with the known long-term commitments and values of the client. In appropriate circumstances, the lawyer may seek guidance from an appropriate diagnostician.

[7] If a legal representative has not been appointed, the lawyer should consider whether appointment of a guardian ad litem, conservator or guardian is necessary to protect the client's interests. Thus, if a client with diminished capacity has substantial property that should be sold for the client's benefit, effective completion of the transaction may require appointment of a legal representative. In addition, rules of procedure in litigation sometimes provide that minors or persons with diminished capacity must be represented by a guardian or next friend if they do not have a general guardian. In many circumstances, however, appointment of a legal representative may be more expensive or traumatic for the client than circumstances in fact require. Evaluation of such circumstances is a matter entrusted to the professional judgment of the lawyer. In considering alternatives, however, the lawyer should be aware of any law that requires the lawyer to advocate the least restrictive action on behalf of the client.

Disclosure of the Client's Condition

[8] Disclosure of the client's diminished capacity could adversely affect the client's interests. For example, raising the question of diminished capacity could, in some circumstances, lead to proceedings for involuntary commitment. Information relating to the representation is protected by Rule 1.6. Therefore, unless authorized to do so, the lawyer may not disclose such information. When taking protective action pursuant to paragraph (b), the lawyer is impliedly authorized to make the necessary disclosures, even when the client directs the lawyer to the contrary. Nevertheless, given the risks of disclosure, paragraph (c) limits what the lawyer may disclose in consulting with other individuals or entities or seeking the appointment of a legal representative. At the very least, the lawyer should determine whether it is likely that the person or entity consulted with will act adversely to the client's interests before discussing matters related to the client. The lawyer's position in such cases is an unavoidably difficult one.

Emergency Legal Assistance

[9] In an emergency where the health, safety or a financial interest of a person with seriously diminished capacity is threatened with imminent and irreparable harm, a lawyer may take legal action on behalf of such a person even though the person is unable to establish a client-lawyer relationship or to make or express considered judgments about the matter, when the person or another acting in good faith on that person's behalf has consulted with the lawyer. Even in such an emergency, however, the lawyer should not act unless the lawyer reasonably believes that the person has no other lawyer, agent or other representative available. The lawyer should take legal action on behalf of the person only to the extent reasonably necessary to maintain the status quo or otherwise avoid imminent and irreparable harm. A lawyer who undertakes to represent a person in such an exigent situation has the same duties under these Rules as the lawyer would with respect to a client.

[10] A lawyer who acts on behalf of a person with seriously diminished capacity in an emergency should keep the confidences of the person as if dealing with a client, disclosing them only to the extent necessary to accomplish the intended protective action. The lawyer should disclose to any tribunal involved and to any other counsel involved the nature of his or her relationship with the person. The lawyer should take steps to regularize the relationship or implement other protective solutions as soon as possible. Normally, a lawyer would not seek compensation for such emergency actions taken.

Definitional Cross-References

"Reasonably" *See* Rule 1.0(h)
"Reasonably believes" *See* Rule 1.0(i)
"Substantial" *See* Rule 1.0(l)

RULE 1.15: SAFEKEEPING PROPERTY

(a) A lawyer shall hold property of clients or third persons that is in a lawyer's possession in connection with a representation separate from the lawyer's own property. Funds shall be kept in a separate account maintained in the state where the lawyer's office is situated, or elsewhere with the consent of the client or third person. Other property shall be identified as such and appropriately safeguarded. Complete records of such account funds and other property shall be kept by the lawyer and shall be preserved for a period of [five years] after termination of the representation.

(b) A lawyer may deposit the lawyer's own funds in a client trust account for the sole purpose of paying bank service charges on that account, but only in an amount necessary for that purpose.

(c) A lawyer shall deposit into a client trust account legal fees and expenses that have been paid in advance, to be withdrawn by the lawyer only as fees are earned or expenses incurred.

(d) Upon receiving funds or other property in which a client or third person has an interest, a lawyer shall promptly notify the client or third person. Except as stated in this Rule or otherwise permitted by law or by agreement with the client, a lawyer shall promptly deliver to the client or third person any funds or other property that the client or third person is entitled to receive and, upon request by the client or third person, shall promptly render a full accounting regarding such property.

(e) When in the course of representation a lawyer is in possession of property in which two or more persons (one of whom may be the lawyer) claim interests, the property shall be kept separate by the lawyer until the dispute is resolved. The lawyer shall promptly distribute all portions of the property as to which the interests are not in dispute.

Comment

[1] A lawyer should hold property of others with the care required of a professional fiduciary. Securities should be kept in a safe deposit box, except when some other form of safekeeping is warranted by special circumstances. All property that is the property of clients or third persons, including prospective clients, must be kept separate from the lawyer's business and personal property and, if monies, in one or more trust accounts. Separate trust accounts may be warranted when administering estate monies or acting in similar fiduciary capacities. A lawyer should maintain on a current basis books and records in accordance with generally accepted accounting practice and comply with any recordkeeping rules established by law or court order. See, e.g., ABA Model Rules for Client Trust Account Records.

[2] While normally it is impermissible to commingle the lawyer's own funds with client funds, paragraph (b) provides that it is permissible

when necessary to pay bank service charges on that account. Accurate records must be kept regarding which part of the funds are the lawyer's.

[3] Lawyers often receive funds from which the lawyer's fee will be paid. The lawyer is not required to remit to the client funds that the lawyer reasonably believes represent fees owed. However, a lawyer may not hold funds to coerce a client into accepting the lawyer's contention. The disputed portion of the funds must be kept in a trust account and the lawyer should suggest means for prompt resolution of the dispute, such as arbitration. The undisputed portion of the funds shall be promptly distributed.

[4] Paragraph (e) also recognizes that third parties may have lawful claims against specific funds or other property in a lawyer's custody, such as a client's creditor who has a lien on funds recovered in a personal injury action. A lawyer may have a duty under applicable law to protect such third-party claims against wrongful interference by the client. In such cases, when the third-party claim is not frivolous under applicable law, the lawyer must refuse to surrender the property to the client until the claims are resolved. A lawyer should not unilaterally assume to arbitrate a dispute between the client and the third party, but, when there are substantial grounds for dispute as to the person entitled to the funds, the lawyer may file an action to have a court resolve the dispute.

[5] The obligations of a lawyer under this Rule are independent of those arising from activity other than rendering legal services. For example, a lawyer who serves only as an escrow agent is governed by the applicable law relating to fiduciaries even though the lawyer does not render legal services in the transaction and is not governed by this Rule.

[6] A lawyers' fund for client protection provides a means through the collective efforts of the bar to reimburse persons who have lost money or property as a result of dishonest conduct of a lawyer. Where such a fund has been established, a lawyer must participate where it is mandatory, and, even when it is voluntary, the lawyer should participate.

RULE 1.16: DECLINING OR TERMINATING REPRESENTATION

(a) Except as stated in paragraph (c), a lawyer shall not represent a client or, where representation has commenced, shall withdraw from the representation of a client if:

(1) the representation will result in violation of the Rules of Professional Conduct or other law;

(2) the lawyer's physical or mental condition materially impairs the lawyer's ability to represent the client; or

(3) the lawyer is discharged.

(b) Except as stated in paragraph (c), a lawyer may withdraw from representing a client if:

(1) withdrawal can be accomplished without material adverse effect on the interests of the client;

(2) the client persists in a course of action involving the lawyer's services that the lawyer reasonably believes is criminal or fraudulent;

(3) the client has used the lawyer's services to perpetrate a crime or fraud;

(4) the client insists upon taking action that the lawyer considers repugnant or with which the lawyer has a fundamental disagreement;

(5) the client fails substantially to fulfill an obligation to the lawyer regarding the lawyer's services and has been given reasonable warning that the lawyer will withdraw unless the obligation is fulfilled;

(6) the representation will result in an unreasonable financial burden on the lawyer or has been rendered unreasonably difficult by the client; or

(7) other good cause for withdrawal exists.

(c) A lawyer must comply with applicable law requiring notice to or permission of a tribunal when terminating a representation. When ordered to do so by a tribunal, a lawyer shall continue representation notwithstanding good cause for terminating the representation.

(d) Upon termination of representation, a lawyer shall take steps to the extent reasonably practicable to protect a client's interests, such as giving reasonable notice to the client, allowing time for employment of other counsel, surrendering papers and property to which the client is entitled and refunding any advance payment of fee or expense that has not been earned or incurred. The lawyer may retain papers relating to the client to the extent permitted by other law.

Comment

[1] A lawyer should not accept representation in a matter unless it can be performed competently, promptly, without improper conflict of in-

terest and to completion. Ordinarily, a representation in a matter is completed when the agreed-upon assistance has been concluded. See Rules 1.2(c) and 6.5. See also Rule 1.3, Comment [4].

Mandatory Withdrawal

[2] A lawyer ordinarily must decline or withdraw from representation if the client demands that the lawyer engage in conduct that is illegal or violates the Rules of Professional Conduct or other law. The lawyer is not obliged to decline or withdraw simply because the client suggests such a course of conduct; a client may make such a suggestion in the hope that a lawyer will not be constrained by a professional obligation.

[3] When a lawyer has been appointed to represent a client, withdrawal ordinarily requires approval of the appointing authority. See also Rule 6.2. Similarly, court approval or notice to the court is often required by applicable law before a lawyer withdraws from pending litigation. Difficulty may be encountered if withdrawal is based on the client's demand that the lawyer engage in unprofessional conduct. The court may request an explanation for the withdrawal, while the lawyer may be bound to keep confidential the facts that would constitute such an explanation. The lawyer's statement that professional considerations require termination of the representation ordinarily should be accepted as sufficient. Lawyers should be mindful of their obligations to both clients and the court under Rules 1.6 and 3.3.

Discharge

[4] A client has a right to discharge a lawyer at any time, with or without cause, subject to liability for payment for the lawyer's services. Where future dispute about the withdrawal may be anticipated, it may be advisable to prepare a written statement reciting the circumstances.

[5] Whether a client can discharge appointed counsel may depend on applicable law. A client seeking to do so should be given a full explanation of the consequences. These consequences may include a decision by the appointing authority that appointment of successor counsel is unjustified, thus requiring self-representation by the client.

[6] If the client has severely diminished capacity, the client may lack the legal capacity to discharge the lawyer, and in any event the discharge may be seriously adverse to the client's interests. The lawyer should make special effort to help the client consider the consequences and may take reasonably necessary protective action as provided in Rule 1.14.

Optional Withdrawal

[7] A lawyer may withdraw from representation in some circumstances. The lawyer has the option to withdraw if it can be accomplished without material adverse effect on the client's interests. Withdrawal is also justified if the client persists in a course of action that the lawyer reasonably believes is criminal or fraudulent, for a lawyer is not required to be associated with such conduct even if the lawyer does not further it. Withdrawal is also permitted if the lawyer's services were misused in the past even if that would materially prejudice the client. The lawyer may also withdraw where the client insists on taking action that the lawyer considers repugnant or with which the lawyer has a fundamental disagreement.

[8] A lawyer may withdraw if the client refuses to abide by the terms of an agreement relating to the representation, such as an agreement concerning fees or court costs or an agreement limiting the objectives of the representation.

Assisting the Client upon Withdrawal

[9] Even if the lawyer has been unfairly discharged by the client, a lawyer must take all reasonable steps to mitigate the consequences to the client. The lawyer may retain papers as security for a fee only to the extent permitted by law. See Rule 1.15.

Definitional Cross-References

"Fraud" and "Fraudulent" *See* Rule 1.0(d)
"Reasonable" *See* Rule 1.0(h)
"Reasonably believes" *See* Rule 1.0(i)
"Tribunal" *See* Rule 1.0(m)

RULE 1.17: SALE OF
LAW PRACTICE

A lawyer or a law firm may sell or purchase a law practice, or an area of law practice, including good will, if the following conditions are satisfied:

(a) The seller ceases to engage in the private practice of law, or in the area of practice that has been sold, [in the geographic area] [in the jurisdiction] (a jurisdiction may elect either version) in which the practice has been conducted;

(b) The entire practice, or the entire area of practice, is sold to one or more lawyers or law firms;

(c) The seller gives written notice to each of the seller's clients regarding:

(1) the proposed sale;

(2) the client's right to retain other counsel or to take possession of the file; and

(3) the fact that the client's consent to the transfer of the client's files will be presumed if the client does not take any action or does not otherwise object within ninety (90) days of receipt of the notice.

If a client cannot be given notice, the representation of that client may be transferred to the purchaser only upon entry of an order so authorizing by a court having jurisdiction. The seller may disclose to the court in camera information relating to the representation only to the extent necessary to obtain an order authorizing the transfer of a file.

(d) The fees charged clients shall not be increased by reason of the sale.

Comment

[1] The practice of law is a profession, not merely a business. Clients are not commodities that can be purchased and sold at will. Pursuant to this Rule, when a lawyer or an entire firm ceases to practice, or ceases to practice in an area of law, and other lawyers or firms take over the representation, the selling lawyer or firm may obtain compensation for the reasonable value of the practice as may withdrawing partners of law firms. See Rules 5.4 and 5.6.

Termination of Practice by the Seller

[2] The requirement that all of the private practice, or all of an area of practice, be sold is satisfied if the seller in good faith makes the entire practice, or the area of practice, available for sale to the purchasers. The fact that a number of the seller's clients decide not to be represented by the purchasers but take their matters elsewhere, therefore, does not result in a violation. Return to private practice as a result of an unanticipated change in circumstances does not necessarily result in a violation. For example, a lawyer who has sold the practice to accept an appointment to judicial office does not violate the requirement that the sale be attendant

to cessation of practice if the lawyer later resumes private practice upon being defeated in a contested or a retention election for the office or resigns from a judiciary position.

[3] The requirement that the seller cease to engage in the private practice of law does not prohibit employment as a lawyer on the staff of a public agency or a legal services entity that provides legal services to the poor, or as in-house counsel to a business.

[4] The Rule permits a sale of an entire practice attendant upon retirement from the private practice of law within the jurisdiction. Its provisions, therefore, accommodate the lawyer who sells the practice on the occasion of moving to another state. Some states are so large that a move from one locale therein to another is tantamount to leaving the jurisdiction in which the lawyer has engaged in the practice of law. To also accommodate lawyers so situated, states may permit the sale of the practice when the lawyer leaves the geographical area rather than the jurisdiction. The alternative desired should be indicated by selecting one of the two provided for in Rule 1.17(a).

[5] This Rule also permits a lawyer or law firm to sell an area of practice. If an area of practice is sold and the lawyer remains in the active practice of law, the lawyer must cease accepting any matters in the area of practice that has been sold, either as counsel or co-counsel or by assuming joint responsibility for a matter in connection with the division of a fee with another lawyer as would otherwise be permitted by Rule 1.5(e). For example, a lawyer with a substantial number of estate planning matters and a substantial number of probate administration cases may sell the estate planning portion of the practice but remain in the practice of law by concentrating on probate administration; however, that practitioner may not thereafter accept any estate planning matters. Although a lawyer who leaves a jurisdiction or geographical area typically would sell the entire practice, this Rule permits the lawyer to limit the sale to one or more areas of the practice, thereby preserving the lawyer's right to continue practice in the areas of the practice that were not sold.

Sale of Entire Practice or Entire Area of Practice

[6] The Rule requires that the seller's entire practice, or an entire area of practice, be sold. The prohibition against sale of less than an entire practice area protects those clients whose matters are less lucrative and who might find it difficult to secure other counsel if a sale could be lim-

ited to substantial fee-generating matters. The purchasers are required to undertake all client matters in the practice or practice area, subject to client consent. This requirement is satisfied, however, even if a purchaser is unable to undertake a particular client matter because of a conflict of interest.

Client Confidences, Consent and Notice

[7] Negotiations between seller and prospective purchaser prior to disclosure of information relating to a specific representation of an identifiable client no more violate the confidentiality provisions of Model Rule 1.6 than do preliminary discussions concerning the possible association of another lawyer or mergers between firms, with respect to which client consent is not required. See Rule 1.6(b)(7). Providing the purchaser access to detailed information relating to the representation, such as the client's file, however, requires client consent. The Rule provides that before such information can be disclosed by the seller to the purchaser the client must be given actual written notice of the contemplated sale, including the identity of the purchaser, and must be told that the decision to consent or make other arrangements must be made within 90 days. If nothing is heard from the client within that time, consent to the sale is presumed.

[8] A lawyer or law firm ceasing to practice cannot be required to remain in practice because some clients cannot be given actual notice of the proposed purchase. Since these clients cannot themselves consent to the purchase or direct any other disposition of their files, the Rule requires an order from a court having jurisdiction authorizing their transfer or other disposition. The court can be expected to determine whether reasonable efforts to locate the client have been exhausted, and whether the absent client's legitimate interests will be served by authorizing the transfer of the file so that the purchaser may continue the representation. Preservation of client confidences requires that the petition for a court order be considered in camera. (A procedure by which such an order can be obtained needs to be established in jurisdictions in which it presently does not exist).

[9] All elements of client autonomy, including the client's absolute right to discharge a lawyer and transfer the representation to another, survive the sale of the practice or area of practice.

Fee Arrangements Between Client and Purchaser

[10] The sale may not be financed by increases in fees charged the clients of the practice. Existing arrangements between the seller and the client as to fees and the scope of the work must be honored by the purchaser.

Other Applicable Ethical Standards

[11] Lawyers participating in the sale of a law practice or a practice area are subject to the ethical standards applicable to involving another lawyer in the representation of a client. These include, for example, the seller's obligation to exercise competence in identifying a purchaser qualified to assume the practice and the purchaser's obligation to undertake the representation competently (see Rule 1.1); the obligation to avoid disqualifying conflicts, and to secure the client's informed consent for those conflicts that can be agreed to (see Rule 1.7 regarding conflicts and Rule 1.0(e) for the definition of informed consent); and the obligation to protect information relating to the representation (see Rules 1.6 and 1.9).

[12] If approval of the substitution of the purchasing lawyer for the selling lawyer is required by the rules of any tribunal in which a matter is pending, such approval must be obtained before the matter can be included in the sale (see Rule 1.16).

Applicability of the Rule

[13] This Rule applies to the sale of a law practice of a deceased, disabled or disappeared lawyer. Thus, the seller may be represented by a non-lawyer representative not subject to these Rules. Since, however, no lawyer may participate in a sale of a law practice which does not conform to the requirements of this Rule, the representatives of the seller as well as the purchasing lawyer can be expected to see to it that they are met.

[14] Admission to or retirement from a law partnership or professional association, retirement plans and similar arrangements, and a sale of tangible assets of a law practice, do not constitute a sale or purchase governed by this Rule.

[15] This Rule does not apply to the transfers of legal representation between lawyers when such transfers are unrelated to the sale of a practice or an area of practice.

Definitional Cross-References

"Law firm" *See* Rule 1.0(c)

"Written" *See* Rule 1.0(n)

RULE 1.18: DUTIES TO PROSPECTIVE CLIENT

(a) A person who consults with a lawyer about the possibility of forming a client-lawyer relationship with respect to a matter is a prospective client.

(b) Even when no client-lawyer relationship ensues, a lawyer who has learned information from a prospective client shall not use or reveal that information, except as Rule 1.9 would permit with respect to information of a former client.

(c) A lawyer subject to paragraph (b) shall not represent a client with interests materially adverse to those of a prospective client in the same or a substantially related matter if the lawyer received information from the prospective client that could be significantly harmful to that person in the matter, except as provided in paragraph (d). If a lawyer is disqualified from representation under this paragraph, no lawyer in a firm with which that lawyer is associated may knowingly undertake or continue representation in such a matter, except as provided in paragraph (d).

(d) When the lawyer has received disqualifying information as defined in paragraph (c), representation is permissible if:

(1) both the affected client and the prospective client have given informed consent, confirmed in writing; or:

(2) the lawyer who received the information took reasonable measures to avoid exposure to more disqualifying information than was reasonably necessary to determine whether to represent the prospective client; and

(i) the disqualified lawyer is timely screened from any participation in the matter and is apportioned no part of the fee therefrom; and

(ii) written notice is promptly given to the prospective client.

Comment

[1] Prospective clients, like clients, may disclose information to a lawyer, place documents or other property in the lawyer's custody, or rely on the lawyer's advice. A lawyer's consultations with a prospective client usually are limited in time and depth and leave both the prospective client and the lawyer free (and sometimes required) to proceed no further. Hence, prospective clients should receive some but not all of the protection afforded clients.

[2] A person becomes a prospective client by consulting with a lawyer about the possibility of forming a client-lawyer relationship with respect to a matter. Whether communications, including written, oral, or electronic communications, constitute a consultation depends on the circumstances. For example, a consultation is likely to have occurred if a lawyer, either in person or through the lawyer's advertising in any medium, specifically requests or invites the submission of information about a potential representation without clear and reasonably understandable warnings and cautionary statements that limit the lawyer's obligations, and a person provides information in response. See also Comment [4]. In contrast, a consultation does not occur if a person provides information to a lawyer in response to advertising that merely describes the lawyer's education, experience, areas of practice, and contact information, or provides legal information of general interest. Such a person communicates information unilaterally to a lawyer, without any reasonable expectation that the lawyer is willing to discuss the possibility of forming a client-lawyer relationship, and is thus not a "prospective client." Moreover, a person who communicates with a lawyer for the purpose of disqualifying the lawyer is not a "prospective client."

[3] It is often necessary for a prospective client to reveal information to the lawyer during an initial consultation prior to the decision about formation of a client-lawyer relationship. The lawyer often must learn such information to determine whether there is a conflict of interest with an existing client and whether the matter is one that the lawyer is willing to undertake. Paragraph (b) prohibits the lawyer from using or revealing that information, except as permitted by Rule 1.9, even if the client or lawyer decides not to proceed with the representation. The duty exists regardless of how brief the initial conference may be.

[4] In order to avoid acquiring disqualifying information from a prospective client, a lawyer considering whether or not to undertake a new matter should limit the initial consultation to only such information as reasonably appears necessary for that purpose. Where the information indicates that a conflict of interest or other reason for non-representation exists, the lawyer should so inform the prospective client or decline the representation. If the prospective client wishes to retain the lawyer, and if consent is possible under Rule 1.7, then consent from all affected present or former clients must be obtained before accepting the representation.

[5] A lawyer may condition a consultation with a prospective client on the person's informed consent that no information disclosed during

the consultation will prohibit the lawyer from representing a different client in the matter. See Rule 1.0(e) for the definition of informed consent. If the agreement expressly so provides, the prospective client may also consent to the lawyer's subsequent use of information received from the prospective client.

[6] Even in the absence of an agreement, under paragraph (c), the lawyer is not prohibited from representing a client with interests adverse to those of the prospective client in the same or a substantially related matter unless the lawyer has received from the prospective client information that could be significantly harmful if used in the matter.

[7] Under paragraph (c), the prohibition in this Rule is imputed to other lawyers as provided in Rule 1.10, but, under paragraph (d)(1), imputation may be avoided if the lawyer obtains the informed consent, confirmed in writing, of both the prospective and affected clients. In the alternative, imputation may be avoided if the conditions of paragraph (d)(2) are met and all disqualified lawyers are timely screened and written notice is promptly given to the prospective client. See Rule 1.0(k) (requirements for screening procedures). Paragraph (d)(2)(i) does not prohibit the screened lawyer from receiving a salary or partnership share established by prior independent agreement, but that lawyer may not receive compensation directly related to the matter in which the lawyer is disqualified.

[8] Notice, including a general description of the subject matter about which the lawyer was consulted, and of the screening procedures employed, generally should be given as soon as practicable after the need for screening becomes apparent.

[9] For the duty of competence of a lawyer who gives assistance on the merits of a matter to a prospective client, see Rule 1.1. For a lawyer's duties when a prospective client entrusts valuables or papers to the lawyer's care, see Rule 1.15.

Definitional Cross-References

"Confirmed in writing" *See* Rule 1.0(b)
"Firm" *See* Rule 1.0(c)
"Informed consent" *See* Rule 1.0(e)
"Knowingly" *See* Rule 1.0(f)
"Reasonable" and "Reasonably" *See* Rule 1.0(h)
"Screened" *See* Rule 1.0(k)
"Written" *See* Rule 1.0(n)

COUNSELOR

RULE 2.1: ADVISOR

In representing a client, a lawyer shall exercise
independent professional judgment and render candid advice.
In rendering advice, a lawyer may refer not only to law but
to other considerations such as moral, economic, social and
political factors, that may be relevant to the client's situation.

Comment

Scope of Advice

[1] A client is entitled to straightforward advice expressing the lawyer's honest assessment. Legal advice often involves unpleasant facts and alternatives that a client may be disinclined to confront. In presenting advice, a lawyer endeavors to sustain the client's morale and may put advice in as acceptable a form as honesty permits. However, a lawyer should not be deterred from giving candid advice by the prospect that the advice will be unpalatable to the client.

[2] Advice couched in narrow legal terms may be of little value to a client, especially where practical considerations, such as cost or effects on other people, are predominant. Purely technical legal advice, therefore, can sometimes be inadequate. It is proper for a lawyer to refer to relevant moral and ethical considerations in giving advice. Although a lawyer is not a moral advisor as such, moral and ethical considerations impinge upon most legal questions and may decisively influence how the law will be applied.

[3] A client may expressly or impliedly ask the lawyer for purely technical advice. When such a request is made by a client experienced in legal matters, the lawyer may accept it at face value. When such a request is made by a client inexperienced in legal matters, however, the lawyer's responsibility as advisor may include indicating that more may be involved than strictly legal considerations.

[4] Matters that go beyond strictly legal questions may also be in the domain of another profession. Family matters can involve problems within the professional competence of psychiatry, clinical psychology or social work; business matters can involve problems within the competence of the accounting profession or of financial specialists. Where consultation with a professional in another field is itself something a

competent lawyer would recommend, the lawyer should make such a recommendation. At the same time, a lawyer's advice at its best often consists of recommending a course of action in the face of conflicting recommendations of experts.

Offering Advice

[5] In general, a lawyer is not expected to give advice until asked by the client. However, when a lawyer knows that a client proposes a course of action that is likely to result in substantial adverse legal consequences to the client, the lawyer's duty to the client under Rule 1.4 may require that the lawyer offer advice if the client's course of action is related to the representation. Similarly, when a matter is likely to involve litigation, it may be necessary under Rule 1.4 to inform the client of forms of dispute resolution that might constitute reasonable alternatives to litigation. A lawyer ordinarily has no duty to initiate investigation of a client's affairs or to give advice that the client has indicated is unwanted, but a lawyer may initiate advice to a client when doing so appears to be in the client's interest.

RULE 2.2 (DELETED 2002)

RULE 2.3: EVALUATION FOR USE BY THIRD PERSONS

(a) A lawyer may provide an evaluation of a matter affecting a client for the use of someone other than the client if the lawyer reasonably believes that making the evaluation is compatible with other aspects of the lawyer's relationship with the client.

(b) When the lawyer knows or reasonably should know that the evaluation is likely to affect the client's interests materially and adversely, the lawyer shall not provide the evaluation unless the client gives informed consent.

(c) Except as disclosure is authorized in connection with a report of an evaluation, information relating to the evaluation is otherwise protected by Rule 1.6.

Comment
Definition

[1] An evaluation may be performed at the client's direction or when impliedly authorized in order to carry out the representation. See Rule 1.2. Such an evaluation may be for the primary purpose of establishing information for the benefit of third parties; for example, an opinion concerning the title of property rendered at the behest of a vendor for the information of a prospective purchaser, or at the behest of a borrower for the information of a prospective lender. In some situations, the evaluation may be required by a government agency; for example, an opinion concerning the legality of the securities registered for sale under the securities laws. In other instances, the evaluation may be required by a third person, such as a purchaser of a business.

[2] A legal evaluation should be distinguished from an investigation of a person with whom the lawyer does not have a client-lawyer relationship. For example, a lawyer retained by a purchaser to analyze a vendor's title to property does not have a client-lawyer relationship with the vendor. So also, an investigation into a person's affairs by a government lawyer or by special counsel employed by the government, is not an evaluation as that term is used in this Rule. The question is whether the lawyer is retained by the person whose affairs are being examined. When the lawyer is retained by that person, the general rules concerning loyalty to client and preservation of confidences apply, which is not the case if the lawyer is retained by someone else. For this reason, it is essential to identify the person by whom the lawyer is retained. This should be made clear not only to the person under examination, but also to others to whom the results are to be made available.

Duties Owed to Third Person and Client

[3] When the evaluation is intended for the information or use of a third person, a legal duty to that person may or may not arise. That legal question is beyond the scope of this Rule. However, since such an evaluation involves a departure from the normal client-lawyer relationship, careful analysis of the situation is required. The lawyer must be satisfied as a matter of professional judgment that making the evaluation is compatible with other functions undertaken in behalf of the client. For example, if the lawyer is acting as advocate in defending the client against charges of fraud, it would normally be incompatible with that responsi-

bility for the lawyer to perform an evaluation for others concerning the same or a related transaction. Assuming no such impediment is apparent, however, the lawyer should advise the client of the implications of the evaluation, particularly the lawyer's responsibilities to third persons and the duty to disseminate the findings.

Access to and Disclosure of Information

[4] The quality of an evaluation depends on the freedom and extent of the investigation upon which it is based. Ordinarily a lawyer should have whatever latitude of investigation seems necessary as a matter of professional judgment. Under some circumstances, however, the terms of the evaluation may be limited. For example, certain issues or sources may be categorically excluded, or the scope of search may be limited by time constraints or the noncooperation of persons having relevant information. Any such limitations that are material to the evaluation should be described in the report. If after a lawyer has commenced an evaluation, the client refuses to comply with the terms upon which it was understood the evaluation was to have been made, the lawyer's obligations are determined by law, having reference to the terms of the client's agreement and the surrounding circumstances. In no circumstances is the lawyer permitted to knowingly make a false statement of material fact or law in providing an evaluation under this Rule. See Rule 4.1.

Obtaining Client's Informed Consent

[5] Information relating to an evaluation is protected by Rule 1.6. In many situations, providing an evaluation to a third party poses no significant risk to the client; thus, the lawyer may be impliedly authorized to disclose information to carry out the representation. See Rule 1.6(a). Where, however, it is reasonably likely that providing the evaluation will affect the client's interests materially and adversely, the lawyer must first obtain the client's consent after the client has been adequately informed concerning the important possible effects on the client's interests. See Rules 1.6(a) and 1.0(e).

Financial Auditors' Requests for Information

[6] When a question concerning the legal situation of a client arises at the instance of the client's financial auditor and the question is referred to the lawyer, the lawyer's response may be made in accordance with procedures recognized in the legal profession. Such a procedure is set forth

in the American Bar Association Statement of Policy Regarding Lawyers' Responses to Auditors' Requests for Information, adopted in 1975.

Definitional Cross-References

"Informed consent" *See* Rule 1.0(e)
"Knows" *See* Rule 1.0(f)
"Reasonably believes" *See* Rule 1.0(i)
"Reasonably should know" *See* Rule 1.0(j)

RULE 2.4: LAWYER SERVING AS THIRD-PARTY NEUTRAL

(a) A lawyer serves as a third-party neutral when the lawyer assists two or more persons who are not clients of the lawyer to reach a resolution of a dispute or other matter that has arisen between them. Service as a third-party neutral may include service as an arbitrator, a mediator or in such other capacity as will enable the lawyer to assist the parties to resolve the matter.

(b) A lawyer serving as a third-party neutral shall inform unrepresented parties that the lawyer is not representing them. When the lawyer knows or reasonably should know that a party does not understand the lawyer's role in the matter, the lawyer shall explain the difference between the lawyer's role as a third-party neutral and a lawyer's role as one who represents a client.

Comment

[1] Alternative dispute resolution has become a substantial part of the civil justice system. Aside from representing clients in dispute-resolution processes, lawyers often serve as third-party neutrals. A third-party neutral is a person, such as a mediator, arbitrator, conciliator or evaluator, who assists the parties, represented or unrepresented, in the resolution of a dispute or in the arrangement of a transaction. Whether a third-party neutral serves primarily as a facilitator, evaluator or decisionmaker depends on the particular process that is either selected by the parties or mandated by a court.

[2] The role of a third-party neutral is not unique to lawyers, although, in some court-connected contexts, only lawyers are allowed to serve in this role or to handle certain types of cases. In performing this role, the lawyer may be subject to court rules or other law that apply ei-

ther to third-party neutrals generally or to lawyers serving as third-party neutrals. Lawyer-neutrals may also be subject to various codes of ethics, such as the Code of Ethics for Arbitrators in Commercial Disputes prepared by a joint committee of the American Bar Association and the American Arbitration Association or the Model Standards of Conduct for Mediators jointly prepared by the American Bar Association, the American Arbitration Association and the Society of Professionals in Dispute Resolution.

[3] Unlike nonlawyers who serve as third-party neutrals, lawyers serving in this role may experience unique problems as a result of differences between the role of a third-party neutral and a lawyer's service as a client representative. The potential for confusion is significant when the parties are unrepresented in the process. Thus, paragraph (b) requires a lawyer-neutral to inform unrepresented parties that the lawyer is not representing them. For some parties, particularly parties who frequently use dispute-resolution processes, this information will be sufficient. For others, particularly those who are using the process for the first time, more information will be required. Where appropriate, the lawyer should inform unrepresented parties of the important differences between the lawyer's role as third-party neutral and a lawyer's role as a client representative, including the inapplicability of the attorney-client evidentiary privilege. The extent of disclosure required under this paragraph will depend on the particular parties involved and the subject matter of the proceeding, as well as the particular features of the dispute-resolution process selected.

[4] A lawyer who serves as a third-party neutral subsequently may be asked to serve as a lawyer representing a client in the same matter. The conflicts of interest that arise for both the individual lawyer and the lawyer's law firm are addressed in Rule 1.12.

[5] Lawyers who represent clients in alternative dispute-resolution processes are governed by the Rules of Professional Conduct. When the dispute-resolution process takes place before a tribunal, as in binding arbitration (see Rule 1.0(m)), the lawyer's duty of candor is governed by Rule 3.3. Otherwise, the lawyer's duty of candor toward both the third-party neutral and other parties is governed by Rule 4.1.

Definitional Cross-References

"Knows" *See* Rule 1.0(f)
"Reasonably should know" *See* Rule 1.0(j)

ADVOCATE

RULE 3.1: MERITORIOUS
CLAIMS AND CONTENTIONS

A lawyer shall not bring or defend a proceeding, or assert
or controvert an issue therein, unless there is a basis in law and
fact for doing so that is not frivolous, which includes a good faith
argument for an extension, modification or reversal of existing
law. A lawyer for the defendant in a criminal proceeding, or the
respondent in a proceeding that could result in incarceration,
may nevertheless so defend the proceeding as to require that
every element of the case be established.

Comment

[1] The advocate has a duty to use legal procedure for the fullest
benefit of the client's cause, but also a duty not to abuse legal procedure.
The law, both procedural and substantive, establishes the limits within
which an advocate may proceed. However, the law is not always clear
and never is static. Accordingly, in determining the proper scope of advocacy, account must be taken of the law's ambiguities and potential for
change.

[2] The filing of an action or defense or similar action taken for a client is not frivolous merely because the facts have not first been fully substantiated or because the lawyer expects to develop vital evidence only
by discovery. What is required of lawyers, however, is that they inform
themselves about the facts of their clients' cases and the applicable law
and determine that they can make good faith arguments in support of
their clients' positions. Such action is not frivolous even though the lawyer believes that the client's position ultimately will not prevail. The action is frivolous, however, if the lawyer is unable either to make a good
faith argument on the merits of the action taken or to support the action
taken by a good faith argument for an extension, modification or reversal
of existing law.

[3] The lawyer's obligations under this Rule are subordinate to federal or state constitutional law that entitles a defendant in a criminal matter to the assistance of counsel in presenting a claim or contention that
otherwise would be prohibited by this Rule.

RULE 3.2: EXPEDITING LITIGATION

A lawyer shall make reasonable efforts to expedite litigation consistent with the interests of the client.

Comment

[1] Dilatory practices bring the administration of justice into disrepute. Although there will be occasions when a lawyer may properly seek a postponement for personal reasons, it is not proper for a lawyer to routinely fail to expedite litigation solely for the convenience of the advocates. Nor will a failure to expedite be reasonable if done for the purpose of frustrating an opposing party's attempt to obtain rightful redress or repose. It is not a justification that similar conduct is often tolerated by the bench and bar. The question is whether a competent lawyer acting in good faith would regard the course of action as having some substantial purpose other than delay. Realizing financial or other benefit from otherwise improper delay in litigation is not a legitimate interest of the client.

Definitional Cross-References

"Reasonable" *See* Rule 1.0(h)

RULE 3.3: CANDOR TOWARD THE TRIBUNAL

(a) A lawyer shall not knowingly:

(1) make a false statement of fact or law to a tribunal or fail to correct a false statement of material fact or law previously made to the tribunal by the lawyer;

(2) fail to disclose to the tribunal legal authority in the controlling jurisdiction known to the lawyer to be directly adverse to the position of the client and not disclosed by opposing counsel; or

(3) offer evidence that the lawyer knows to be false. If a lawyer, the lawyer's client, or a witness called by the lawyer, has offered material evidence and the lawyer comes to know of its falsity, the lawyer shall take reasonable remedial measures, including, if necessary, disclosure to the tribunal. A lawyer may refuse to offer evidence, other than the testimony of a defendant in a criminal matter, that the lawyer reasonably believes is false.

(b) A lawyer who represents a client in an adjudicative
proceeding and who knows that a person intends to engage,
is engaging or has engaged in criminal or fraudulent conduct
related to the proceeding shall take reasonable remedial
measures, including, if necessary, disclosure to the tribunal.

(c) The duties stated in paragraphs (a) and (b) continue to
the conclusion of the proceeding, and apply even if compliance
requires disclosure of information otherwise protected by Rule 1.6.

(d) In an ex parte proceeding, a lawyer shall inform the
tribunal of all material facts known to the lawyer that will
enable the tribunal to make an informed decision, whether
or not the facts are adverse.

Comment

[1] This Rule governs the conduct of a lawyer who is representing
a client in the proceedings of a tribunal. See Rule 1.0(m) for the definition of "tribunal." It also applies when the lawyer is representing a client
in an ancillary proceeding conducted pursuant to the tribunal's adjudicative authority, such as a deposition. Thus, for example, paragraph (a)
(3) requires a lawyer to take reasonable remedial measures if the lawyer
comes to know that a client who is testifying in a deposition has offered
evidence that is false.

[2] This Rule sets forth the special duties of lawyers as officers of the
court to avoid conduct that undermines the integrity of the adjudicative
process. A lawyer acting as an advocate in an adjudicative proceeding
has an obligation to present the client's case with persuasive force. Performance of that duty while maintaining confidences of the client, however, is qualified by the advocate's duty of candor to the tribunal. Consequently, although a lawyer in an adversary proceeding is not required to
present an impartial exposition of the law or to vouch for the evidence
submitted in a cause, the lawyer must not allow the tribunal to be misled
by false statements of law or fact or evidence that the lawyer knows to be
false.

Representations by a Lawyer

[3] An advocate is responsible for pleadings and other documents
prepared for litigation, but is usually not required to have personal
knowledge of matters asserted therein, for litigation documents ordinarily present assertions by the client, or by someone on the client's behalf,

and not assertions by the lawyer. Compare Rule 3.1. However, an assertion purporting to be on the lawyer's own knowledge, as in an affidavit by the lawyer or in a statement in open court, may properly be made only when the lawyer knows the assertion is true or believes it to be true on the basis of a reasonably diligent inquiry. There are circumstances where failure to make a disclosure is the equivalent of an affirmative misrepresentation. The obligation prescribed in Rule 1.2(d) not to counsel a client to commit or assist the client in committing a fraud applies in litigation. Regarding compliance with Rule 1.2(d), see the Comment to that Rule. See also the Comment to Rule 8.4(b).

Legal Argument

[4] Legal argument based on a knowingly false representation of law constitutes dishonesty toward the tribunal. A lawyer is not required to make a disinterested exposition of the law, but must recognize the existence of pertinent legal authorities. Furthermore, as stated in paragraph (a)(2), an advocate has a duty to disclose directly adverse authority in the controlling jurisdiction that has not been disclosed by the opposing party. The underlying concept is that legal argument is a discussion seeking to determine the legal premises properly applicable to the case.

Offering Evidence

[5] Paragraph (a)(3) requires that the lawyer refuse to offer evidence that the lawyer knows to be false, regardless of the client's wishes. This duty is premised on the lawyer's obligation as an officer of the court to prevent the trier of fact from being misled by false evidence. A lawyer does not violate this Rule if the lawyer offers the evidence for the purpose of establishing its falsity.

[6] If a lawyer knows that the client intends to testify falsely or wants the lawyer to introduce false evidence, the lawyer should seek to persuade the client that the evidence should not be offered. If the persuasion is ineffective and the lawyer continues to represent the client, the lawyer must refuse to offer the false evidence. If only a portion of a witness's testimony will be false, the lawyer may call the witness to testify but may not elicit or otherwise permit the witness to present the testimony that the lawyer knows is false.

[7] The duties stated in paragraphs (a) and (b) apply to all lawyers, including defense counsel in criminal cases. In some jurisdictions, however, courts have required counsel to present the accused as a witness

or to give a narrative statement if the accused so desires, even if counsel knows that the testimony or statement will be false. The obligation of the advocate under the Rules of Professional Conduct is subordinate to such requirements. See also Comment [9].

[8] The prohibition against offering false evidence only applies if the lawyer knows that the evidence is false. A lawyer's reasonable belief that evidence is false does not preclude its presentation to the trier of fact. A lawyer's knowledge that evidence is false, however, can be inferred from the circumstances. See Rule 1.0(f). Thus, although a lawyer should resolve doubts about the veracity of testimony or other evidence in favor of the client, the lawyer cannot ignore an obvious falsehood.

[9] Although paragraph (a)(3) only prohibits a lawyer from offering evidence the lawyer knows to be false, it permits the lawyer to refuse to offer testimony or other proof that the lawyer reasonably believes is false. Offering such proof may reflect adversely on the lawyer's ability to discriminate in the quality of evidence and thus impair the lawyer's effectiveness as an advocate. Because of the special protections historically provided criminal defendants, however, this Rule does not permit a lawyer to refuse to offer the testimony of such a client where the lawyer reasonably believes but does not know that the testimony will be false. Unless the lawyer knows the testimony will be false, the lawyer must honor the client's decision to testify. See also Comment [7].

Remedial Measures

[10] Having offered material evidence in the belief that it was true, a lawyer may subsequently come to know that the evidence is false. Or, a lawyer may be surprised when the lawyer's client, or another witness called by the lawyer, offers testimony the lawyer knows to be false, either during the lawyer's direct examination or in response to cross-examination by the opposing lawyer. In such situations or if the lawyer knows of the falsity of testimony elicited from the client during a deposition, the lawyer must take reasonable remedial measures. In such situations, the advocate's proper course is to remonstrate with the client confidentially, advise the client of the lawyer's duty of candor to the tribunal and seek the client's cooperation with respect to the withdrawal or correction of the false statements or evidence. If that fails, the advocate must take further remedial action. If withdrawal from the representation is not permitted or will not undo the effect of the false evidence, the advocate must make such disclosure to the tribunal as is reasonably necessary to remedy

the situation, even if doing so requires the lawyer to reveal information that otherwise would be protected by Rule 1.6. It is for the tribunal then to determine what should be done—making a statement about the matter to the trier of fact, ordering a mistrial or perhaps nothing.

[11] The disclosure of a client's false testimony can result in grave consequences to the client, including not only a sense of betrayal but also loss of the case and perhaps a prosecution for perjury. But the alternative is that the lawyer cooperate in deceiving the court, thereby subverting the truth-finding process which the adversary system is designed to implement. See Rule 1.2(d). Furthermore, unless it is clearly understood that the lawyer will act upon the duty to disclose the existence of false evidence, the client can simply reject the lawyer's advice to reveal the false evidence and insist that the lawyer keep silent. Thus the client could in effect coerce the lawyer into being a party to fraud on the court.

Preserving Integrity of Adjudicative Process

[12] Lawyers have a special obligation to protect a tribunal against criminal or fraudulent conduct that undermines the integrity of the adjudicative process, such as bribing, intimidating or otherwise unlawfully communicating with a witness, juror, court official or other participant in the proceeding, unlawfully destroying or concealing documents or other evidence or failing to disclose information to the tribunal when required by law to do so. Thus, paragraph (b) requires a lawyer to take reasonable remedial measures, including disclosure if necessary, whenever the lawyer knows that a person, including the lawyer's client, intends to engage, is engaging or has engaged in criminal or fraudulent conduct related to the proceeding.

Duration of Obligation

[13] A practical time limit on the obligation to rectify false evidence or false statements of law and fact has to be established. The conclusion of the proceeding is a reasonably definite point for the termination of the obligation. A proceeding has concluded within the meaning of this Rule when a final judgment in the proceeding has been affirmed on appeal or the time for review has passed.

Ex Parte Proceedings

[14] Ordinarily, an advocate has the limited responsibility of presenting one side of the matters that a tribunal should consider in reaching a

decision; the conflicting position is expected to be presented by the opposing party. However, in any ex parte proceeding, such as an application for a temporary restraining order, there is no balance of presentation by opposing advocates. The object of an ex parte proceeding is nevertheless to yield a substantially just result. The judge has an affirmative responsibility to accord the absent party just consideration. The lawyer for the represented party has the correlative duty to make disclosures of material facts known to the lawyer and that the lawyer reasonably believes are necessary to an informed decision.

Withdrawal

[15] Normally, a lawyer's compliance with the duty of candor imposed by this Rule does not require that the lawyer withdraw from the representation of a client whose interests will be or have been adversely affected by the lawyer's disclosure. The lawyer may, however, be required by Rule 1.16(a) to seek permission of the tribunal to withdraw if the lawyer's compliance with this Rule's duty of candor results in such an extreme deterioration of the client-lawyer relationship that the lawyer can no longer competently represent the client. Also see Rule 1.16(b) for the circumstances in which a lawyer will be permitted to seek a tribunal's permission to withdraw. In connection with a request for permission to withdraw that is premised on a client's misconduct, a lawyer may reveal information relating to the representation only to the extent reasonably necessary to comply with this Rule or as otherwise permitted by Rule 1.6.

Definitional Cross-References

"Fraudulent" *See* Rule 1.0(d)
"Knowingly" and "Known" and "Knows" *See* Rule 1.0(f)
"Reasonable" *See* Rule 1.0(h)
"Reasonably believes" *See* Rule 1.0(i)
"Tribunal" *See* Rule 1.0(m)

RULE 3.4: FAIRNESS TO OPPOSING PARTY AND COUNSEL

A lawyer shall not:
(a) unlawfully obstruct another party's access to evidence or unlawfully alter, destroy or conceal a document or other material

having potential evidentiary value. A lawyer shall not counsel or assist another person to do any such act;

(b) falsify evidence, counsel or assist a witness to testify falsely, or offer an inducement to a witness that is prohibited by law;

(c) knowingly disobey an obligation under the rules of a tribunal, except for an open refusal based on an assertion that no valid obligation exists;

(d) in pretrial procedure, make a frivolous discovery request or fail to make reasonably diligent effort to comply with a legally proper discovery request by an opposing party;

(e) in trial, allude to any matter that the lawyer does not reasonably believe is relevant or that will not be supported by admissible evidence, assert personal knowledge of facts in issue except when testifying as a witness, or state a personal opinion as to the justness of a cause, the credibility of a witness, the culpability of a civil litigant or the guilt or innocence of an accused; or

(f) request a person other than a client to refrain from voluntarily giving relevant information to another party unless:

(1) the person is a relative or an employee or other agent of a client; and

(2) the lawyer reasonably believes that the person's interests will not be adversely affected by refraining from giving such information.

Comment

[1] The procedure of the adversary system contemplates that the evidence in a case is to be marshalled competitively by the contending parties. Fair competition in the adversary system is secured by prohibitions against destruction or concealment of evidence, improperly influencing witnesses, obstructive tactics in discovery procedure, and the like.

[2] Documents and other items of evidence are often essential to establish a claim or defense. Subject to evidentiary privileges, the right of an opposing party, including the government, to obtain evidence through discovery or subpoena is an important procedural right. The exercise of that right can be frustrated if relevant material is altered, concealed or destroyed. Applicable law in many jurisdictions makes it an offense to destroy material for purpose of impairing its availability in a pending proceeding or one whose commencement can be foreseen. Falsifying evi-

dence is also generally a criminal offense. Paragraph (a) applies to evidentiary material generally, including computerized information. Applicable law may permit a lawyer to take temporary possession of physical evidence of client crimes for the purpose of conducting a limited examination that will not alter or destroy material characteristics of the evidence. In such a case, applicable law may require the lawyer to turn the evidence over to the police or other prosecuting authority, depending on the circumstances.

[3] With regard to paragraph (b), it is not improper to pay a witness's expenses or to compensate an expert witness on terms permitted by law. The common law rule in most jurisdictions is that it is improper to pay an occurrence witness any fee for testifying and that it is improper to pay an expert witness a contingent fee.

[4] Paragraph (f) permits a lawyer to advise employees of a client to refrain from giving information to another party, for the employees may identify their interests with those of the client. See also Rule 4.2.

Definitional Cross-References

"Knowingly" *See* Rule 1.0(f)
"Reasonably" *See* Rule 1.0(h)
"Reasonably believes" *See* Rule 1.0(i)
"Tribunal" *See* Rule 1.0(m)

RULE 3.5: IMPARTIALITY AND DECORUM OF THE TRIBUNAL

A lawyer shall not:

(a) seek to influence a judge, juror, prospective juror or other official by means prohibited by law;

(b) communicate ex parte with such a person during the proceeding unless authorized to do so by law or court order;

(c) communicate with a juror or prospective juror after discharge of the jury if:

(1) the communication is prohibited by law or court order;

(2) the juror has made known to the lawyer a desire not to communicate; or

(3) the communication involves misrepresentation, coercion, duress or harassment; or

(d) engage in conduct intended to disrupt a tribunal.

Comment

[1] Many forms of improper influence upon a tribunal are proscribed by criminal law. Others are specified in the ABA Model Code of Judicial Conduct, with which an advocate should be familiar. A lawyer is required to avoid contributing to a violation of such provisions.

[2] During a proceeding a lawyer may not communicate ex parte with persons serving in an official capacity in the proceeding, such as judges, masters or jurors, unless authorized to do so by law or court order.

[3] A lawyer may on occasion want to communicate with a juror or prospective juror after the jury has been discharged. The lawyer may do so unless the communication is prohibited by law or a court order but must respect the desire of the juror not to talk with the lawyer. The lawyer may not engage in improper conduct during the communication.

[4] The advocate's function is to present evidence and argument so that the cause may be decided according to law. Refraining from abusive or obstreperous conduct is a corollary of the advocate's right to speak on behalf of litigants. A lawyer may stand firm against abuse by a judge but should avoid reciprocation; the judge's default is no justification for similar dereliction by an advocate. An advocate can present the cause, protect the record for subsequent review and preserve professional integrity by patient firmness no less effectively than by belligerence or theatrics.

[5] The duty to refrain from disruptive conduct applies to any proceeding of a tribunal, including a deposition. See Rule 1.0(m).

Definitional Cross-References

"Known" *See* Rule 1.0(f)
"Tribunal" *See* Rule 1.0(m)

RULE 3.6: TRIAL PUBLICITY

(a) A lawyer who is participating or has participated in the investigation or litigation of a matter shall not make an extrajudicial statement that the lawyer knows or reasonably should know will be disseminated by means of public communication and will have a substantial likelihood of materially prejudicing an adjudicative proceeding in the matter.

(b) Notwithstanding paragraph (a), a lawyer may state:

(1) the claim, offense or defense involved and, except when prohibited by law, the identity of the persons involved;

(2) information contained in a public record;

(3) that an investigation of a matter is in progress;

(4) the scheduling or result of any step in litigation;

(5) a request for assistance in obtaining evidence and information necessary thereto;

(6) a warning of danger concerning the behavior of a person involved, when there is reason to believe that there exists the likelihood of substantial harm to an individual or to the public interest; and

(7) in a criminal case, in addition to subparagraphs (1) through (6):

(i) the identity, residence, occupation and family status of the accused;

(ii) if the accused has not been apprehended, information necessary to aid in apprehension of that person;

(iii) the fact, time and place of arrest; and

(iv) the identity of investigating and arresting officers or agencies and the length of the investigation.

(c) Notwithstanding paragraph (a), a lawyer may make a statement that a reasonable lawyer would believe is required to protect a client from the substantial undue prejudicial effect of recent publicity not initiated by the lawyer or the lawyer's client. A statement made pursuant to this paragraph shall be limited to such information as is necessary to mitigate the recent adverse publicity.

(d) No lawyer associated in a firm or government agency with a lawyer subject to paragraph (a) shall make a statement prohibited by paragraph (a).

Comment

[1] It is difficult to strike a balance between protecting the right to a fair trial and safeguarding the right of free expression. Preserving the right to a fair trial necessarily entails some curtailment of the information that may be disseminated about a party prior to trial, particularly where trial by jury is involved. If there were no such limits, the result would be the practical nullification of the protective effect of the rules of forensic decorum and the exclusionary rules of evidence. On the other hand, there are vital social interests served by the free dissemination of information about events having legal consequences and about legal proceedings

themselves. The public has a right to know about threats to its safety and measures aimed at assuring its security. It also has a legitimate interest in the conduct of judicial proceedings, particularly in matters of general public concern. Furthermore, the subject matter of legal proceedings is often of direct significance in debate and deliberation over questions of public policy.

[2] Special rules of confidentiality may validly govern proceedings in juvenile, domestic relations and mental disability proceedings, and perhaps other types of litigation. Rule 3.4(c) requires compliance with such rules.

[3] The Rule sets forth a basic general prohibition against a lawyer's making statements that the lawyer knows or should know will have a substantial likelihood of materially prejudicing an adjudicative proceeding. Recognizing that the public value of informed commentary is great and the likelihood of prejudice to a proceeding by the commentary of a lawyer who is not involved in the proceeding is small, the Rule applies only to lawyers who are, or who have been involved in the investigation or litigation of a case, and their associates.

[4] Paragraph (b) identifies specific matters about which a lawyer's statements would not ordinarily be considered to present a substantial likelihood of material prejudice, and should not in any event be considered prohibited by the general prohibition of paragraph (a). Paragraph (b) is not intended to be an exhaustive listing of the subjects upon which a lawyer may make a statement, but statements on other matters may be subject to paragraph (a).

[5] There are, on the other hand, certain subjects that are more likely than not to have a material prejudicial effect on a proceeding, particularly when they refer to a civil matter triable to a jury, a criminal matter, or any other proceeding that could result in incarceration. These subjects relate to:

(1) the character, credibility, reputation or criminal record of a party, suspect in a criminal investigation or witness, or the identity of a witness, or the expected testimony of a party or witness;

(2) in a criminal case or proceeding that could result in incarceration, the possibility of a plea of guilty to the offense or the existence or contents of any confession, admission, or statement given by a defendant or suspect or that person's refusal or failure to make a statement;

(3) the performance or results of any examination or test or the re-

fusal or failure of a person to submit to an examination or test, or the identity or nature of physical evidence expected to be presented;

(4) any opinion as to the guilt or innocence of a defendant or suspect in a criminal case or proceeding that could result in incarceration;

(5) information that the lawyer knows or reasonably should know is likely to be inadmissible as evidence in a trial and that would, if disclosed, create a substantial risk of prejudicing an impartial trial; or

(6) the fact that a defendant has been charged with a crime, unless there is included therein a statement explaining that the charge is merely an accusation and that the defendant is presumed innocent until and unless proven guilty.

[6] Another relevant factor in determining prejudice is the nature of the proceeding involved. Criminal jury trials will be most sensitive to extrajudicial speech. Civil trials may be less sensitive. Non-jury hearings and arbitration proceedings may be even less affected. The Rule will still place limitations on prejudicial comments in these cases, but the likelihood of prejudice may be different depending on the type of proceeding.

[7] Finally, extrajudicial statements that might otherwise raise a question under this Rule may be permissible when they are made in response to statements made publicly by another party, another party's lawyer, or third persons, where a reasonable lawyer would believe a public response is required in order to avoid prejudice to the lawyer's client. When prejudicial statements have been publicly made by others, responsive statements may have the salutary effect of lessening any resulting adverse impact on the adjudicative proceeding. Such responsive statements should be limited to contain only such information as is necessary to mitigate undue prejudice created by the statements made by others.

[8] See Rule 3.8(f) for additional duties of prosecutors in connection with extrajudicial statements about criminal proceedings.

Definitional Cross-References

"Firm" *See* Rule 1.0(c)
"Knows" *See* Rule 1.0(f)
"Reasonable" *See* Rule 1.0(h)
"Reasonably should know" *See* Rule 1.0(j)
"Substantial" *See* Rule 1.0(l)

RULE 3.7: LAWYER AS WITNESS

(a) A lawyer shall not act as advocate at a trial in which the lawyer is likely to be a necessary witness unless:

(1) the testimony relates to an uncontested issue;

(2) the testimony relates to the nature and value of legal services rendered in the case; or

(3) disqualification of the lawyer would work substantial hardship on the client.

(b) A lawyer may act as advocate in a trial in which another lawyer in the lawyer's firm is likely to be called as a witness unless precluded from doing so by Rule 1.7 or Rule 1.9.

Comment

[1] Combining the roles of advocate and witness can prejudice the tribunal and the opposing party and can also involve a conflict of interest between the lawyer and client.

Advocate-Witness Rule

[2] The tribunal has proper objection when the trier of fact may be confused or misled by a lawyer serving as both advocate and witness. The opposing party has proper objection where the combination of roles may prejudice that party's rights in the litigation. A witness is required to testify on the basis of personal knowledge, while an advocate is expected to explain and comment on evidence given by others. It may not be clear whether a statement by an advocate-witness should be taken as proof or as an analysis of the proof.

[3] To protect the tribunal, paragraph (a) prohibits a lawyer from simultaneously serving as advocate and necessary witness except in those circumstances specified in paragraphs (a)(1) through (a)(3). Paragraph (a)(1) recognizes that if the testimony will be uncontested, the ambiguities in the dual role are purely theoretical. Paragraph (a)(2) recognizes that where the testimony concerns the extent and value of legal services rendered in the action in which the testimony is offered, permitting the lawyers to testify avoids the need for a second trial with new counsel to resolve that issue. Moreover, in such a situation the judge has firsthand knowledge of the matter in issue; hence, there is less dependence on the adversary process to test the credibility of the testimony.

[4] Apart from these two exceptions, paragraph (a)(3) recognizes that a balancing is required between the interests of the client and those of

the tribunal and the opposing party. Whether the tribunal is likely to be misled or the opposing party is likely to suffer prejudice depends on the nature of the case, the importance and probable tenor of the lawyer's testimony, and the probability that the lawyer's testimony will conflict with that of other witnesses. Even if there is risk of such prejudice, in determining whether the lawyer should be disqualified, due regard must be given to the effect of disqualification on the lawyer's client. It is relevant that one or both parties could reasonably foresee that the lawyer would probably be a witness. The conflict of interest principles stated in Rules 1.7, 1.9 and 1.10 have no application to this aspect of the problem.

[5] Because the tribunal is not likely to be misled when a lawyer acts as advocate in a trial in which another lawyer in the lawyer's firm will testify as a necessary witness, paragraph (b) permits the lawyer to do so except in situations involving a conflict of interest.

Conflict of Interest

[6] In determining if it is permissible to act as advocate in a trial in which the lawyer will be a necessary witness, the lawyer must also consider that the dual role may give rise to a conflict of interest that will require compliance with Rules 1.7 or 1.9. For example, if there is likely to be substantial conflict between the testimony of the client and that of the lawyer the representation involves a conflict of interest that requires compliance with Rule 1.7. This would be true even though the lawyer might not be prohibited by paragraph (a) from simultaneously serving as advocate and witness because the lawyer's disqualification would work a substantial hardship on the client. Similarly, a lawyer who might be permitted to simultaneously serve as an advocate and a witness by paragraph (a)(3) might be precluded from doing so by Rule 1.9. The problem can arise whether the lawyer is called as a witness on behalf of the client or is called by the opposing party. Determining whether or not such a conflict exists is primarily the responsibility of the lawyer involved. If there is a conflict of interest, the lawyer must secure the client's informed consent, confirmed in writing. In some cases, the lawyer will be precluded from seeking the client's consent. See Rule 1.7. See Rule 1.0(b) for the definition of "confirmed in writing" and Rule 1.0(e) for the definition of "informed consent."

[7] Paragraph (b) provides that a lawyer is not disqualified from serving as an advocate because a lawyer with whom the lawyer is associated in a firm is precluded from doing so by paragraph (a). If, however,

the testifying lawyer would also be disqualified by Rule 1.7 or Rule 1.9 from representing the client in the matter, other lawyers in the firm will be precluded from representing the client by Rule 1.10 unless the client gives informed consent under the conditions stated in Rule 1.7.

Definitional Cross-References

"Firm" *See* Rule 1.0(c)
"Substantial" *See* Rule 1.0(l)

RULE 3.8: SPECIAL RESPONSIBILITIES OF A PROSECUTOR

The prosecutor in a criminal case shall:

(a) refrain from prosecuting a charge that the prosecutor knows is not supported by probable cause;

(b) make reasonable efforts to assure that the accused has been advised of the right to, and the procedure for obtaining, counsel and has been given reasonable opportunity to obtain counsel;

(c) not seek to obtain from an unrepresented accused a waiver of important pretrial rights, such as the right to a preliminary hearing;

(d) make timely disclosure to the defense of all evidence or information known to the prosecutor that tends to negate the guilt of the accused or mitigates the offense, and, in connection with sentencing, disclose to the defense and to the tribunal all unprivileged mitigating information known to the prosecutor, except when the prosecutor is relieved of this responsibility by a protective order of the tribunal;

(e) not subpoena a lawyer in a grand jury or other criminal proceeding to present evidence about a past or present client unless the prosecutor reasonably believes:

(1) the information sought is not protected from disclosure by any applicable privilege;

(2) the evidence sought is essential to the successful completion of an ongoing investigation or prosecution; and

(3) there is no other feasible alternative to obtain the information;

(f) except for statements that are necessary to inform the public of the nature and extent of the prosecutor's action and that serve a legitimate law enforcement purpose, refrain from making extrajudicial comments that have a substantial likelihood of heightening public condemnation of the accused and exercise reasonable care to prevent investigators, law enforcement personnel, employees or other persons assisting or associated with the prosecutor in a criminal case from making an extrajudicial statement that the prosecutor would be prohibited from making under Rule 3.6 or this Rule.

(g) When a prosecutor knows of new, credible and material evidence creating a reasonable likelihood that a convicted defendant did not commit an offense of which the defendant was convicted, the prosecutor shall:

(1) promptly disclose that evidence to an appropriate court or authority, and

(2) if the conviction was obtained in the prosecutor's jurisdiction,

(i) promptly disclose that evidence to the defendant unless a court authorizes delay, and

(ii) undertake further investigation, or make reasonable efforts to cause an investigation, to determine whether the defendant was convicted of an offense that the defendant did not commit.

(h) When a prosecutor knows of clear and convincing evidence establishing that a defendant in the prosecutor's jurisdiction was convicted of an offense that the defendant did not commit, the prosecutor shall seek to remedy the conviction.

Comment

[1] A prosecutor has the responsibility of a minister of justice and not simply that of an advocate. This responsibility carries with it specific obligations to see that the defendant is accorded procedural justice, that guilt is decided upon the basis of sufficient evidence, and that special precautions are taken to prevent and to rectify the conviction of innocent persons. The extent of mandated remedial action is a matter of debate and varies in different jurisdictions. Many jurisdictions have adopted the ABA Standards for Criminal Justice Relating to the Prosecution Function, which are the product of prolonged and careful deliberation by lawyers experienced in both criminal prosecution and defense. Competent representation of the sovereignty may require a prosecutor to undertake some procedural and remedial measures as a matter of obligation. Applicable

law may require other measures by the prosecutor and knowing disregard of those obligations or a systematic abuse of prosecutorial discretion could constitute a violation of Rule 8.4.

[2] In some jurisdictions, a defendant may waive a preliminary hearing and thereby lose a valuable opportunity to challenge probable cause. Accordingly, prosecutors should not seek to obtain waivers of preliminary hearings or other important pretrial rights from unrepresented accused persons. Paragraph (c) does not apply, however, to an accused appearing *pro se* with the approval of the tribunal. Nor does it forbid the lawful questioning of an uncharged suspect who has knowingly waived the rights to counsel and silence.

[3] The exception in paragraph (d) recognizes that a prosecutor may seek an appropriate protective order from the tribunal if disclosure of information to the defense could result in substantial harm to an individual or to the public interest.

[4] Paragraph (e) is intended to limit the issuance of lawyer subpoenas in grand jury and other criminal proceedings to those situations in which there is a genuine need to intrude into the client-lawyer relationship.

[5] Paragraph (f) supplements Rule 3.6, which prohibits extrajudicial statements that have a substantial likelihood of prejudicing an adjudicatory proceeding. In the context of a criminal prosecution, a prosecutor's extrajudicial statement can create the additional problem of increasing public condemnation of the accused. Although the announcement of an indictment, for example, will necessarily have severe consequences for the accused, a prosecutor can, and should, avoid comments which have no legitimate law enforcement purpose and have a substantial likelihood of increasing public opprobrium of the accused. Nothing in this Comment is intended to restrict the statements which a prosecutor may make which comply with Rule 3.6(b) or 3.6(c).

[6] Like other lawyers, prosecutors are subject to Rules 5.1 and 5.3, which relate to responsibilities regarding lawyers and nonlawyers who work for or are associated with the lawyer's office. Paragraph (f) reminds the prosecutor of the importance of these obligations in connection with the unique dangers of improper extrajudicial statements in a criminal case. In addition, paragraph (f) requires a prosecutor to exercise reasonable care to prevent persons assisting or associated with the prosecutor from making improper extrajudicial statements, even when such persons are not under the direct supervision of the prosecutor. Ordinarily,

the reasonable care standard will be satisfied if the prosecutor issues the appropriate cautions to law enforcement personnel and other relevant individuals.

[7] When a prosecutor knows of new, credible and material evidence creating a reasonable likelihood that a person outside the prosecutor's jurisdiction was convicted of a crime that the person did not commit, paragraph (g) requires prompt disclosure to the court or other appropriate authority, such as the chief prosecutor of the jurisdiction where the conviction occurred. If the conviction was obtained in the prosecutor's jurisdiction, paragraph (g) requires the prosecutor to examine the evidence and undertake further investigation to determine whether the defendant is in fact innocent or make reasonable efforts to cause another appropriate authority to undertake the necessary investigation, and to promptly disclose the evidence to the court and, absent court-authorized delay, to the defendant. Consistent with the objectives of Rules 4.2 and 4.3, disclosure to a represented defendant must be made through the defendant's counsel, and, in the case of an unrepresented defendant, would ordinarily be accompanied by a request to a court for the appointment of counsel to assist the defendant in taking such legal measures as may be appropriate.

[8] Under paragraph (h), once the prosecutor knows of clear and convincing evidence that the defendant was convicted of an offense that the defendant did not commit, the prosecutor must seek to remedy the conviction. Necessary steps may include disclosure of the evidence to the defendant, requesting that the court appoint counsel for an unrepresented indigent defendant and, where appropriate, notifying the court that the prosecutor has knowledge that the defendant did not commit the offense of which the defendant was convicted.

[9] A prosecutor's independent judgment, made in good faith, that the new evidence is not of such nature as to trigger the obligations of sections (g) and (h), though subsequently determined to have been erroneous, does not constitute a violation of this Rule.

Definitional Cross-References

"Known" and "Knows" *See* Rule 1.0(f)
"Reasonable" *See* Rule 1.0(h)
"Reasonably believes" *See* Rule 1.0(i)
"Substantial" *See* Rule 1.0(l)
"Tribunal" *See* Rule 1.0(m)

RULE 3.9: ADVOCATE IN NONADJUDICATIVE PROCEEDINGS

A lawyer representing a client before a legislative body or administrative agency in a nonadjudicative proceeding shall disclose that the appearance is in a representative capacity and shall conform to the provisions of Rules 3.3(a) through (c), 3.4(a) through (c), and 3.5.

Comment

[1] In representation before bodies such as legislatures, municipal councils, and executive and administrative agencies acting in a rule-making or policy-making capacity, lawyers present facts, formulate issues and advance argument in the matters under consideration. The decision-making body, like a court, should be able to rely on the integrity of the submissions made to it. A lawyer appearing before such a body must deal with it honestly and in conformity with applicable rules of procedure. See Rules 3.3(a) through (c), 3.4(a) through (c) and 3.5.

[2] Lawyers have no exclusive right to appear before nonadjudicative bodies, as they do before a court. The requirements of this Rule therefore may subject lawyers to regulations inapplicable to advocates who are not lawyers. However, legislatures and administrative agencies have a right to expect lawyers to deal with them as they deal with courts.

[3] This Rule only applies when a lawyer represents a client in connection with an official hearing or meeting of a governmental agency or a legislative body to which the lawyer or the lawyer's client is presenting evidence or argument. It does not apply to representation of a client in a negotiation or other bilateral transaction with a governmental agency or in connection with an application for a license or other privilege or the client's compliance with generally applicable reporting requirements, such as the filing of income-tax returns. Nor does it apply to the representation of a client in connection with an investigation or examination of the client's affairs conducted by government investigators or examiners. Representation in such matters is governed by Rules 4.1 through 4.4.

TRANSACTIONS WITH PERSONS OTHER THAN CLIENTS

RULE 4.1: TRUTHFULNESS IN STATEMENTS TO OTHERS

In the course of representing a client a lawyer shall not knowingly:

(a) make a false statement of material fact or law to a third person; or

(b) fail to disclose a material fact when disclosure is necessary to avoid assisting a criminal or fraudulent act by a client, unless disclosure is prohibited by Rule 1.6.

Comment

Misrepresentation

[1] A lawyer is required to be truthful when dealing with others on a client's behalf, but generally has no affirmative duty to inform an opposing party of relevant facts. A misrepresentation can occur if the lawyer incorporates or affirms a statement of another person that the lawyer knows is false. Misrepresentations can also occur by partially true but misleading statements or omissions that are the equivalent of affirmative false statements. For dishonest conduct that does not amount to a false statement or for misrepresentations by a lawyer other than in the course of representing a client, see Rule 8.4.

Statements of Fact

[2] This Rule refers to statements of fact. Whether a particular statement should be regarded as one of fact can depend on the circumstances. Under generally accepted conventions in negotiation, certain types of statements ordinarily are not taken as statements of material fact. Estimates of price or value placed on the subject of a transaction and a party's intentions as to an acceptable settlement of a claim are ordinarily in this category, and so is the existence of an undisclosed principal except where nondisclosure of the principal would constitute fraud. Lawyers should be mindful of their obligations under applicable law to avoid criminal and tortious misrepresentation.

Crime or Fraud by Client

[3] Under Rule 1.2(d), a lawyer is prohibited from counseling or assisting a client in conduct that the lawyer knows is criminal or fraudulent. Paragraph (b) states a specific application of the principle set forth in Rule 1.2(d) and addresses the situation where a client's crime or fraud takes the form of a lie or misrepresentation. Ordinarily, a lawyer can avoid assisting a client's crime or fraud by withdrawing from the representation. Sometimes it may be necessary for the lawyer to give notice of the fact of withdrawal and to disaffirm an opinion, document, affirmation or the like. In extreme cases, substantive law may require a lawyer to disclose information relating to the representation to avoid being deemed to have assisted the client's crime or fraud. If the lawyer can avoid assisting a client's crime or fraud only by disclosing this information, then under paragraph (b) the lawyer is required to do so, unless the disclosure is prohibited by Rule 1.6.

Definitional Cross-References

"Fraudulent" *See* Rule 1.0(d)
"Knowingly" *See* Rule 1.0(f)

RULE 4.2: COMMUNICATION WITH PERSON REPRESENTED BY COUNSEL

In representing a client, a lawyer shall not communicate about the subject of the representation with a person the lawyer knows to be represented by another lawyer in the matter, unless the lawyer has the consent of the other lawyer or is authorized to do so by law or a court order.

Comment

[1] This Rule contributes to the proper functioning of the legal system by protecting a person who has chosen to be represented by a lawyer in a matter against possible overreaching by other lawyers who are participating in the matter, interference by those lawyers with the client-lawyer relationship and the uncounselled disclosure of information relating to the representation.

[2] This Rule applies to communications with any person who is represented by counsel concerning the matter to which the communication relates.

[3] The Rule applies even though the represented person initiates or consents to the communication. A lawyer must immediately terminate communication with a person if, after commencing communication, the lawyer learns that the person is one with whom communication is not permitted by this Rule.

[4] This Rule does not prohibit communication with a represented person, or an employee or agent of such a person, concerning matters outside the representation. For example, the existence of a controversy between a government agency and a private party, or between two organizations, does not prohibit a lawyer for either from communicating with nonlawyer representatives of the other regarding a separate matter. Nor does this Rule preclude communication with a represented person who is seeking advice from a lawyer who is not otherwise representing a client in the matter. A lawyer may not make a communication prohibited by this Rule through the acts of another. See Rule 8.4(a). Parties to a matter may communicate directly with each other, and a lawyer is not prohibited from advising a client concerning a communication that the client is legally entitled to make. Also, a lawyer having independent justification or legal authorization for communicating with a represented person is permitted to do so.

[5] Communications authorized by law may include communications by a lawyer on behalf of a client who is exercising a constitutional or other legal right to communicate with the government. Communications authorized by law may also include investigative activities of lawyers representing governmental entities, directly or through investigative agents, prior to the commencement of criminal or civil enforcement proceedings. When communicating with the accused in a criminal matter, a government lawyer must comply with this Rule in addition to honoring the constitutional rights of the accused. The fact that a communication does not violate a state or federal constitutional right is insufficient to establish that the communication is permissible under this Rule.

[6] A lawyer who is uncertain whether a communication with a represented person is permissible may seek a court order. A lawyer may also seek a court order in exceptional circumstances to authorize a communication that would otherwise be prohibited by this Rule, for example, where communication with a person represented by counsel is necessary to avoid reasonably certain injury.

[7] In the case of a represented organization, this Rule prohibits communications with a constituent of the organization who supervises, di-

rects or regularly consults with the organization's lawyer concerning the matter or has authority to obligate the organization with respect to the matter or whose act or omission in connection with the matter may be imputed to the organization for purposes of civil or criminal liability. Consent of the organization's lawyer is not required for communication with a former constituent. If a constituent of the organization is represented in the matter by his or her own counsel, the consent by that counsel to a communication will be sufficient for purposes of this Rule. Compare Rule 3.4(f). In communicating with a current or former constituent of an organization, a lawyer must not use methods of obtaining evidence that violate the legal rights of the organization. See Rule 4.4.

[8] The prohibition on communications with a represented person only applies in circumstances where the lawyer knows that the person is in fact represented in the matter to be discussed. This means that the lawyer has actual knowledge of the fact of the representation; but such actual knowledge may be inferred from the circumstances. See Rule 1.0(f). Thus, the lawyer cannot evade the requirement of obtaining the consent of counsel by closing eyes to the obvious.

[9] In the event the person with whom the lawyer communicates is not known to be represented by counsel in the matter, the lawyer's communications are subject to Rule 4.3.

Definitional Cross-References

"Knows" *See* Rule 1.0(f)

RULE 4.3: DEALING WITH UNREPRESENTED PERSON

In dealing on behalf of a client with a person who is not represented by counsel, a lawyer shall not state or imply that the lawyer is disinterested. When the lawyer knows or reasonably should know that the unrepresented person misunderstands the lawyer's role in the matter, the lawyer shall make reasonable efforts to correct the misunderstanding. The lawyer shall not give legal advice to an unrepresented person, other than the advice to secure counsel, if the lawyer knows or reasonably should know that the interests of such a person are or have a reasonable possibility of being in conflict with the interests of the client.

Comment

[1] An unrepresented person, particularly one not experienced in dealing with legal matters, might assume that a lawyer is disinterested in loyalties or is a disinterested authority on the law even when the lawyer represents a client. In order to avoid a misunderstanding, a lawyer will typically need to identify the lawyer's client and, where necessary, explain that the client has interests opposed to those of the unrepresented person. For misunderstandings that sometimes arise when a lawyer for an organization deals with an unrepresented constituent, see Rule 1.13(f).

[2] The Rule distinguishes between situations involving unrepresented persons whose interests may be adverse to those of the lawyer's client and those in which the person's interests are not in conflict with the client's. In the former situation, the possibility that the lawyer will compromise the unrepresented person's interests is so great that the Rule prohibits the giving of any advice, apart from the advice to obtain counsel. Whether a lawyer is giving impermissible advice may depend on the experience and sophistication of the unrepresented person, as well as the setting in which the behavior and comments occur. This Rule does not prohibit a lawyer from negotiating the terms of a transaction or settling a dispute with an unrepresented person. So long as the lawyer has explained that the lawyer represents an adverse party and is not representing the person, the lawyer may inform the person of the terms on which the lawyer's client will enter into an agreement or settle a matter, prepare documents that require the person's signature and explain the lawyer's own view of the meaning of the document or the lawyer's view of the underlying legal obligations.

Definitional Cross-References

"Knows" *See* Rule 1.0(f)
"Reasonable" *See* Rule 1.0(h)
"Reasonably should know" *See* Rule 1.0(j)

RULE 4.4: RESPECT FOR RIGHTS OF THIRD PERSONS

(a) In representing a client, a lawyer shall not use means that have no substantial purpose other than to embarrass, delay, or burden a third person, or use methods of obtaining evidence that violate the legal rights of such a person.

(b) A lawyer who receives a document or electronically stored information relating to the representation of the lawyer's client and knows or reasonably should know that the document or electronically stored information was inadvertently sent shall promptly notify the sender.

Comment

[1] Responsibility to a client requires a lawyer to subordinate the interests of others to those of the client, but that responsibility does not imply that a lawyer may disregard the rights of third persons. It is impractical to catalogue all such rights, but they include legal restrictions on methods of obtaining evidence from third persons and unwarranted intrusions into privileged relationships, such as the client-lawyer relationship.

[2] Paragraph (b) recognizes that lawyers sometimes receive a document or electronically stored information that was mistakenly sent or produced by opposing parties or their lawyers. A document or electronically stored information is inadvertently sent when it is accidentally transmitted, such as when an email or letter is misaddressed or a document or electronically stored information is accidentally included with information that was intentionally transmitted. If a lawyer knows or reasonably should know that such a document or electronically stored information was sent inadvertently, then this Rule requires the lawyer to promptly notify the sender in order to permit that person to take protective measures. Whether the lawyer is required to take additional steps, such as returning the document or deleting electronically stored information, is a matter of law beyond the scope of these Rules, as is the question of whether the privileged status of a document or electronically stored information has been waived. Similarly, this Rule does not address the legal duties of a lawyer who receives a document or electronically stored information that the lawyer knows or reasonably should know may have been inappropriately obtained by the sending person. For purposes of this Rule, "document or electronically stored information" includes, in addition to paper documents, email and other forms of electronically stored information, including embedded data (commonly referred to as "metadata"), that is subject to being read or put into readable form. Metadata in electronic documents creates an obligation under this Rule only if the receiving lawyer knows or reasonably should know that the metadata was inadvertently sent to the receiving lawyer.

[3] Some lawyers may choose to return a document or delete electronically stored information unread, for example, when the lawyer learns before receiving it that it was inadvertently sent. Where a lawyer is not required by applicable law to do so, the decision to voluntarily return such a document or delete electronically stored information is a matter of professional judgment ordinarily reserved to the lawyer. See Rules 1.2 and 1.4.

Definitional Cross-References

"Knows" *See* Rule 1.0(f)
"Reasonably should know" *See* Rule 1.0(j)
"Substantial" *See* Rule 1.0(l)

LAW FIRMS AND ASSOCIATIONS

RULE 5.1: RESPONSIBILITIES OF PARTNERS, MANAGERS, AND SUPERVISORY LAWYERS

(a) A partner in a law firm, and a lawyer who individually or together with other lawyers possesses comparable managerial authority in a law firm, shall make reasonable efforts to ensure that the firm has in effect measures giving reasonable assurance that all lawyers in the firm conform to the Rules of Professional Conduct.

(b) A lawyer having direct supervisory authority over another lawyer shall make reasonable efforts to ensure that the other lawyer conforms to the Rules of Professional Conduct.

(c) A lawyer shall be responsible for another lawyer's violation of the Rules of Professional Conduct if:

(1) the lawyer orders or, with knowledge of the specific conduct, ratifies the conduct involved; or

(2) the lawyer is a partner or has comparable managerial authority in the law firm in which the other lawyer practices, or has direct supervisory authority over the other lawyer, and knows of the conduct at a time when its consequences can be avoided or mitigated but fails to take reasonable remedial action.

Comment

[1] Paragraph (a) applies to lawyers who have managerial authority over the professional work of a firm. See Rule 1.0(c). This includes mem-

bers of a partnership, the shareholders in a law firm organized as a professional corporation, and members of other associations authorized to practice law; lawyers having comparable managerial authority in a legal services organization or a law department of an enterprise or government agency; and lawyers who have intermediate managerial responsibilities in a firm. Paragraph (b) applies to lawyers who have supervisory authority over the work of other lawyers in a firm.

[2] Paragraph (a) requires lawyers with managerial authority within a firm to make reasonable efforts to establish internal policies and procedures designed to provide reasonable assurance that all lawyers in the firm will conform to the Rules of Professional Conduct. Such policies and procedures include those designed to detect and resolve conflicts of interest, identify dates by which actions must be taken in pending matters, account for client funds and property and ensure that inexperienced lawyers are properly supervised.

[3] Other measures that may be required to fulfill the responsibility prescribed in paragraph (a) can depend on the firm's structure and the nature of its practice. In a small firm of experienced lawyers, informal supervision and periodic review of compliance with the required systems ordinarily will suffice. In a large firm, or in practice situations in which difficult ethical problems frequently arise, more elaborate measures may be necessary. Some firms, for example, have a procedure whereby junior lawyers can make confidential referral of ethical problems directly to a designated senior partner or special committee. See Rule 5.2. Firms, whether large or small, may also rely on continuing legal education in professional ethics. In any event, the ethical atmosphere of a firm can influence the conduct of all its members, and the partners may not assume that all lawyers associated with the firm will inevitably conform to the Rules.

[4] Paragraph (c) expresses a general principle of personal responsibility for acts of another. See also Rule 8.4(a).

[5] Paragraph (c)(2) defines the duty of a partner or other lawyer having comparable managerial authority in a law firm, as well as a lawyer who has direct supervisory authority over performance of specific legal work by another lawyer. Whether a lawyer has supervisory authority in particular circumstances is a question of fact. Partners and lawyers with comparable authority have at least indirect responsibility for all work being done by the firm, while a partner or manager in charge of a particular matter ordinarily also has supervisory responsibility for the work of other firm lawyers engaged in the matter. Appropriate remedial

action by a partner or managing lawyer would depend on the immediacy of that lawyer's involvement and the seriousness of the misconduct. A supervisor is required to intervene to prevent avoidable consequences of misconduct if the supervisor knows that the misconduct occurred. Thus, if a supervising lawyer knows that a subordinate misrepresented a matter to an opposing party in negotiation, the supervisor as well as the subordinate has a duty to correct the resulting misapprehension.

[6] Professional misconduct by a lawyer under supervision could reveal a violation of paragraph (b) on the part of the supervisory lawyer even though it does not entail a violation of paragraph (c) because there was no direction, ratification or knowledge of the violation.

[7] Apart from this Rule and Rule 8.4(a), a lawyer does not have disciplinary liability for the conduct of a partner, associate or subordinate. Whether a lawyer may be liable civilly or criminally for another lawyer's conduct is a question of law beyond the scope of these Rules.

[8] The duties imposed by this Rule on managing and supervising lawyers do not alter the personal duty of each lawyer in a firm to abide by the Rules of Professional Conduct. See Rule 5.2(a).

Definitional Cross-References

"Firm" and "Law firm" *See* Rule 1.0(c)
"Knows" *See* Rule 1.0(f)
"Partner" *See* Rule 1.0(g)
"Reasonable" *See* Rule 1.0(h)

RULE 5.2: RESPONSIBILITIES OF A SUBORDINATE LAWYER

(a) A lawyer is bound by the Rules of Professional Conduct notwithstanding that the lawyer acted at the direction of another person.

(b) A subordinate lawyer does not violate the Rules of Professional Conduct if that lawyer acts in accordance with a supervisory lawyer's reasonable resolution of an arguable question of professional duty.

Comment

[1] Although a lawyer is not relieved of responsibility for a violation by the fact that the lawyer acted at the direction of a supervisor, that fact

may be relevant in determining whether a lawyer had the knowledge required to render conduct a violation of the Rules. For example, if a subordinate filed a frivolous pleading at the direction of a supervisor, the subordinate would not be guilty of a professional violation unless the subordinate knew of the document's frivolous character.

[2] When lawyers in a supervisor-subordinate relationship encounter a matter involving professional judgment as to ethical duty, the supervisor may assume responsibility for making the judgment. Otherwise a consistent course of action or position could not be taken. If the question can reasonably be answered only one way, the duty of both lawyers is clear and they are equally responsible for fulfilling it. However, if the question is reasonably arguable, someone has to decide upon the course of action. That authority ordinarily reposes in the supervisor, and a subordinate may be guided accordingly. For example, if a question arises whether the interests of two clients conflict under Rule 1.7, the supervisor's reasonable resolution of the question should protect the subordinate professionally if the resolution is subsequently challenged.

Definitional Cross-References

"Reasonable" *See* Rule 1.0(h)

RULE 5.3: RESPONSIBILITIES
REGARDING NONLAWYER ASSISTANCE

With respect to a nonlawyer employed or retained by or associated with a lawyer:

(a) a partner, and a lawyer who individually or together with other lawyers possesses comparable managerial authority in a law firm shall make reasonable efforts to ensure that the firm has in effect measures giving reasonable assurance that the person's conduct is compatible with the professional obligations of the lawyer;

(b) a lawyer having direct supervisory authority over the nonlawyer shall make reasonable efforts to ensure that the person's conduct is compatible with the professional obligations of the lawyer; and

(c) a lawyer shall be responsible for conduct of such a person that would be a violation of the Rules of Professional Conduct if engaged in by a lawyer if:

(1) the lawyer orders or, with the knowledge of the specific conduct, ratifies the conduct involved; or

(2) the lawyer is a partner or has comparable managerial authority in the law firm in which the person is employed, or has direct supervisory authority over the person, and knows of the conduct at a time when its consequences can be avoided or mitigated but fails to take reasonable remedial action.

Comment

[1] Paragraph (a) requires lawyers with managerial authority within a law firm to make reasonable efforts to ensure that the firm has in effect measures giving reasonable assurance that nonlawyers in the firm and nonlawyers outside the firm who work on firm matters act in a way compatible with the professional obligations of the lawyer. See Comment [6] to Rule 1.1 (retaining lawyers outside the firm) and Comment [1] to Rule 5.1 (responsibilities with respect to lawyers within a firm). Paragraph (b) applies to lawyers who have supervisory authority over such nonlawyers within or outside the firm. Paragraph (c) specifies the circumstances in which a lawyer is responsible for the conduct of such nonlawyers within or outside the firm that would be a violation of the Rules of Professional Conduct if engaged in by a lawyer.

Nonlawyers Within the Firm

[2] Lawyers generally employ assistants in their practice, including secretaries, investigators, law student interns, and paraprofessionals. Such assistants, whether employees or independent contractors, act for the lawyer in rendition of the lawyer's professional services. A lawyer must give such assistants appropriate instruction and supervision concerning the ethical aspects of their employment, particularly regarding the obligation not to disclose information relating to representation of the client, and should be responsible for their work product. The measures employed in supervising nonlawyers should take account of the fact that they do not have legal training and are not subject to professional discipline.

Nonlawyers Outside the Firm

[3] A lawyer may use nonlawyers outside the firm to assist the lawyer in rendering legal services to the client. Examples include the retention of an investigative or paraprofessional service, hiring a document

management company to create and maintain a database for complex litigation, sending client documents to a third party for printing or scanning, and using an Internet-based service to store client information. When using such services outside the firm, a lawyer must make reasonable efforts to ensure that the services are provided in a manner that is compatible with the lawyer's professional obligations. The extent of this obligation will depend upon the circumstances, including the education, experience and reputation of the nonlawyer; the nature of the services involved; the terms of any arrangements concerning the protection of client information; and the legal and ethical environments of the jurisdictions in which the services will be performed, particularly with regard to confidentiality. See also Rules 1.1 (competence), 1.2 (allocation of authority), 1.4 (communication with client), 1.6 (confidentiality), 5.4(a) (professional independence of the lawyer), and 5.5(a) (unauthorized practice of law). When retaining or directing a nonlawyer outside the firm, a lawyer should communicate directions appropriate under the circumstances to give reasonable assurance that the nonlawyer's conduct is compatible with the professional obligations of the lawyer.

[4] Where the client directs the selection of a particular nonlawyer service provider outside the firm, the lawyer ordinarily should agree with the client concerning the allocation of responsibility for monitoring as between the client and the lawyer. See Rule 1.2. When making such an allocation in a matter pending before a tribunal, lawyers and parties may have additional obligations that are a matter of law beyond the scope of these Rules.

Definitional Cross-References

"Firm" and "Law firm" *See* Rule 1.0(c)
"Knows" *See* Rule 1.0(f)
"Partner" *See* Rule 1.0(g)
"Reasonable" *See* Rule 1.0(h)

RULE 5.4: PROFESSIONAL INDEPENDENCE OF A LAWYER

(a) A lawyer or law firm shall not share legal fees with a nonlawyer, except that:

(1) an agreement by a lawyer with the lawyer's firm, partner, or associate may provide for the payment of money,

over a reasonable period of time after the lawyer's death, to the lawyer's estate or to one or more specified persons;

(2) a lawyer who purchases the practice of a deceased, disabled, or disappeared lawyer may, pursuant to the provisions of Rule 1.17, pay to the estate or other representative of that lawyer the agreed-upon purchase price;

(3) a lawyer or law firm may include nonlawyer employees in a compensation or retirement plan, even though the plan is based in whole or in part on a profit-sharing arrangement; and

(4) a lawyer may share court-awarded legal fees with a nonprofit organization that employed, retained or recommended employment of the lawyer in the matter.

(b) A lawyer shall not form a partnership with a nonlawyer if any of the activities of the partnership consist of the practice of law.

(c) A lawyer shall not permit a person who recommends, employs, or pays the lawyer to render legal services for another to direct or regulate the lawyer's professional judgment in rendering such legal services.

(d) A lawyer shall not practice with or in the form of a professional corporation or association authorized to practice law for a profit, if:

(1) a nonlawyer owns any interest therein, except that a fiduciary representative of the estate of a lawyer may hold the stock or interest of the lawyer for a reasonable time during administration;

(2) a nonlawyer is a corporate director or officer thereof or occupies the position of similar responsibility in any form of association other than a corporation; or

(3) a nonlawyer has the right to direct or control the professional judgment of a lawyer.

Comment

[1] The provisions of this Rule express traditional limitations on sharing fees. These limitations are to protect the lawyer's professional independence of judgment. Where someone other than the client pays the lawyer's fee or salary, or recommends employment of the lawyer, that arrangement does not modify the lawyer's obligation to the client. As stated in paragraph (c), such arrangements should not interfere with the lawyer's professional judgment.

[2] This Rule also expresses traditional limitations on permitting a third party to direct or regulate the lawyer's professional judgment in rendering legal services to another. See also Rule 1.8(f) (lawyer may accept compensation from a third party as long as there is no interference with the lawyer's independent professional judgment and the client gives informed consent).

Definitional Cross-References

"Firm" and "Law firm" *See* Rule 1.0(c)
"Partner" *See* Rule 1.0(g)

RULE 5.5: UNAUTHORIZED PRACTICE OF LAW; MULTIJURISDICTIONAL PRACTICE OF LAW

(a) A lawyer shall not practice law in a jurisdiction in violation of the regulation of the legal profession in that jurisdiction, or assist another in doing so.

(b) A lawyer who is not admitted to practice in this jurisdiction shall not:

(1) except as authorized by these Rules or other law, establish an office or other systematic and continuous presence in this jurisdiction for the practice of law; or

(2) hold out to the public or otherwise represent that the lawyer is admitted to practice law in this jurisdiction.

(c) A lawyer admitted in another United States jurisdiction, and not disbarred or suspended from practice in any jurisdiction, may provide legal services on a temporary basis in this jurisdiction that:

(1) are undertaken in association with a lawyer who is admitted to practice in this jurisdiction and who actively participates in the matter;

(2) are in or reasonably related to a pending or potential proceeding before a tribunal in this or another jurisdiction, if the lawyer, or a person the lawyer is assisting, is authorized by law or order to appear in such proceeding or reasonably expects to be so authorized;

(3) are in or reasonably related to a pending or potential arbitration, mediation, or other alternative dispute resolution proceeding in this or another jurisdiction, if the services arise out of or are reasonably related to the lawyer's practice in a

jurisdiction in which the lawyer is admitted to practice and
are not services for which the forum requires pro hac vice
admission; or

(4) are not within paragraphs (c)(2) or (c)(3) and arise
out of or are reasonably related to the lawyer's practice in
a jurisdiction in which the lawyer is admitted to practice.

(d) A lawyer admitted in another United States jurisdiction or
in a foreign jurisdiction, and not disbarred or suspended from
practice in any jurisdiction or the equivalent thereof, or a person
otherwise lawfully practicing as an in-house counsel under the
laws of a foreign jurisdiction, may provide legal services through
an office or other systematic and continuous presence in this
jurisdiction that:

(1) are provided to the lawyer's employer or its
organizational affiliates; are not services for which the forum
requires pro hac vice admission; and, when performed by
a foreign lawyer and requires advice on the law of this or
another jurisdiction or of the United States, such advice shall
be based upon the advice of a lawyer who is duly licensed
and authorized by the jurisdiction to provide such advice; or

(2) are services that the lawyer is authorized by federal law
or other law or rule to provide in this jurisdiction.

(e) For purposes of paragraph (d):

(1) the foreign lawyer must be a member in good standing
of a recognized legal profession in a foreign jurisdiction,
the members of which are admitted to practice as lawyers or
counselors at law or the equivalent, and subject to effective
regulation and discipline by a duly constituted professional
body or a public authority; or

(2) the person otherwise lawfully practicing as an in-house
counsel under the laws of a foreign jurisdiction must be
authorized to practice under this Rule by, in the exercise of its
discretion, [the highest court of this jurisdiction].

Comment

[1] A lawyer may practice law only in a jurisdiction in which the
lawyer is authorized to practice. A lawyer may be admitted to practice
law in a jurisdiction on a regular basis or may be authorized by court
rule or order or by law to practice for a limited purpose or on a restricted
basis. Paragraph (a) applies to unauthorized practice of law by a lawyer,
whether through the lawyer's direct action or by the lawyer assisting an-

other person. For example, a lawyer may not assist a person in practicing law in violation of the rules governing professional conduct in that person's jurisdiction.

[2] The definition of the practice of law is established by law and varies from one jurisdiction to another. Whatever the definition, limiting the practice of law to members of the bar protects the public against rendition of legal services by unqualified persons. This Rule does not prohibit a lawyer from employing the services of paraprofessionals and delegating functions to them, so long as the lawyer supervises the delegated work and retains responsibility for their work. See Rule 5.3.

[3] A lawyer may provide professional advice and instruction to nonlawyers whose employment requires knowledge of the law; for example, claims adjusters, employees of financial or commercial institutions, social workers, accountants and persons employed in government agencies. Lawyers also may assist independent nonlawyers, such as paraprofessionals, who are authorized by the law of a jurisdiction to provide particular law-related services. In addition, a lawyer may counsel nonlawyers who wish to proceed pro se.

[4] Other than as authorized by law or this Rule, a lawyer who is not admitted to practice generally in this jurisdiction violates paragraph (b)(1) if the lawyer establishes an office or other systematic and continuous presence in this jurisdiction for the practice of law. Presence may be systematic and continuous even if the lawyer is not physically present here. Such a lawyer must not hold out to the public or otherwise represent that the lawyer is admitted to practice law in this jurisdiction. See also Rule 7.1.

[5] There are occasions in which a lawyer admitted to practice in another United States jurisdiction, and not disbarred or suspended from practice in any jurisdiction, may provide legal services on a temporary basis in this jurisdiction under circumstances that do not create an unreasonable risk to the interests of their clients, the public or the courts. Paragraph (c) identifies four such circumstances. The fact that conduct is not so identified does not imply that the conduct is or is not authorized. With the exception of paragraphs (d)(1) and (d)(2), this Rule does not authorize a U.S. or foreign lawyer to establish an office or other systematic and continuous presence in this jurisdiction without being admitted to practice generally here.

[6] There is no single test to determine whether a lawyer's services are provided on a "temporary basis" in this jurisdiction, and may therefore be permissible under paragraph (c). Services may be "temporary"

even though the lawyer provides services in this jurisdiction on a recurring basis, or for an extended period of time, as when the lawyer is representing a client in a single lengthy negotiation or litigation.

[7] Paragraphs (c) and (d) apply to lawyers who are admitted to practice law in any United States jurisdiction, which includes the District of Columbia and any state, territory or commonwealth of the United States. Paragraph (d) also applies to lawyers admitted in a foreign jurisdiction. The word "admitted" in paragraphs (c), (d) and (e) contemplates that the lawyer is authorized to practice in the jurisdiction in which the lawyer is admitted and excludes a lawyer who while technically admitted is not authorized to practice, because, for example, the lawyer is on inactive status.

[8] Paragraph (c)(1) recognizes that the interests of clients and the public are protected if a lawyer admitted only in another jurisdiction associates with a lawyer licensed to practice in this jurisdiction. For this paragraph to apply, however, the lawyer admitted to practice in this jurisdiction must actively participate in and share responsibility for the representation of the client.

[9] Lawyers not admitted to practice generally in a jurisdiction may be authorized by law or order of a tribunal or an administrative agency to appear before the tribunal or agency. This authority may be granted pursuant to formal rules governing admission pro hac vice or pursuant to informal practice of the tribunal or agency. Under paragraph (c)(2), a lawyer does not violate this Rule when the lawyer appears before a tribunal or agency pursuant to such authority. To the extent that a court rule or other law of this jurisdiction requires a lawyer who is not admitted to practice in this jurisdiction to obtain admission pro hac vice before appearing before a tribunal or administrative agency, this Rule requires the lawyer to obtain that authority.

[10] Paragraph (c)(2) also provides that a lawyer rendering services in this jurisdiction on a temporary basis does not violate this Rule when the lawyer engages in conduct in anticipation of a proceeding or hearing in a jurisdiction in which the lawyer is authorized to practice law or in which the lawyer reasonably expects to be admitted pro hac vice. Examples of such conduct include meetings with the client, interviews of potential witnesses, and the review of documents. Similarly, a lawyer admitted only in another jurisdiction may engage in conduct temporarily in this jurisdiction in connection with pending litigation in another jurisdiction in which the lawyer is or reasonably expects to be authorized to appear, including taking depositions in this jurisdiction.

[11] When a lawyer has been or reasonably expects to be admitted to appear before a court or administrative agency, paragraph (c)(2) also permits conduct by lawyers who are associated with that lawyer in the matter, but who do not expect to appear before the court or administrative agency. For example, subordinate lawyers may conduct research, review documents, and attend meetings with witnesses in support of the lawyer responsible for the litigation.

[12] Paragraph (c)(3) permits a lawyer admitted to practice law in another jurisdiction to perform services on a temporary basis in this jurisdiction if those services are in or reasonably related to a pending or potential arbitration, mediation, or other alternative dispute resolution proceeding in this or another jurisdiction, if the services arise out of or are reasonably related to the lawyer's practice in a jurisdiction in which the lawyer is admitted to practice. The lawyer, however, must obtain admission pro hac vice in the case of a court-annexed arbitration or mediation or otherwise if court rules or law so require.

[13] Paragraph (c)(4) permits a lawyer admitted in another jurisdiction to provide certain legal services on a temporary basis in this jurisdiction that arise out of or are reasonably related to the lawyer's practice in a jurisdiction in which the lawyer is admitted but are not within paragraphs (c)(2) or (c)(3). These services include both legal services and services that nonlawyers may perform but that are considered the practice of law when performed by lawyers.

[14] Paragraphs (c)(3) and (c)(4) require that the services arise out of or be reasonably related to the lawyer's practice in a jurisdiction in which the lawyer is admitted. A variety of factors evidence such a relationship. The lawyer's client may have been previously represented by the lawyer, or may be resident in or have substantial contacts with the jurisdiction in which the lawyer is admitted. The matter, although involving other jurisdictions, may have a significant connection with that jurisdiction. In other cases, significant aspects of the lawyer's work might be conducted in that jurisdiction or a significant aspect of the matter may involve the law of that jurisdiction. The necessary relationship might arise when the client's activities or the legal issues involve multiple jurisdictions, such as when the officers of a multinational corporation survey potential business sites and seek the services of their lawyer in assessing the relative merits of each. In addition, the services may draw on the lawyer's recognized expertise developed through the regular practice of law on behalf of clients in matters involving a particular body of federal, nationally-uniform,

foreign, or international law. Lawyers desiring to provide pro bono legal services on a temporary basis in a jurisdiction that has been affected by a major disaster, but in which they are not otherwise authorized to practice law, as well as lawyers from the affected jurisdiction who seek to practice law temporarily in another jurisdiction, but in which they are not otherwise authorized to practice law, should consult the [*Model Court Rule on Provision of Legal Services Following Determination of Major Disaster*].

[15] Paragraph (d) identifies two circumstances in which a lawyer who is admitted to practice in another United States or a foreign jurisdiction, and is not disbarred or suspended from practice in any jurisdiction, or the equivalent thereof, may establish an office or other systematic and continuous presence in this jurisdiction for the practice of law. Pursuant to paragraph (c) of this Rule, a lawyer admitted in any U.S. jurisdiction may also provide legal services in this jurisdiction on a temporary basis. See also *Model Rule on Temporary Practice by Foreign Lawyers*. Except as provided in paragraphs (d)(1) and (d)(2), a lawyer who is admitted to practice law in another United States or foreign jurisdiction and who establishes an office or other systematic or continuous presence in this jurisdiction must become admitted to practice law generally in this jurisdiction.

[16] Paragraph (d)(1) applies to a U.S. or foreign lawyer who is employed by a client to provide legal services to the client or its organizational affiliates, i.e., entities that control, are controlled by, or are under common control with the employer. This paragraph does not authorize the provision of personal legal services to the employer's officers or employees. The paragraph applies to in-house corporate lawyers, government lawyers and others who are employed to render legal services to the employer. The lawyer's ability to represent the employer outside the jurisdiction in which the lawyer is licensed generally serves the interests of the employer and does not create an unreasonable risk to the client and others because the employer is well situated to assess the lawyer's qualifications and the quality of the lawyer's work. To further decrease any risk to the client, when advising on the domestic law of a United States jurisdiction or on the law of the United States, the foreign lawyer authorized to practice under paragraph (d)(1) of this Rule needs to base that advice on the advice of a lawyer licensed and authorized by the jurisdiction to provide it.

[17] If an employed lawyer establishes an office or other systematic presence in this jurisdiction for the purpose of rendering legal services to

the employer, the lawyer may be subject to registration or other requirements, including assessments for client protection funds and mandatory continuing legal education. See *Model Rule for Registration of In-House Counsel.*

[18] Paragraph (d)(2) recognizes that a U.S. or foreign lawyer may provide legal services in a jurisdiction in which the lawyer is not licensed when authorized to do so by federal or other law, which includes statute, court rule, executive regulation or judicial precedent. See, e.g., *Model Rule on Practice Pending Admission.*

[19] A lawyer who practices law in this jurisdiction pursuant to paragraphs (c) or (d) or otherwise is subject to the disciplinary authority of this jurisdiction. See Rule 8.5(a).

[20] In some circumstances, a lawyer who practices law in this jurisdiction pursuant to paragraphs (c) or (d) may have to inform the client that the lawyer is not licensed to practice law in this jurisdiction. For example, that may be required when the representation occurs primarily in this jurisdiction and requires knowledge of the law of this jurisdiction. See Rule 1.4(b).

[21] Paragraphs (c) and (d) do not authorize communications advertising legal services in this jurisdiction by lawyers who are admitted to practice in other jurisdictions. Whether and how lawyers may communicate the availability of their services in this jurisdiction is governed by Rules 7.1 to 7.3.

Definitional Cross-References

"Reasonably" *See* Rule 1.0(h)
"Tribunal" *See* Rule 1.0(m)

Rule 5.6: Restrictions on Right to Practice

A lawyer shall not participate in offering or making:

(a) a partnership, shareholders, operating, employment, or other similar type of agreement that restricts the right of a lawyer to practice after termination of the relationship, except an agreement concerning benefits upon retirement; or

(b) an agreement in which a restriction on the lawyer's right to practice is part of the settlement of a client controversy.

Comment

[1] An agreement restricting the right of lawyers to practice after leaving a firm not only limits their professional autonomy but also limits the freedom of clients to choose a lawyer. Paragraph (a) prohibits such agreements except for restrictions incident to provisions concerning retirement benefits for service with the firm.

[2] Paragraph (b) prohibits a lawyer from agreeing not to represent other persons in connection with settling a claim on behalf of a client.

[3] This Rule does not apply to prohibit restrictions that may be included in the terms of the sale of a law practice pursuant to Rule 1.17.

RULE 5.7: RESPONSIBILITIES REGARDING LAW-RELATED SERVICES

(a) A lawyer shall be subject to the Rules of Professional Conduct with respect to the provision of law-related services, as defined in paragraph (b), if the law-related services are provided:

(1) by the lawyer in circumstances that are not distinct from the lawyer's provision of legal services to clients; or

(2) in other circumstances by an entity controlled by the lawyer individually or with others if the lawyer fails to take reasonable measures to assure that a person obtaining the law-related services knows that the services are not legal services and that the protections of the client-lawyer relationship do not exist.

(b) The term "law-related services" denotes services that might reasonably be performed in conjunction with and in substance are related to the provision of legal services, and that are not prohibited as unauthorized practice of law when provided by a nonlawyer.

Comment

[1] When a lawyer performs law-related services or controls an organization that does so, there exists the potential for ethical problems. Principal among these is the possibility that the person for whom the law-related services are performed fails to understand that the services may not carry with them the protections normally afforded as part of the client-lawyer relationship. The recipient of the law-related services may

expect, for example, that the protection of client confidences, prohibitions against representation of persons with conflicting interests, and obligations of a lawyer to maintain professional independence apply to the provision of law-related services when that may not be the case.

[2] Rule 5.7 applies to the provision of law-related services by a lawyer even when the lawyer does not provide any legal services to the person for whom the law-related services are performed and whether the law-related services are performed through a law firm or a separate entity. The Rule identifies the circumstances in which all of the Rules of Professional Conduct apply to the provision of law-related services. Even when those circumstances do not exist, however, the conduct of a lawyer involved in the provision of law-related services is subject to those Rules that apply generally to lawyer conduct, regardless of whether the conduct involves the provision of legal services. See, e.g., Rule 8.4.

[3] When law-related services are provided by a lawyer under circumstances that are not distinct from the lawyer's provision of legal services to clients, the lawyer in providing the law-related services must adhere to the requirements of the Rules of Professional Conduct as provided in paragraph (a)(1). Even when the law-related and legal services are provided in circumstances that are distinct from each other, for example through separate entities or different support staff within the law firm, the Rules of Professional Conduct apply to the lawyer as provided in paragraph (a)(2) unless the lawyer takes reasonable measures to assure that the recipient of the law-related services knows that the services are not legal services and that the protections of the client-lawyer relationship do not apply.

[4] Law-related services also may be provided through an entity that is distinct from that through which the lawyer provides legal services. If the lawyer individually or with others has control of such an entity's operations, the Rule requires the lawyer to take reasonable measures to assure that each person using the services of the entity knows that the services provided by the entity are not legal services and that the Rules of Professional Conduct that relate to the client-lawyer relationship do not apply. A lawyer's control of an entity extends to the ability to direct its operation. Whether a lawyer has such control will depend upon the circumstances of the particular case.

[5] When a client-lawyer relationship exists with a person who is referred by a lawyer to a separate law-related service entity controlled by the lawyer, individually or with others, the lawyer must comply with Rule 1.8(a).

[6] In taking the reasonable measures referred to in paragraph (a)(2) to assure that a person using law-related services understands the practical effect or significance of the inapplicability of the Rules of Professional Conduct, the lawyer should communicate to the person receiving the law-related services, in a manner sufficient to assure that the person understands the significance of the fact, that the relationship of the person to the business entity will not be a client-lawyer relationship. The communication should be made before entering into an agreement for provision of or providing law-related services, and preferably should be in writing.

[7] The burden is upon the lawyer to show that the lawyer has taken reasonable measures under the circumstances to communicate the desired understanding. For instance, a sophisticated user of law-related services, such as a publicly held corporation, may require a lesser explanation than someone unaccustomed to making distinctions between legal services and law-related services, such as an individual seeking tax advice from a lawyer-accountant or investigative services in connection with a lawsuit.

[8] Regardless of the sophistication of potential recipients of law-related services, a lawyer should take special care to keep separate the provision of law-related and legal services in order to minimize the risk that the recipient will assume that the law-related services are legal services. The risk of such confusion is especially acute when the lawyer renders both types of services with respect to the same matter. Under some circumstances the legal and law-related services may be so closely entwined that they cannot be distinguished from each other, and the requirement of disclosure and consultation imposed by paragraph (a)(2) of the Rule cannot be met. In such a case a lawyer will be responsible for assuring that both the lawyer's conduct and, to the extent required by Rule 5.3, that of nonlawyer employees in the distinct entity that the lawyer controls complies in all respects with the Rules of Professional Conduct.

[9] A broad range of economic and other interests of clients may be served by lawyers' engaging in the delivery of law-related services. Examples of law-related services include providing title insurance, financial planning, accounting, trust services, real estate counseling, legislative lobbying, economic analysis, social work, psychological counseling, tax preparation, and patent, medical or environmental consulting.

[10] When a lawyer is obliged to accord the recipients of such services the protections of those Rules that apply to the client-lawyer re-

lationship, the lawyer must take special care to heed the proscriptions of the Rules addressing conflict of interest (Rules 1.7 through 1.11, especially Rules 1.7(a)(2) and 1.8(a), (b) and (f)), and to scrupulously adhere to the requirements of Rule 1.6 relating to disclosure of confidential information. The promotion of the law-related services must also in all respects comply with Rules 7.1 through 7.3, dealing with advertising and solicitation. In that regard, lawyers should take special care to identify the obligations that may be imposed as a result of a jurisdiction's decisional law.

[11] When the full protections of all of the Rules of Professional Conduct do not apply to the provision of law-related services, principles of law external to the Rules, for example, the law of principal and agent, govern the legal duties owed to those receiving the services. Those other legal principles may establish a different degree of protection for the recipient with respect to confidentiality of information, conflicts of interest and permissible business relationships with clients. See also Rule 8.4 (Misconduct).

Definitional Cross-References

"Knows" *See* Rule 1.0(f)
"Reasonable" *See* Rule 1.0(h)

PUBLIC SERVICE

RULE 6.1: VOLUNTARY PRO BONO PUBLICO SERVICE

Every lawyer has a professional responsibility to provide legal services to those unable to pay. A lawyer should aspire to render at least (50) hours of pro bono publico legal services per year. In fulfilling this responsibility, the lawyer should:

(a) provide a substantial majority of the (50) hours of legal services without fee or expectation of fee to:

(1) persons of limited means; or

(2) charitable, religious, civic, community, governmental and educational organizations in matters that are designed primarily to address the needs of persons of limited means; and

(b) provide any additional services through:

(1) delivery of legal services at no fee or substantially reduced fee to individuals, groups or organizations seeking

to secure or protect civil rights, civil liberties or public rights, or charitable, religious, civic, community, governmental and educational organizations in matters in furtherance of their organizational purposes, where the payment of standard legal fees would significantly deplete the organization's economic resources or would be otherwise inappropriate;

    (2) delivery of legal services at a substantially reduced fee to persons of limited means; or

    (3) participation in activities for improving the law, the legal system or the legal profession.

In addition, a lawyer should voluntarily contribute financial support to organizations that provide legal services to persons of limited means.

Comment

[1] Every lawyer, regardless of professional prominence or professional work load, has a responsibility to provide legal services to those unable to pay, and personal involvement in the problems of the disadvantaged can be one of the most rewarding experiences in the life of a lawyer. The American Bar Association urges all lawyers to provide a minimum of 50 hours of pro bono services annually. States, however, may decide to choose a higher or lower number of hours of annual service (which may be expressed as a percentage of a lawyer's professional time) depending upon local needs and local conditions. It is recognized that in some years a lawyer may render greater or fewer hours than the annual standard specified, but during the course of his or her legal career, each lawyer should render on average per year, the number of hours set forth in this Rule. Services can be performed in civil matters or in criminal or quasi-criminal matters for which there is no government obligation to provide funds for legal representation, such as post-conviction death penalty appeal cases.

[2] Paragraphs (a)(1) and (2) recognize the critical need for legal services that exists among persons of limited means by providing that a substantial majority of the legal services rendered annually to the disadvantaged be furnished without fee or expectation of fee. Legal services under these paragraphs consist of a full range of activities, including individual and class representation, the provision of legal advice, legislative lobbying, administrative rule making and the provision of free training or mentoring to those who represent persons of limited means. The variety of these activities should facilitate participation by government

lawyers, even when restrictions exist on their engaging in the outside practice of law.

[3] Persons eligible for legal services under paragraphs (a)(1) and (2) are those who qualify for participation in programs funded by the Legal Services Corporation and those whose incomes and financial resources are slightly above the guidelines utilized by such programs but nevertheless, cannot afford counsel. Legal services can be rendered to individuals or to organizations such as homeless shelters, battered women's centers and food pantries that serve those of limited means. The term "governmental organizations" includes, but is not limited to, public protection programs and sections of governmental or public sector agencies.

[4] Because service must be provided without fee or expectation of fee, the intent of the lawyer to render free legal services is essential for the work performed to fall within the meaning of paragraphs (a)(1) and (2). Accordingly, services rendered cannot be considered pro bono if an anticipated fee is uncollected, but the award of statutory attorneys' fees in a case originally accepted as pro bono would not disqualify such services from inclusion under this section. Lawyers who do receive fees in such cases are encouraged to contribute an appropriate portion of such fees to organizations or projects that benefit persons of limited means.

[5] While it is possible for a lawyer to fulfill the annual responsibility to perform pro bono services exclusively through activities described in paragraphs (a)(1) and (2), to the extent that any hours of service remained unfulfilled, the remaining commitment can be met in a variety of ways as set forth in paragraph (b). Constitutional, statutory or regulatory restrictions may prohibit or impede government and public sector lawyers and judges from performing the pro bono services outlined in paragraphs (a)(1) and (2). Accordingly, where those restrictions apply, government and public sector lawyers and judges may fulfill their pro bono responsibility by performing services outlined in paragraph (b).

[6] Paragraph (b)(1) includes the provision of certain types of legal services to those whose incomes and financial resources place them above limited means. It also permits the pro bono lawyer to accept a substantially reduced fee for services. Examples of the types of issues that may be addressed under this paragraph include First Amendment claims, Title VII claims and environmental protection claims. Additionally, a wide range of organizations may be represented, including social service, medical research, cultural and religious groups.

[7] Paragraph (b)(2) covers instances in which lawyers agree to and receive a modest fee for furnishing legal services to persons of limited means. Participation in judicare programs and acceptance of court appointments in which the fee is substantially below a lawyer's usual rate are encouraged under this section.

[8] Paragraph (b)(3) recognizes the value of lawyers engaging in activities that improve the law, the legal system or the legal profession. Serving on bar association committees, serving on boards of pro bono or legal services programs, taking part in Law Day activities, acting as a continuing legal education instructor, a mediator or an arbitrator and engaging in legislative lobbying to improve the law, the legal system or the profession are a few examples of the many activities that fall within this paragraph.

[9] Because the provision of pro bono services is a professional responsibility, it is the individual ethical commitment of each lawyer. Nevertheless, there may be times when it is not feasible for a lawyer to engage in pro bono services. At such times a lawyer may discharge the pro bono responsibility by providing financial support to organizations providing free legal services to persons of limited means. Such financial support should be reasonably equivalent to the value of the hours of service that would have otherwise been provided. In addition, at times it may be more feasible to satisfy the pro bono responsibility collectively, as by a firm's aggregate pro bono activities.

[10] Because the efforts of individual lawyers are not enough to meet the need for free legal services that exists among persons of limited means, the government and the profession have instituted additional programs to provide those services. Every lawyer should financially support such programs, in addition to either providing direct pro bono services or making financial contributions when pro bono service is not feasible.

[11] Law firms should act reasonably to enable and encourage all lawyers in the firm to provide the pro bono legal services called for by this Rule.

[12] The responsibility set forth in this Rule is not intended to be enforced through disciplinary process.

Definitional Cross-References

"Substantial" *See* Rule 1.0(l)

Rule 6.2: Accepting Appointments

A lawyer shall not seek to avoid appointment by a tribunal to represent a person except for good cause, such as:

(a) representing the client is likely to result in violation of the Rules of Professional Conduct or other law;

(b) representing the client is likely to result in an unreasonable financial burden on the lawyer; or

(c) the client or the cause is so repugnant to the lawyer as to be likely to impair the client-lawyer relationship or the lawyer's ability to represent the client.

Comment

[1] A lawyer ordinarily is not obliged to accept a client whose character or cause the lawyer regards as repugnant. The lawyer's freedom to select clients is, however, qualified. All lawyers have a responsibility to assist in providing pro bono publico service. See Rule 6.1. An individual lawyer fulfills this responsibility by accepting a fair share of unpopular matters or indigent or unpopular clients. A lawyer may also be subject to appointment by a court to serve unpopular clients or persons unable to afford legal services.

Appointed Counsel

[2] For good cause a lawyer may seek to decline an appointment to represent a person who cannot afford to retain counsel or whose cause is unpopular. Good cause exists if the lawyer could not handle the matter competently, see Rule 1.1, or if undertaking the representation would result in an improper conflict of interest, for example, when the client or the cause is so repugnant to the lawyer as to be likely to impair the client-lawyer relationship or the lawyer's ability to represent the client. A lawyer may also seek to decline an appointment if acceptance would be unreasonably burdensome, for example, when it would impose a financial sacrifice so great as to be unjust.

[3] An appointed lawyer has the same obligations to the client as retained counsel, including the obligations of loyalty and confidentiality, and is subject to the same limitations on the client-lawyer relationship, such as the obligation to refrain from assisting the client in violation of the Rules.

Definitional Cross-References

"Tribunal" *See* Rule 1.0(m)

RULE 6.3: MEMBERSHIP IN
LEGAL SERVICES ORGANIZATION

A lawyer may serve as a director, officer or member of a legal services organization, apart from the law firm in which the lawyer practices, notwithstanding that the organization serves persons having interests adverse to a client of the lawyer. The lawyer shall not knowingly participate in a decision or action of the organization:

(a) if participating in the decision or action would be incompatible with the lawyer's obligations to a client under Rule 1.7; or

(b) where the decision or action could have a material adverse effect on the representation of a client of the organization whose interests are adverse to a client of the lawyer.

Comment

[1] Lawyers should be encouraged to support and participate in legal service organizations. A lawyer who is an officer or a member of such an organization does not thereby have a client-lawyer relationship with persons served by the organization. However, there is potential conflict between the interests of such persons and the interests of the lawyer's clients. If the possibility of such conflict disqualified a lawyer from serving on the board of a legal services organization, the profession's involvement in such organizations would be severely curtailed.

[2] It may be necessary in appropriate cases to reassure a client of the organization that the representation will not be affected by conflicting loyalties of a member of the board. Established, written policies in this respect can enhance the credibility of such assurances.

Definitional Cross-References

"Law firm" *See* Rule 1.0(c)
"Knowingly" *See* Rule 1.0(f)

RULE 6.4: LAW REFORM ACTIVITIES
AFFECTING CLIENT INTERESTS

A lawyer may serve as a director, officer or member of an organization involved in reform of the law or its administration notwithstanding that the reform may affect the interests of a client of the lawyer. When the lawyer knows that the interests of a client may be materially benefitted by a decision in which the lawyer participates, the lawyer shall disclose that fact but need not identify the client.

Comment

[1] Lawyers involved in organizations seeking law reform generally do not have a client-lawyer relationship with the organization. Otherwise, it might follow that a lawyer could not be involved in a bar association law reform program that might indirectly affect a client. See also Rule 1.2(b). For example, a lawyer specializing in antitrust litigation might be regarded as disqualified from participating in drafting revisions of rules governing that subject. In determining the nature and scope of participation in such activities, a lawyer should be mindful of obligations to clients under other Rules, particularly Rule 1.7. A lawyer is professionally obligated to protect the integrity of the program by making an appropriate disclosure within the organization when the lawyer knows a private client might be materially benefitted.

Definitional Cross-References
"Knows" *See* Rule 1.0(f)

RULE 6.5: NONPROFIT AND COURT-ANNEXED LIMITED LEGAL SERVICES PROGRAMS

(a) A lawyer who, under the auspices of a program sponsored by a nonprofit organization or court, provides short-term limited legal services to a client without expectation by either the lawyer or the client that the lawyer will provide continuing representation in the matter:

(1) is subject to Rules 1.7 and 1.9(a) only if the lawyer knows that the representation of the client involves a conflict of interest; and

(2) is subject to Rule 1.10 only if the lawyer knows that another lawyer associated with the lawyer in a law firm is disqualified by Rule 1.7 or 1.9(a) with respect to the matter.

(b) Except as provided in paragraph (a)(2), Rule 1.10 is inapplicable to a representation governed by this Rule.

Comment

[1] Legal services organizations, courts and various nonprofit organizations have established programs through which lawyers provide short-term limited legal services—such as advice or the completion of legal forms—that will assist persons to address their legal problems without further representation by a lawyer. In these programs, such as legal-advice hotlines, advice-only clinics or pro se counseling programs, a client-lawyer relationship is established, but there is no expectation that the lawyer's representation of the client will continue beyond the limited consultation. Such programs are normally operated under circumstances in which it is not feasible for a lawyer to systematically screen for conflicts of interest as is generally required before undertaking a representation. See, e.g., Rules 1.7, 1.9 and 1.10.

[2] A lawyer who provides short-term limited legal services pursuant to this Rule must secure the client's informed consent to the limited scope of the representation. See Rule 1.2(c). If a short-term limited representation would not be reasonable under the circumstances, the lawyer may offer advice to the client but must also advise the client of the need for further assistance of counsel. Except as provided in this Rule, the Rules of Professional Conduct, including Rules 1.6 and 1.9(c), are applicable to the limited representation.

[3] Because a lawyer who is representing a client in the circumstances addressed by this Rule ordinarily is not able to check systematically for conflicts of interest, paragraph (a) requires compliance with Rules 1.7 or 1.9(a) only if the lawyer knows that the representation presents a conflict of interest for the lawyer, and with Rule 1.10 only if the lawyer knows that another lawyer in the lawyer's firm is disqualified by Rules 1.7 or 1.9(a) in the matter.

[4] Because the limited nature of the services significantly reduces the risk of conflicts of interest with other matters being handled by the lawyer's firm, paragraph (b) provides that Rule 1.10 is inapplicable to a representation governed by this Rule except as provided by paragraph (a)(2). Paragraph (a)(2) requires the participating lawyer to comply with Rule 1.10 when the lawyer knows that the lawyer's firm is disqualified by Rules 1.7 or 1.9(a). By virtue of paragraph (b), however, a lawyer's participation in a short-term limited legal services program will not preclude the lawyer's firm from undertaking or continuing the representation of a client with interests adverse to a client being represented under

the program's auspices. Nor will the personal disqualification of a lawyer participating in the program be imputed to other lawyers participating in the program.

[5] If, after commencing a short-term limited representation in accordance with this Rule, a lawyer undertakes to represent the client in the matter on an ongoing basis, Rules 1.7, 1.9(a) and 1.10 become applicable.

Definitional Cross-References

"Law firm" *See* Rule 1.0(c)
"Knows" *See* Rule 1.0(f)

INFORMATION ABOUT LEGAL SERVICES

RULE 7.1: COMMUNICATIONS CONCERNING A LAWYER'S SERVICES

A lawyer shall not make a false or misleading communication about the lawyer or the lawyer's services. A communication is false or misleading if it contains a material misrepresentation of fact or law, or omits a fact necessary to make the statement considered as a whole not materially misleading.

Comment

[1] This Rule governs all communications about a lawyer's services, including advertising. Whatever means are used to make known a lawyer's services, statements about them must be truthful.

[2] Misleading truthful statements are prohibited by this Rule. A truthful statement is misleading if it omits a fact necessary to make the lawyer's communication considered as a whole not materially misleading. A truthful statement is misleading if a substantial likelihood exists that it will lead a reasonable person to formulate a specific conclusion about the lawyer or the lawyer's services for which there is no reasonable factual foundation. A truthful statement is also misleading if presented in a way that creates a substantial likelihood that a reasonable person would believe the lawyer's communication requires that person to take further action when, in fact, no action is required.

[3] A communication that truthfully reports a lawyer's achievements on behalf of clients or former clients may be misleading if presented so as to lead a reasonable person to form an unjustified expectation that the

same results could be obtained for other clients in similar matters without reference to the specific factual and legal circumstances of each client's case. Similarly, an unsubstantiated claim about a lawyer's or law firm's services or fees, or an unsubstantiated comparison of the lawyer's or law firm's services or fees with those of other lawyers or law firms, may be misleading if presented with such specificity as would lead a reasonable person to conclude that the comparison or claim can be substantiated. The inclusion of an appropriate disclaimer or qualifying language may preclude a finding that a statement is likely to create unjustified expectations or otherwise mislead the public.

[4] It is professional misconduct for a lawyer to engage in conduct involving dishonesty, fraud, deceit or misrepresentation. Rule 8.4(c). See also Rule 8.4(e) for the prohibition against stating or implying an ability to improperly influence a government agency or official or to achieve results by means that violate the Rules of Professional Conduct or other law.

[5] Firm names, letterhead and professional designations are communications concerning a lawyer's services. A firm may be designated by the names of all or some of its current members, by the names of deceased members where there has been a succession in the firm's identity or by a trade name if it is not false or misleading. A lawyer or law firm also may be designated by a distinctive website address, social media username or comparable professional designation that is not misleading. A law firm name or designation is misleading if it implies a connection with a government agency, with a deceased lawyer who was not a former member of the firm, with a lawyer not associated with the firm or a predecessor firm, with a nonlawyer or with a public or charitable legal services organization. If a firm uses a trade name that includes a geographical name such as "Springfield Legal Clinic," an express statement explaining that it is not a public legal aid organization may be required to avoid a misleading implication.

[6] A law firm with offices in more than one jurisdiction may use the same name or other professional designation in each jurisdiction.

[7] Lawyers may not imply or hold themselves out as practicing together in one firm when they are not a firm, as defined in Rule 1.0(c), because to do so would be false and misleading.

[8] It is misleading to use the name of a lawyer holding a public office in the name of a law firm, or in communications on the law firm's behalf, during any substantial period in which the lawyer is not actively and regularly practicing with the firm.

RULE 7.2: COMMUNICATIONS CONCERNING A LAWYER'S SERVICES: SPECIFIC RULES

(a) A lawyer may communicate information regarding the lawyer's services through any media.

(b) A lawyer shall not compensate, give or promise anything of value to a person for recommending the lawyer's services except that a lawyer may:

(1) pay the reasonable costs of advertisements or communications permitted by this Rule;

(2) pay the usual charges of a legal service plan or a not-for-profit or qualified lawyer referral service;

(3) pay for a law practice in accordance with Rule 1.17;

(4) refer clients to another lawyer or a nonlawyer professional pursuant to an agreement not otherwise prohibited under these Rules that provides for the other person to refer clients or customers to the lawyer, if:

(i) the reciprocal referral agreement is not exclusive; and

(ii) the client is informed of the existence and nature of the agreement; and

(5) give nominal gifts as an expression of appreciation that are neither intended nor reasonably expected to be a form of compensation for recommending a lawyer's services.

(c) A lawyer shall not state or imply that a lawyer is certified as a specialist in a particular field of law, unless:

(1) the lawyer has been certified as a specialist by an organization that has been approved by an appropriate authority of the state or the District of Columbia or a U.S. Territory or that has been accredited by the American Bar Association; and

(2) the name of the certifying organization is clearly identified in the communication.

(d) Any communication made under this Rule must include the name and contact information of at least one lawyer or law firm responsible for its content.

Comment

[1] This Rule permits public dissemination of information concerning a lawyer's or law firm's name, address, email address, website, and telephone number; the kinds of services the lawyer will undertake; the

basis on which the lawyer's fees are determined, including prices for specific services and payment and credit arrangements; a lawyer's foreign language ability; names of references and, with their consent, names of clients regularly represented; and other information that might invite the attention of those seeking legal assistance.

Paying Others to Recommend a Lawyer

[2] Except as permitted under paragraphs (b)(1)-(b)(5), lawyers are not permitted to pay others for recommending the lawyer's services. A communication contains a recommendation if it endorses or vouches for a lawyer's credentials, abilities, competence, character, or other professional qualities. Directory listings and group advertisements that list lawyers by practice area, without more, do not constitute impermissible "recommendations."

[3] Paragraph (b)(1) allows a lawyer to pay for advertising and communications permitted by this Rule, including the costs of print directory listings, on-line directory listings, newspaper ads, television and radio airtime, domain-name registrations, sponsorship fees, Internet-based advertisements, and group advertising. A lawyer may compensate employees, agents and vendors who are engaged to provide marketing or client development services, such as publicists, public-relations personnel, business-development staff, television and radio station employees or spokespersons and website designers.

[4] Paragraph (b)(5) permits lawyers to give nominal gifts as an expression of appreciation to a person for recommending the lawyer's services or referring a prospective client. The gift may not be more than a token item as might be given for holidays, or other ordinary social hospitality. A gift is prohibited if offered or given in consideration of any promise, agreement or understanding that such a gift would be forthcoming or that referrals would be made or encouraged in the future.

[5] A lawyer may pay others for generating client leads, such as Internet-based client leads, as long as the lead generator does not recommend the lawyer, any payment to the lead generator is consistent with Rules 1.5(e) (division of fees) and 5.4 (professional independence of the lawyer), and the lead generator's communications are consistent with Rule 7.1 (communications concerning a lawyer's services). To comply with Rule 7.1, a lawyer must not pay a lead generator that states, implies, or creates a reasonable impression that it is recommending the lawyer, is making the referral without payment from the lawyer, or has analyzed a

person's legal problems when determining which lawyer should receive the referral. See Comment [2] (definition of "recommendation"). See also Rule 5.3 (duties of lawyers and law firms with respect to the conduct of nonlawyers); Rule 8.4(a) (duty to avoid violating the Rules through the acts of another).

[6] A lawyer may pay the usual charges of a legal service plan or a not-for-profit or qualified lawyer referral service. A legal service plan is a prepaid or group legal service plan or a similar delivery system that assists people who seek to secure legal representation. A lawyer referral service, on the other hand, is any organization that holds itself out to the public as a lawyer referral service. Qualified referral services are consumer-oriented organizations that provide unbiased referrals to lawyers with appropriate experience in the subject matter of the representation and afford other client protections, such as complaint procedures or malpractice insurance requirements. Consequently, this Rule only permits a lawyer to pay the usual charges of a not-for-profit or qualified lawyer referral service. A qualified lawyer referral service is one that is approved by an appropriate regulatory authority as affording adequate protections for the public. See, e.g., the American Bar Association's Model Supreme Court Rules Governing Lawyer Referral Services and Model Lawyer Referral and Information Service Quality Assurance Act.

[7] A lawyer who accepts assignments or referrals from a legal service plan or referrals from a lawyer referral service must act reasonably to assure that the activities of the plan or service are compatible with the lawyer's professional obligations. Legal service plans and lawyer referral services may communicate with the public, but such communication must be in conformity with these Rules. Thus, advertising must not be false or misleading, as would be the case if the communications of a group advertising program or a group legal services plan would mislead the public to think that it was a lawyer referral service sponsored by a state agency or bar association.

[8] A lawyer also may agree to refer clients to another lawyer or a nonlawyer professional, in return for the undertaking of that person to refer clients or customers to the lawyer. Such reciprocal referral arrangements must not interfere with the lawyer's professional judgment as to making referrals or as to providing substantive legal services. See Rules 2.1 and 5.4(c). Except as provided in Rule 1.5(e), a lawyer who receives referrals from a lawyer or nonlawyer professional must not pay anything solely for the referral, but the lawyer does not violate paragraph (b) of

this Rule by agreeing to refer clients to the other lawyer or nonlawyer professional, so long as the reciprocal referral agreement is not exclusive and the client is informed of the referral agreement. Conflicts of interest created by such arrangements are governed by Rule 1.7. Reciprocal referral agreements should not be of indefinite duration and should be reviewed periodically to determine whether they comply with these Rules. This Rule does not restrict referrals or divisions of revenues or net income among lawyers within firms comprised of multiple entities.

Communications about Fields of Practice

[9] Paragraph (c) of this Rule permits a lawyer to communicate that the lawyer does or does not practice in particular areas of law. A lawyer is generally permitted to state that the lawyer "concentrates in" or is a "specialist," practices a "specialty," or "specializes in" particular fields based on the lawyer's experience, specialized training or education, but such communications are subject to the "false and misleading" standard applied in Rule 7.1 to communications concerning a lawyer's services.

[10] The Patent and Trademark Office has a long-established policy of designating lawyers practicing before the Office. The designation of Admiralty practice also has a long historical tradition associated with maritime commerce and the federal courts. A lawyer's communications about these practice areas are not prohibited by this Rule.

[11] This Rule permits a lawyer to state that the lawyer is certified as a specialist in a field of law if such certification is granted by an organization approved by an appropriate authority of a state, the District of Columbia or a U.S. Territory or accredited by the American Bar Association or another organization, such as a state supreme court or a state bar association, that has been approved by the authority of the state, the District of Columbia or a U.S. Territory to accredit organizations that certify lawyers as specialists. Certification signifies that an objective entity has recognized an advanced degree of knowledge and experience in the specialty area greater than is suggested by general licensure to practice law. Certifying organizations may be expected to apply standards of experience, knowledge and proficiency to ensure that a lawyer's recognition as a specialist is meaningful and reliable. To ensure that consumers can obtain access to useful information about an organization granting certification, the name of the certifying organization must be included in any communication regarding the certification.

Required Contact Information

[12] This Rule requires that any communication about a lawyer or law firm's services include the name of, and contact information for, the lawyer or law firm. Contact information includes a website address, a telephone number, an email address or a physical office location.

RULE 7.3: SOLICITATION OF CLIENTS

(a) "Solicitation" or "solicit" denotes a communication initiated by or on behalf of a lawyer or law firm that is directed to a specific person the lawyer knows or reasonably should know needs legal services in a particular matter and that offers to provide, or reasonably can be understood as offering to provide, legal services for that matter.

(b) A lawyer shall not solicit professional employment by live person-to-person contact when a significant motive for the lawyer's doing so is the lawyer's or law firm's pecuniary gain, unless the contact is with a:

(1) lawyer;

(2) person who has a family, close personal, or prior business or professional relationship with the lawyer or law firm; or

(3) person who routinely uses for business purposes the type of legal services offered by the lawyer.

(c) A lawyer shall not solicit professional employment even when not otherwise prohibited by paragraph (b), if:

(1) the target of the solicitation has made known to the lawyer a desire not to be solicited by the lawyer; or

(2) the solicitation involves coercion, duress or harassment.

(d) This Rule does not prohibit communications authorized by law or ordered by a court or other tribunal.

(e) Notwithstanding the prohibitions in this Rule, a lawyer may participate with a prepaid or group legal service plan operated by an organization not owned or directed by the lawyer that uses live person-to-person contact to enroll members or sell subscriptions for the plan from persons who are not known to need legal services in a particular matter covered by the plan.

Comment

[1] Paragraph (b) prohibits a lawyer from soliciting professional employment by live person-to-person contact when a significant motive for the lawyer's doing so is the lawyer's or the law firm's pecuniary gain. A lawyer's communication is not a solicitation if it is directed to the general public, such as through a billboard, an Internet banner advertisement, a website or a television commercial, or if it is in response to a request for information or is automatically generated in response to electronic searches.

[2] "Live person-to-person contact" means in-person, face-to-face, live telephone and other real-time visual or auditory person-to-person communications where the person is subject to a direct personal encounter without time for reflection. Such person-to-person contact does not include chat rooms, text messages or other written communications that recipients may easily disregard. A potential for overreaching exists when a lawyer, seeking pecuniary gain, solicits a person known to be in need of legal services. This form of contact subjects a person to the private importuning of the trained advocate in a direct interpersonal encounter. The person, who may already feel overwhelmed by the circumstances giving rise to the need for legal services, may find it difficult to fully evaluate all available alternatives with reasoned judgment and appropriate selfinterest in the face of the lawyer's presence and insistence upon an immediate response. The situation is fraught with the possibility of undue influence, intimidation, and overreaching.

[3] The potential for overreaching inherent in live person-to-person contact justifies its prohibition, since lawyers have alternative means of conveying necessary information. In particular, communications can be mailed or transmitted by email or other electronic means that do not violate other laws. These forms of communications make it possible for the public to be informed about the need for legal services, and about the qualifications of available lawyers and law firms, without subjecting the public to live person-to-person persuasion that may overwhelm a person's judgment.

[4] The contents of live person-to-person contact can be disputed and may not be subject to thirdparty scrutiny. Consequently, they are much more likely to approach (and occasionally cross) the dividing line between accurate representations and those that are false and misleading.

[5] There is far less likelihood that a lawyer would engage in overreaching against a former client, or a person with whom the lawyer has a close personal, family, business or professional relationship, or in situ-

ations in which the lawyer is motivated by considerations other than the lawyer's pecuniary gain. Nor is there a serious potential for overreaching when the person contacted is a lawyer or is known to routinely use the type of legal services involved for business purposes. Examples include persons who routinely hire outside counsel to represent the entity; entrepreneurs who regularly engage business, employment law or intellectual property lawyers; small business proprietors who routinely hire lawyers for lease or contract issues; and other people who routinely retain lawyers for business transactions or formations. Paragraph (b) is not intended to prohibit a lawyer from participating in constitutionally protected activities of public or charitable legal-service organizations or bona fide political, social, civic, fraternal, employee or trade organizations whose purposes include providing or recommending legal services to their members or beneficiaries.

[6] A solicitation that contains false or misleading information within the meaning of Rule 7.1, that involves coercion, duress or harassment within the meaning of Rule 7.3(c)(2), or that involves contact with someone who has made known to the lawyer a desire not to be solicited by the lawyer within the meaning of Rule 7.3(c)(1) is prohibited. Live, person-to-person contact of individuals who may be especially vulnerable to coercion or duress is ordinarily not appropriate, for example, the elderly, those whose first language is not English, or the disabled.

[7] This Rule does not prohibit a lawyer from contacting representatives of organizations or groups that may be interested in establishing a group or prepaid legal plan for their members, insureds, beneficiaries or other third parties for the purpose of informing such entities of the availability of and details concerning the plan or arrangement which the lawyer or lawyer's firm is willing to offer. This form of communication is not directed to people who are seeking legal services for themselves. Rather, it is usually addressed to an individual acting in a fiduciary capacity seeking a supplier of legal services for others who may, if they choose, become prospective clients of the lawyer. Under these circumstances, the activity which the lawyer undertakes in communicating with such representatives and the type of information transmitted to the individual are functionally similar to and serve the same purpose as advertising permitted under Rule 7.2.

[8] Communications authorized by law or ordered by a court or tribunal include a notice to potential members of a class in class action litigation.

[9] Paragraph (e) of this Rule permits a lawyer to participate with an organization which uses personal contact to enroll members for its group or prepaid legal service plan, provided that the personal contact is not undertaken by any lawyer who would be a provider of legal services through the plan. The organization must not be owned by or directed (whether as manager or otherwise) by any lawyer or law firm that participates in the plan. For example, paragraph (e) would not permit a lawyer to create an organization controlled directly or indirectly by the lawyer and use the organization for the person-to-person solicitation of legal employment of the lawyer through memberships in the plan or otherwise. The communication permitted by these organizations must not be directed to a person known to need legal services in a particular matter, but must be designed to inform potential plan members generally of another means of affordable legal services. Lawyers who participate in a legal service plan must reasonably assure that the plan sponsors are in compliance with Rules 7.1, 7.2 and 7.3(c).

RULE 7.4 (DELETED 2018)

RULE 7.5 (DELETED 2018)

RULE 7.6: POLITICAL CONTRIBUTIONS TO OBTAIN GOVERNMENT LEGAL ENGAGEMENTS OR APPOINTMENTS BY JUDGES

A lawyer or law firm shall not accept a government legal engagement or an appointment by a judge if the lawyer or law firm makes a political contribution or solicits political contributions for the purpose of obtaining or being considered for that type of legal engagement or appointment.

Comment

[1] Lawyers have a right to participate fully in the political process, which includes making and soliciting political contributions to candidates for judicial and other public office. Nevertheless, when lawyers make or solicit political contributions in order to obtain an engagement for legal work awarded by a government agency, or to obtain appoint-

ment by a judge, the public may legitimately question whether the lawyers engaged to perform the work are selected on the basis of competence and merit. In such a circumstance, the integrity of the profession is undermined.

[2] The term "political contribution" denotes any gift, subscription, loan, advance or deposit of anything of value made directly or indirectly to a candidate, incumbent, political party or campaign committee to influence or provide financial support for election to or retention in judicial or other government office. Political contributions in initiative and referendum elections are not included. For purposes of this Rule, the term "political contribution" does not include uncompensated services.

[3] Subject to the exceptions below, (i) the term "government legal engagement" denotes any engagement to provide legal services that a public official has the direct or indirect power to award; and (ii) the term "appointment by a judge" denotes an appointment to a position such as referee, commissioner, special master, receiver, guardian or other similar position that is made by a judge. Those terms do not, however, include (a) substantially uncompensated services; (b) engagements or appointments made on the basis of experience, expertise, professional qualifications and cost following a request for proposal or other process that is free from influence based upon political contributions; and (c) engagements or appointments made on a rotational basis from a list compiled without regard to political contributions.

[4] The term "lawyer or law firm" includes a political action committee or other entity owned or controlled by a lawyer or law firm.

[5] Political contributions are for the purpose of obtaining or being considered for a government legal engagement or appointment by a judge if, but for the desire to be considered for the legal engagement or appointment, the lawyer or law firm would not have made or solicited the contributions. The purpose may be determined by an examination of the circumstances in which the contributions occur. For example, one or more contributions that in the aggregate are substantial in relation to other contributions by lawyers or law firms, made for the benefit of an official in a position to influence award of a government legal engagement, and followed by an award of the legal engagement to the contributing or soliciting lawyer or the lawyer's firm would support an inference that the purpose of the contributions was to obtain the engagement, absent other factors that weigh against existence of the proscribed purpose. Those factors may include among others that the contribution or solicitation was

made to further a political, social, or economic interest or because of an existing personal, family, or professional relationship with a candidate.

[6] If a lawyer makes or solicits a political contribution under circumstances that constitute bribery or another crime, Rule 8.4(b) is implicated.

Definitional Cross-References

"Law firm" *See* Rule 1.0(c)

MAINTAINING THE INTEGRITY OF THE PROFESSION

RULE 8.1: BAR ADMISSION AND DISCIPLINARY MATTERS

An applicant for admission to the bar, or a lawyer in connection with a bar admission application or in connection with a disciplinary matter, shall not:

(a) knowingly make a false statement of material fact; or

(b) fail to disclose a fact necessary to correct a misapprehension known by the person to have arisen in the matter, or knowingly fail to respond to a lawful demand for information from an admissions or disciplinary authority, except that this Rule does not require disclosure of information otherwise protected by Rule 1.6.

Comment

[1] The duty imposed by this Rule extends to persons seeking admission to the bar as well as to lawyers. Hence, if a person makes a material false statement in connection with an application for admission, it may be the basis for subsequent disciplinary action if the person is admitted, and in any event may be relevant in a subsequent admission application. The duty imposed by this Rule applies to a lawyer's own admission or discipline as well as that of others. Thus, it is a separate professional offense for a lawyer to knowingly make a misrepresentation or omission in connection with a disciplinary investigation of the lawyer's own conduct. Paragraph (b) of this Rule also requires correction of any prior misstatement in the matter that the applicant or lawyer may have made and affirmative clarification of any misunderstanding on the part of the admissions or disciplinary authority of which the person involved becomes aware.

[2] This Rule is subject to the provisions of the Fifth Amendment of the United States Constitution and corresponding provisions of state constitutions. A person relying on such a provision in response to a question, however, should do so openly and not use the right of nondisclosure as a justification for failure to comply with this Rule.

[3] A lawyer representing an applicant for admission to the bar, or representing a lawyer who is the subject of a disciplinary inquiry or proceeding, is governed by the Rules applicable to the client-lawyer relationship, including Rule 1.6 and, in some cases, Rule 3.3.

Definitional Cross-References

"Knowingly" and "Known" *See* Rule 1.0(f)

RULE 8.2: JUDICIAL AND LEGAL OFFICIALS

(a) A lawyer shall not make a statement that the lawyer knows to be false or with reckless disregard as to its truth or falsity concerning the qualifications or integrity of a judge, adjudicatory officer or public legal officer, or of a candidate for election or appointment to judicial or legal office.

(b) A lawyer who is a candidate for judicial office shall comply with the applicable provisions of the Code of Judicial Conduct.

Comment

[1] Assessments by lawyers are relied on in evaluating the professional or personal fitness of persons being considered for election or appointment to judicial office and to public legal offices, such as attorney general, prosecuting attorney and public defender. Expressing honest and candid opinions on such matters contributes to improving the administration of justice. Conversely, false statements by a lawyer can unfairly undermine public confidence in the administration of justice.

[2] When a lawyer seeks judicial office, the lawyer should be bound by applicable limitations on political activity.

[3] To maintain the fair and independent administration of justice, lawyers are encouraged to continue traditional efforts to defend judges and courts unjustly criticized.

Definitional Cross-References

"Knows" *See* Rule 1.0(f)

RULE 8.3: REPORTING
PROFESSIONAL MISCONDUCT

(a) A lawyer who knows that another lawyer has committed a violation of the Rules of Professional Conduct that raises a substantial question as to that lawyer's honesty, trustworthiness or fitness as a lawyer in other respects, shall inform the appropriate professional authority.

(b) A lawyer who knows that a judge has committed a violation of applicable rules of judicial conduct that raises a substantial question as to the judge's fitness for office shall inform the appropriate authority.

(c) This Rule does not require disclosure of information otherwise protected by Rule 1.6 or information gained by a lawyer or judge while participating in an approved lawyers assistance program.

Comment

[1] Self-regulation of the legal profession requires that members of the profession initiate disciplinary investigation when they know of a violation of the Rules of Professional Conduct. Lawyers have a similar obligation with respect to judicial misconduct. An apparently isolated violation may indicate a pattern of misconduct that only a disciplinary investigation can uncover. Reporting a violation is especially important where the victim is unlikely to discover the offense.

[2] A report about misconduct is not required where it would involve violation of Rule 1.6. However, a lawyer should encourage a client to consent to disclosure where prosecution would not substantially prejudice the client's interests.

[3] If a lawyer were obliged to report every violation of the Rules, the failure to report any violation would itself be a professional offense. Such a requirement existed in many jurisdictions but proved to be unenforceable. This Rule limits the reporting obligation to those offenses that a self-regulating profession must vigorously endeavor to prevent. A measure of judgment is, therefore, required in complying with the provisions of this Rule. The term "substantial" refers to the seriousness of the possible offense and not the quantum of evidence of which the lawyer is aware. A report should be made to the bar disciplinary agency unless some other agency, such as a peer review agency, is more appropriate in the circumstances. Similar considerations apply to the reporting of judicial misconduct.

[4] The duty to report professional misconduct does not apply to a lawyer retained to represent a lawyer whose professional conduct is in question. Such a situation is governed by the Rules applicable to the client-lawyer relationship.

[5] Information about a lawyer's or judge's misconduct or fitness may be received by a lawyer in the course of that lawyer's participation in an approved lawyers or judges assistance program. In that circumstance, providing for an exception to the reporting requirements of paragraphs (a) and (b) of this Rule encourages lawyers and judges to seek treatment through such a program. Conversely, without such an exception, lawyers and judges may hesitate to seek assistance from these programs, which may then result in additional harm to their professional careers and additional injury to the welfare of clients and the public. These Rules do not otherwise address the confidentiality of information received by a lawyer or judge participating in an approved lawyers assistance program; such an obligation, however, may be imposed by the rules of the program or other law.

Definitional Cross-References

"Knows" *See* Rule 1.0(f)

"Substantial" *See* Rule 1.0(l)

RULE 8.4: MISCONDUCT

It is professional misconduct for a lawyer to:

(a) violate or attempt to violate the Rules of Professional Conduct, knowingly assist or induce another to do so, or do so through the acts of another;

(b) commit a criminal act that reflects adversely on the lawyer's honesty, trustworthiness or fitness as a lawyer in other respects;

(c) engage in conduct involving dishonesty, fraud, deceit or misrepresentation;

(d) engage in conduct that is prejudicial to the administration of justice;

(e) state or imply an ability to influence improperly a government agency or official or to achieve results by means that violate the Rules of Professional Conduct or other law;

(f) knowingly assist a judge or judicial officer in conduct that is a violation of applicable rules of judicial conduct or other law; or

(g) engage in conduct that the lawyer knows or reasonably should know is harassment or discrimination on the basis of race, sex, religion, national origin, ethnicity, disability, age, sexual orientation, gender identity, marital status or socioeconomic status in conduct related to the practice of law. This paragraph does not limit the ability of a lawyer to accept, decline or withdraw from a representation in accordance with Rule 1.16. This paragraph does not preclude legitimate advice or advocacy consistent with these Rules.

Comment

[1] Lawyers are subject to discipline when they violate or attempt to violate the Rules of Professional Conduct, knowingly assist or induce another to do so or do so through the acts of another, as when they request or instruct an agent to do so on the lawyer's behalf. Paragraph (a), however, does not prohibit a lawyer from advising a client concerning action the client is legally entitled to take.

[2] Many kinds of illegal conduct reflect adversely on fitness to practice law, such as offenses involving fraud and the offense of willful failure to file an income tax return. However, some kinds of offenses carry no such implication. Traditionally, the distinction was drawn in terms of offenses involving "moral turpitude." That concept can be construed to include offenses concerning some matters of personal morality, such as adultery and comparable offenses, that have no specific connection to fitness for the practice of law. Although a lawyer is personally answerable to the entire criminal law, a lawyer should be professionally answerable only for offenses that indicate lack of those characteristics relevant to law practice. Offenses involving violence, dishonesty, breach of trust, or serious interference with the administration of justice are in that category. A pattern of repeated offenses, even ones of minor significance when considered separately, can indicate indifference to legal obligation.

[3] Discrimination and harassment by lawyers in violation of paragraph (g) undermine confidence in the legal profession and the legal system. Such discrimination includes harmful verbal or physical conduct that manifests bias or prejudice towards others. Harassment includes sexual harassment and derogatory or demeaning verbal or physical conduct. Sexual harassment includes unwelcome sexual advances, requests for sexual favors, and other unwelcome verbal or physical conduct of a sexual nature. The substantive law of antidiscrimination and antiharassment statutes and case law may guide application of paragraph (g).

[4] Conduct related to the practice of law includes representing clients; interacting with witnesses, coworkers, court personnel, lawyers and others while engaged in the practice of law; operating or managing a law firm or law practice; and participating in bar association, business or social activities in connection with the practice of law. Lawyers may engage in conduct undertaken to promote diversity and inclusion without violating this Rule by, for example, implementing initiatives aimed at recruiting, hiring, retaining and advancing diverse employees or sponsoring diverse law student organizations.

[5] A trial judge's finding that peremptory challenges were exercised on a discriminatory basis does not alone establish a violation of paragraph (g). A lawyer does not violate paragraph (g) by limiting the scope or subject matter of the lawyer's practice or by limiting the lawyer's practice to members of underserved populations in accordance with these Rules and other law. A lawyer may charge and collect reasonable fees and expenses for a representation. Rule 1.5(a). Lawyers also should be mindful of their professional obligations under Rule 6.1 to provide legal services to those who are unable to pay, and their obligation under Rule 6.2 not to avoid appointments from a tribunal except for good cause. See Rule 6.2(a), (b) and (c). A lawyer's representation of a client does not constitute an endorsement by the lawyer of the client's views or activities. See Rule 1.2(b).

[6] A lawyer may refuse to comply with an obligation imposed by law upon a good faith belief that no valid obligation exists. The provisions of Rule 1.2(d) concerning a good faith challenge to the validity, scope, meaning or application of the law apply to challenges of legal regulation of the practice of law.

[7] Lawyers holding public office assume legal responsibilities going beyond those of other citizens. A lawyer's abuse of public office can suggest an inability to fulfill the professional role of lawyers. The same is true of abuse of positions of private trust such as trustee, executor, administrator, guardian, agent and officer, director or manager of a corporation or other organization.

Definitional Cross-References

"Fraud" *See* Rule 1.0(d)
"Knowingly and knows" *See* Rule 1.0(f)
"Reasonably should know" *See* Rule 1.0(j)

RULE 8.5: DISCIPLINARY AUTHORITY; CHOICE OF LAW

(a) Disciplinary Authority. A lawyer admitted to practice in this jurisdiction is subject to the disciplinary authority of this jurisdiction, regardless of where the lawyer's conduct occurs. A lawyer not admitted in this jurisdiction is also subject to the disciplinary authority of this jurisdiction if the lawyer provides or offers to provide any legal services in this jurisdiction. A lawyer may be subject to the disciplinary authority of both this jurisdiction and another jurisdiction for the same conduct.

(b) Choice of Law. In any exercise of the disciplinary authority of this jurisdiction, the rules of professional conduct to be applied shall be as follows:

(1) for conduct in connection with a matter pending before a tribunal, the rules of the jurisdiction in which the tribunal sits, unless the rules of the tribunal provide otherwise; and

(2) for any other conduct, the rules of the jurisdiction in which the lawyer's conduct occurred, or, if the predominant effect of the conduct is in a different jurisdiction, the rules of that jurisdiction shall be applied to the conduct. A lawyer shall not be subject to discipline if the lawyer's conduct conforms to the rules of a jurisdiction in which the lawyer reasonably believes the predominant effect of the lawyer's conduct will occur.

Comment
Disciplinary Authority

[1] It is longstanding law that the conduct of a lawyer admitted to practice in this jurisdiction is subject to the disciplinary authority of this jurisdiction. Extension of the disciplinary authority of this jurisdiction to other lawyers who provide or offer to provide legal services in this jurisdiction is for the protection of the citizens of this jurisdiction. Reciprocal enforcement of a jurisdiction's disciplinary findings and sanctions will further advance the purposes of this Rule. See, Rules 6 and 22, ABA *Model Rules for Lawyer Disciplinary Enforcement*. A lawyer who is subject to the disciplinary authority of this jurisdiction under Rule 8.5(a) appoints an official to be designated by this court to receive service of process in this jurisdiction. The fact that the lawyer is subject to the disciplinary authority of this jurisdiction may be a factor in determining whether personal jurisdiction may be asserted over the lawyer for civil matters.

Choice of Law

[2] A lawyer may be potentially subject to more than one set of rules of professional conduct which impose different obligations. The lawyer may be licensed to practice in more than one jurisdiction with differing rules, or may be admitted to practice before a particular court with rules that differ from those of the jurisdiction or jurisdictions in which the lawyer is licensed to practice. Additionally, the lawyer's conduct may involve significant contacts with more than one jurisdiction.

[3] Paragraph (b) seeks to resolve such potential conflicts. Its premise is that minimizing conflicts between rules, as well as uncertainty about which rules are applicable, is in the best interest of both clients and the profession (as well as the bodies having authority to regulate the profession). Accordingly, it takes the approach of (i) providing that any particular conduct of a lawyer shall be subject to only one set of rules of professional conduct, (ii) making the determination of which set of rules applies to particular conduct as straightforward as possible, consistent with recognition of appropriate regulatory interests of relevant jurisdictions, and (iii) providing protection from discipline for lawyers who act reasonably in the face of uncertainty.

[4] Paragraph (b)(1) provides that as to a lawyer's conduct relating to a proceeding pending before a tribunal, the lawyer shall be subject only to the rules of professional conduct of that tribunal. As to all other conduct, including conduct in anticipation of a proceeding not yet pending before a tribunal, paragraph (b)(2) provides that a lawyer shall be subject to the rules of the jurisdiction in which the lawyer's conduct occurred, or, if the predominant effect of the conduct is in another jurisdiction, the rules of that jurisdiction shall be applied to the conduct. In the case of conduct in anticipation of a proceeding that is likely to be before a tribunal, the predominant effect of such conduct could be where the conduct occurred, where the tribunal sits or in another jurisdiction.

[5] When a lawyer's conduct involves significant contacts with more than one jurisdiction, it may not be clear whether the predominant effect of the lawyer's conduct will occur in a jurisdiction other than the one in which the conduct occurred. So long as the lawyer's conduct conforms to the rules of a jurisdiction in which the lawyer reasonably believes the predominant effect will occur, the lawyer shall not be subject to discipline under this Rule. With respect to conflicts of interest, in determining a lawyer's reasonable belief under paragraph (b)(2), a written agreement between the lawyer and client that reasonably specifies a particular jurisdiction as within

the scope of that paragraph may be considered if the agreement was obtained with the client's informed consent confirmed in the agreement.

[6] If two admitting jurisdictions were to proceed against a lawyer for the same conduct, they should, applying this rule, identify the same governing ethics rules. They should take all appropriate steps to see that they do apply the same rule to the same conduct, and in all events should avoid proceeding against a lawyer on the basis of two inconsistent rules.

[7] The choice of law provision applies to lawyers engaged in transnational practice, unless international law, treaties or other agreements between competent regulatory authorities in the affected jurisdictions provide otherwise.

Definitional Cross-References

"Reasonably believes" *See* Rule 1.0(i)
"Tribunal" *See* Rule 1.0(m)

Appendix A

Subject Guide

A

Abuse of process,
Rule 3.1 (Comment)

Accepting appointments,
Rule 6.2

Accounting for funds,
Rule 1.15

Acquiring interest in litigation,
Rule 1.8(i)

contingent fee,
Rule 1.8(i)(2)

Adjudicative officers,

negotiating for private
employment,
Rule 1.12(b)

disqualification of former,
Rule 1.12(a)

Administration of justice,

conduct prejudicial to,
Rule 8.4(d)

interference with,
Rule 8.4 (Comment)

lawyer's duty to seek
improvement in,
Preamble

Administration of law,

participation in,
Rule 6.4

Administrative agencies
and tribunals,

appearance before,
Rule 3.9

Administrator,

fee for representation of,
Rule 1.5 (Comment)

Admiralty practice,

communication of,
Rule 7.2(c) (Comment)

Admission to practice,
Rule 8.1

Advance fee payments,

propriety of,
Rule 1.5 (Comment)

deposit of,
Rule 1.15(c)

Adversary system,

duty of lawyer to,
Preamble

Adverse legal authority,

lawyer's duty to disclose,
Rule 3.3(a)(2)

Advertising. (*See also* Solicitation,
Letterheads, Firm name.)

class action members, to notify,
Rule 7.3(d) (Comment)

communications concerning a
lawyer's services, generally,
Rule 7.1

comparisons with services
of other lawyers,
Rule 7.1 (Comment)

fields of practice,
Rule 7.2

mail,
Rule 7.2(a)
Rule 7.3 (Comment)

N

Nonadjudicative proceedings,
  Rule 3.9

Nonlawyer assistants,
  conflict of interest,
    Rule 1.10 (Comment)
  responsibilities of lawyer,
    Rule 5.3

Nonlawyers,
  division of fees with,
    Rule 5.4(a)
  partnership,
    Rule 5.4(b)
  professional corporation,
    Rule 5.4(d)

Nonprofit legal services program,
  Rule 6.5

Nonprofit organization,
  division of fees with,
    Rule 5.4(a)(4)

Notice of receipt of funds
or other property,
  Rule 1.15(d)

O

Objectives of the representation,
  client's right to determine,
    Rule 1.2(a)

Obstruction of party's access
to evidence,
    Rule 3.3 (Comment),
    Rule 3.4(a)

Officer of legal system,
    Preamble

Opinions,
  evaluation for use by
  third persons,
    Rule 2.3

limit on malpractice liability,
  Rule 1.8 (Comment)

Opposing party,
  communication with
  represented party,
    Rule 4.2
  communication with
  unrepresented party,
    Rule 4.3
  duty of fairness to,
    Rule 3.4

Optional withdrawal,
    Rule 1.16(b)

Organization, representation of,
  board of directors, lawyer on,
    Rule 1.7 (Comment)
  communication with,
    Rule 1.4 (Comment)
  communication with
  constituents of,
    Rule 4.2 (Comment)
  conflict of interest,
    Rule 1.7 (Comment)
  intended conduct,
    Rule 1.6 (Comment)
  constituents, representing,
    Rule 1.13(g)
  identity of client,
    Rule 1.13(a), Rule 1.13(f)
  law department of,
    Rule 1.0 (Comment),
    Rule 1.10 (Comment),
    Rule 5.1 (Comment)
  misconduct, client
  engaged in,
    Rule 1.13(b)

CORRELATION TABLES

TABLES A AND B: RELATED SECTIONS IN THE ABA MODEL CODE OF PROFESSIONAL RESPONSIBILITY

TABLE A*

ABA MODEL RULES	ABA MODEL CODE
Competence	
Rule 1.1	EC 1-1, EC 1-2, EC 6-1, EC 6-2, EC 6-3, EC 6-4, EC 6-5, DR 6-101(A)
Scope of Representation and Allocation of Authority between Client and Lawyer	
Rule 1.2(a)	EC 5-12, EC 7-7, EC 7-8, DR 7-101(A)(1)
Rule 1.2(b)	EC 7-17
Rule 1.2(c)	EC 7-8, EC 7-9, DR 7-101(B)(1)
Rule 1.2(d)	EC 7-1, EC 7-2, EC 7-5, EC 7-22, DR 7-102(A)(6), (7), & (8), DR 7-106
Diligence	
Rule 1.3	EC 2-31, EC 6-4, EC 7-1, EC 7-38, DR 6-101(A)(3), DR 7-101(A)(1) & (3)
Communication	
Rule 1.4(a)	EC 7-8, EC 9-2, DR 2-110(C)(1)(c), DR 6-101(A)(3), DR 9-102(B)(1)
Rule 1.4(b)	EC 7-8
Fees	
Rule 1.5(a)	EC 2-16, EC 2-17, EC 2-18, DR 2-106(A) & (B)
Rule 1.5(b)	EC 2-19
Rule 1.5(c)	EC 2-20, EC 5-7
Rule 1.5(d)	EC 2-20, DR 2-106(C)
Rule 1.5(e)	EC 2-22, DR 2-107(A)

---

* Table A provides cross-references to related provisions, but only in the sense that the provisions consider substantially similar subject matter or reflect similar concerns. A cross-reference does not indicate that a provision of the ABA Model Code of Professional Responsibility has been incorporated by the provision of a Model Rule. The Canons of the Code are not cross-referenced.

ABA MODEL RULES	ABA MODEL CODE

Confidentiality of Information

Rule 1.6(a)	EC 4-1, EC 4-2, EC 4-3, EC 4-4, DR 4-101(A), (B), & (C)
Rule 1.6(b)(1)	EC 4-2, DR 4-101(C)(3), DR 7-102(B)
Rule 1.6(b)(2)	DR 4-101(C)(3)
Rule 1.6(b)(3)	None
Rule 1.6(b)(4)	None
Rule 1.6(b)(5)	DR 4-101(C)(4)
Rule 1.6(b)(6)	DR 4-101(C)(2)
Rule 1.6(b)(7)	None
Rule 1.6(c)	None

Conflict of Interest: Current Clients

Rule 1.7(a)	EC 2-21, EC 5-1, EC 5-2, EC 5-3, EC 5-9, EC 5-11, EC 5-13, EC 5-14, EC 5-15, EC 5-17, EC 5-21, EC 5-22, EC 5-23, DR 5-101(A) & (B), DR 5-102, DR 5-104(A), DR 5-105(A) & (B), DR 5-107(A) & (B)
Rule 1.7(b)	EC 2-21, EC 5-15, EC 5-16, EC 5-17, EC 5-19, EC 5-23, DR 5-101(A) & (B), DR 5-102, DR 5-104(A), DR 5-105(C), DR 5-107(A)

Conflict of Interest: Current Clients: Specific Rules

Rule 1.8(a)	EC 5-3, EC 5-5, DR 5-104(A)
Rule 1.8(b)	EC 4-5, DR 4-101(B)
Rule 1.8(c)	EC 5-1, EC 5-2, EC 5-5, EC 5-6
Rule 1.8(d)	EC 5-1, EC 5-3, EC 5-4, DR 5-104(B)
Rule 1.8(e)	EC 5-1, EC 5-3, EC 5-7, EC 5-8, DR 5-103(B)
Rule 1.8(f)	EC 2-21, EC 5-1, EC 5-22, EC 5-23, DR 5-107(A) & (B)
Rule 1.8(g)	EC 5-1, DR 5-106(A)
Rule 1.8(h)	EC 6-6, DR 6-102(A)
Rule 1.8(i)	EC 5-1, EC 5-7, DR 5-101(A), DR 5-103(A)
Rule 1.8(j)	None
Rule 1.8(k)	None

Duties to Former Clients

Rule 1.9(a)	DR 5-105(C)
Rule 1.9(b)	EC 4-5, EC 4-6
Rule 1.9(c)	None

Imputation of Conflicts of Interest: General Rule

Rule 1.10(a)	EC 4-5, DR 5-105(D)
Rule 1.10(b)	EC 4-5, DR 5-105(D)

ABA MODEL RULES	ABA MODEL CODE
Rule 1.10(c)	DR 5-105(A)
Rule 1.10(d)	None

Special Conflicts of Interest for Former and
Current Government Officers and Employees

Rule 1.11(a)	EC 9-3, DR 9-101(B)
Rule 1.11(b)	None
Rule 1.11(c)	None
Rule 1.11(d)	EC 8-8
Rule 1.11(e)	None

Former Judge, Arbitrator, Mediator or Other Third-Party Neutral

Rule 1.12(a)&(b)	EC 5-20, EC 9-3, DR 9-101(A) & (B)
Rule 1.12(c)	DR 5-105(D)
Rule 1.12(d)	None

Organization as Client

Rule 1.13(a)	EC 5-18, EC 5-24
Rule 1.13(b)	EC 5-18, EC 5-24, DR 5-107(B)
Rule 1.13(c)	EC 5-18, EC 5-24, DR 5-105(D), DR 5-107(B)
Rule 1.13(d)	None
Rule 1.13(e)	None
Rule 1.13(f)	EC 5-16
Rule 1.13(g)	EC 4-4, EC 5-16, DR 5-105(B) & (C)

Client with Diminished Capacity

Rule 1.14(a)	EC 7-11, EC 7-12
Rule 1.14(b)	EC 7-12
Rule 1.14(c)	None

Safekeeping Property

Rule 1.15	EC 5-7, EC 9-5, EC 9-7, DR 5-103(A)(1), DR 9-102

Declining or Terminating Representation

Rule 1.16(a)(1)	EC 2-30, EC 2-31, EC 2-32, DR 2-103(E), DR 2-104(A), DR 2-109(A), DR 2-110(B)(1) & (2)
Rule 1.16(a)(2)	EC 1-6, EC 2-30, EC 2-31, EC 2-32, DR 2-110(B)(3), DR 2-110(C)(4)
Rule 1.16(a)(3)	EC 2-31, EC 2-32, DR 2-110(B)(4)
Rule 1.16(b)(1)	EC 2-32, DR 2-110(A)(2), DR 2-110(C)(5)
Rule 1.16(b)(2)	EC 2-31, EC 2-32, DR 2-110(C)(1)(b) & (c), DR 2-110(C)(2)

ABA MODEL RULES	ABA MODEL CODE
Rule 1.16(b)(3)	EC 2-31, EC 2-32, DR 2-110(C)(2)
Rule 1.16(b)(4)	EC 2-30, EC 2-31, EC 2-32, DR 2-110(C)(1)(d)
Rule 1.16(b)(5)	EC 2-31, EC 2-32, DR 2-110(C)(1)(f)(i)(j)
Rule 1.16(b)(6)	EC 2-32, DR 2-110(C)(1)(d) & (e)
Rule 1.16(b)(7)	EC 2-32, DR 2-110(C)(6)
Rule 1.16(c)	EC 2-32, DR 2-110(A)(1)
Rule 1.16(d)	EC 2-32, DR 2-110(A)(2) & (3)

Sale of Law Practice

Rule 1.17	None

Duties to Prospective Client

Rule 1.18	EC 4-1

Advisor

Rule 2.1	EC 5-11, EC 7-3, EC 7-8, DR 5-107(B)

Evaluation for Use by Third Persons

Rule 2.3	None

Lawyer Serving as Third-Party Neutral

Rule 2.4	EC 5-20

Meritorious Claims and Contentions

Rule 3.1	EC 7-1, EC 7-4, EC 7-5, EC 7-14, EC 7-25, DR 5-102(A)(5), DR 2-109(A)(B)(1), DR 7-102(A)(1) & (2)

Expediting Litigation

Rule 3.2	EC 7-20, DR 1-102(A)(5), DR 7-101(A)(1) & (2)

Candor toward the Tribunal

Rule 3.3(a)(1)	EC 7-4, EC 7-26, EC 7-32, EC 8-5, DR 1-102(A)(4) & (5), DR 7-102(A)(4) & (5)
Rule 3.3(a)(2)	EC 7-23, DR 1-102(A)(5), DR 7-106(B)(1)
Rule 3.3(a)(3)	EC 7-5, EC 7-6, EC 7-26, EC 8-5, DR 1-102(A)(4) & (5), DR 7-102(A)(4), (6), & (7), DR 7-102(B)(1) & (2)
Rule 3.3(b)	EC 7-5, EC 7-26, EC 7-27, EC 7-32, EC 8-5, DR 1-102(A)(4) & (5), DR 7-102(A)(4), (6), & (7), DR 7-102(B)(1) & (2), DR 7-108(G), DR 7-109(A) & (B)
Rule 3.3(c)	EC 8-5, DR 7-102(B)
Rule 3.3(d)	EC 7-24, EC 7-27

ABA MODEL RULES	ABA MODEL CODE

Fairness to Opposing Party and Counsel

Rule 3.4(a)	EC 7-6, EC 7-27, DR 1-102(A)(4) & (5), DR 7-106(C)(7), DR 7-109(A) & (B)
Rule 3.4(b)	EC 7-6, EC 7-28, DR 1-102(A)(4), (5), & (6), DR 7-102(A)(6), DR 7-109(C)
Rule 3.4(c)	EC 7-22, EC 7-25, EC 7-38, DR 1-102(A)(5), DR 7-106(A), DR 7-106(C)(5) & (7)
Rule 3.4(d)	DR 1-102(A)(5), DR 7-106(A), DR 7-106(C)(7)
Rule 3.4(e)	EC 7-24, EC 7-25, DR 1-102(A)(5), DR 7-106(C)(1), (2), (3), & (4)
Rule 3.4(f)	EC 7-27, DR 1-102(A)(5), DR 7-104(A)(2), DR 7-109(B)

Impartiality and Decorum of the Tribunal

Rule 3.5(a)	EC 7-20, EC 7-29, EC 7-31, EC 7-32, EC 7-34, DR 7-106, DR 7-108, DR 7-109, DR 7-110, DR 8-101(A)
Rule 3.5(b)	EC 7-35, DR 7-108, DR 7-110(A) & (B)
Rule 3.5(c)	EC 7-29, EC 7-30, EC 7-31, EC 7-32, DR 7-108
Rule 3.5(d)	EC 7-20, EC 7-25, EC 7-36, EC 7-37, DR 7-101(A)(1), DR 7-106(C)(6)

Trial Publicity

Rule 3.6	EC 7-25, EC 7-33, DR 7-107

Lawyer as Witness

Rule 3.7(a)	EC 5-9, EC 5-10, DR 5-101(B)(1) & (2), DR 5-102
Rule 3.7(b)	EC 5-9, DR 5-101(B), DR 5-102

Special Responsibilities of a Prosecutor

Rule 3.8(a)	EC 7-11, EC 7-13, EC 7-14, DR 7-103(A)
Rule 3.8(b)	EC 7-11, EC 7-13
Rule 3.8(c)	EC 7-11, EC 7-13, EC 7-18
Rule 3.8(d)	EC 7-11, EC 7-13, DR 7-103(B)
Rule 3.8(e)	None
Rule 3.8(f)	EC 7-14
Rule 3.8(g)	None
Rule 3.8(h)	None

Advocate in Nonadjudicative Proceedings

Rule 3.9	EC 7-11, EC 7-15, EC 7-16, EC 8-4, EC 8-5, DR 7-106(B)(2), DR 9-101(C)

ABA MODEL RULES	ABA MODEL CODE

Truthfulness in Statements to Others

| Rule 4.1 | EC 7-5, DR 7-102(A)(3), (4), (5), & (7), DR 7-102(B) |

Communication with Person Represented by Counsel

| Rule 4.2 | EC 2-30, EC 7-18, DR 7-104(A)(1) |

Dealing with Unrepresented Person

| Rule 4.3 | EC 2-3, EC 7-18, DR 7-104(A)(2) |

Respect for Rights of Third Persons

| Rule 4.4(a) | EC 7-10, EC 7-14, EC 7-21, EC 7-25, EC 7-29, EC 7-30, EC 7-37, DR 2-110(B)(1), DR 7-101(A)(1), DR 7-102(A)(1), DR 7-106(C)(2), DR 7-107(D), (E), & (F), DR 7-108(D), (E), & (F) |
| Rule 4.4(b) | None |

Responsibilities of Partners, Managers, and Supervisory Lawyers

| Rule 5.1(a)&(b) | EC 4-5, DR 4-101(D), DR 7-107(J) |
| Rule 5.1(c) | DR 1-102(A)(2), DR 1-103(A), DR 7-108(E) |

Responsibilities of a Subordinate Lawyer

| Rule 5.2 | None |

Responsibilities regarding Nonlawyer Assistance

Rule 5.3(a)	EC 3-6, EC 4-2, EC 4-5, EC 7-28, DR 4-101(D), DR 7-107(J)
Rule 5.3(b)	DR 1-102(A)(2), DR 7-107(J), DR 7-108(B), DR 7-108(E)
Rule 5.3(c)	None

Professional Independence of a Lawyer

Rule 5.4(a)	EC 2-33, EC 3-8, EC 5-24, DR 2-103(D)(1), DR 2-103(D)(2), DR 2-103(D)(4)(a), (d), (e), & (f), DR 3-102(A), DR 5-107(C)(3)
Rule 5.4(b)	EC 2-33, EC 3-8, DR 3-103(A)
Rule 5.4(c)	EC 2-33, EC 5-22, EC 5-23, DR 2-103(C), DR 5-107(B)
Rule 5.4(d)	EC 2-33, EC 3-8, DR 5-107(C)

Unauthorized Practice of Law; Multijurisdictional Practice of Law

| Rule 5.5(a) | DR 3-101(A) & (B) |
| Rule 5.5(b) | None |

ABA MODEL RULES	ABA MODEL CODE
Rule 5.5(c)	None
Rule 5.5(d)	None
Rule 5.5(e)	None

Restrictions on Right to Practice

Rule 5.6	DR 2-108

Responsibilities regarding Law-Related Services

Rule 5.7	None

Voluntary Pro Bono Publico Service

Rule 6.1	EC 1-2, EC 1-4, EC 2-1, EC 2-2, EC 2-16, EC 2-24, EC 2-25, EC 6-2, EC 8-1, EC 8-2, EC 8-3, EC 8-7, EC 8-9

Accepting Appointments

Rule 6.2 (a)	EC 2-1, EC 2-25, EC 2-27, EC 2-28, EC 2-29, EC 8-3
Rule 6.2(b)	EC 2-16, EC 2-25, EC 2-29, EC 2-30
Rule 6.2(c)	EC 2-25, EC 2-27, EC 2-29, EC 2-30

Membership in Legal Services Organization

Rule 6.3	EC 2-33, DR 5-101(A)

Law Reform Activities Affecting Client Interests

Rule 6.4	EC 2-33, DR 5-101(A), DR 8-101

Nonprofit and Court-Annexed Limited Legal Services Programs

Rule 6.5	None

Communications Concerning a Lawyer's Services

Rule 7.1	EC 2-8, EC 2-9, EC 2-10, DR 2-101(A), (B), (C), (E), (F), & (G), DR 2-102(E)

Advertising

Rule 7.2(a)	EC 2-1, EC 2-2, EC 2-6, EC 2-7, EC 2-8, EC 2-15, DR 2-101(B) & (H), DR 2-102(A) & (B), DR 2-103(B), DR 2-104(A)(4) & (5)
Rule 7.2(b)	EC 2-8, EC 2-15, DR 2-101(I), DR 2-103(B), (C), & (D)
Rule 7.2(c)	EC 2-8, EC 2-14, DR 2-105(A)(2) & (3)
Rule 7.2(d)	None

ABA MODEL RULES	ABA MODEL CODE

Solicitation of Clients

Rule 7.3   EC 2-3, EC 2-4, EC 5-6, DR 2-103(A), DR 2-103(C)(1), DR 2-103(D)(4)(b) & (c), DR 2-104(A)(1), (2), (3), & (5)

Communication of Fields of Practice and Specialization

Rule 7.2(c)   EC 2-1, EC 2-7, EC 2-8, EC 2-14, DR 2-101(B)(2), DR 2-102(A)(3), DR 2-102(E), DR 2-105(A)

Firm Names and Letterheads

Rule 7.1 (Comment)   EC 2-11, EC 2-12, EC 2-13, DR 2-102(A)(4), DR 2-102(B), (C), (D), & (E), DR 2-105

Political Contributions to Obtain Government
Legal Engagements or Appointments by Judges

Rule 7.6   None

Bar Admission and Disciplinary Matters

Rule 8.1(a)   EC 1-1, EC 1-2, EC 1-3, DR 1-101(A) & (B)

Rule 8.1(b)   DR 1-102(A)(5), DR 1-103(B)

Judicial and Legal Officials

Rule 8.2(a)   EC 8-6, DR 8-102

Rule 8.2(b)   DR 8-103

Reporting Professional Misconduct

Rule 8.3   EC 1-3, DR 1-103(A)

Misconduct

Rule 8.4(a)   EC 1-5, EC 1-6, EC 9-6, DR 1-102(A)(1) & (2), DR 2-103(E), DR 7-102(A) & (B)

Rule 8.4(b)   EC 1-5, DR 1-102(A)(3) & (6), DR 7-102(A)(8), DR 8-101(A)(3)

Rule 8.4(c)   EC 1-5, EC 9-4, DR 1-102(A)(4), DR 8-101(A)(3)

Rule 8.4(d)   EC 3-9, EC 8-3, DR 1-102(A)(5), DR 3-101(B)

Rule 8.4(e)   EC 1-5, EC 9-2, EC 9-4, EC 9-6, DR 9-101(C)

Rule 8.4(f)   EC 1-5, EC 7-34, EC 9-1, DR 1-102(A)(3), (4), (5), & (6), DR 7-110(A), DR 8-101(A)(2)

Rule 8.4(g)   None

Disciplinary Authority; Choice of Law

Rule 8.5   None

TABLE B*

ABA MODEL CODE	ABA MODEL RULES

Canon 1: Integrity of Profession

EC 1-1	Rules 1.1, 8.1(a)
EC 1-2	Rules 1.1, 6.1, 8.1(a)
EC 1-3	Rules 8.1(a), 8.3
EC 1-4	Rule 6.1
EC 1-5	Rule 8.4(a), (b), (c), (e), & (f)
EC 1-6	Rules 1.16(a)(2), 8.4(a)
DR 1-101	Rule 8.1(a)
DR 1-102(A)(1)	Rule 8.4(a)
DR 1-102(A)(2)	Rules 5.1(c), 5.3(b), 8.4(a)
DR 1-102(A)(3)	Rule 8.4(b) & (f)
DR 1-102(A)(4)	Rules 3.3(a)(1), (3), & (b), 3.4(a) & (b), 8.4(c) & (f)
DR 1-102(A)(5)	Rules 3.1, 3.2, 3.3(a) & (b), 3.4, 8.4(d) & (f)
DR 1-102(A)(6)	Rules 3.4(b), 8.4(b) & (f)
DR 1-103(A)	Rules 5.1(c), 8.3
DR 1-103(B)	Rule 8.1(b)

Canon 2: Making Counsel Available

EC 2-1	Rules 6.1, 6.2(a), 7.2(a), 7.2(c)
EC 2-2	Rules 6.1, 7.2(a)
EC 2-3	Rules 4.3, 7.3
EC 2-4	Rule 7.3
EC 2-5	None
EC 2-6	Rule 7.2(a)
EC 2-7	Rules 7.2(a), 7.2(c)
EC 2-8	Rules 7.1, 7.2(a) & (b), 7.4
EC 2-9	Rule 7.1
EC 2-10	Rule 7.1
EC 2-11	Rule 7.1 (Comment)
EC 2-12	Rule 7.1 (Comment)
EC 2-13	Rule 7.1 (Comment)
EC 2-14	Rule 7.2(c)
EC 2-15	Rule 7.2(a) & (b)
EC 2-16	Rules 1.5(a), 6.1, 6.2(b)

** Table B provides cross-references to related provisions, but only in the sense that the provisions consider substantially similar subject matter or reflect similar concerns. A cross-reference does not indicate that a provision of the ABA Model Code of Professional Responsibility has been incorporated by the provision of a Model Rule. The Canons of the Code are not cross-referenced.

ABA MODEL CODE	ABA MODEL RULES
EC 2-17	Rule 1.5(a)
EC 2-18	Rule 1.5(a)
EC 2-19	Rule 1.5(b)
EC 2-20	Rule 1.5(c) & (d)
EC 2-21	Rules 1.7(a), 1.8(f)
EC 2-22	Rule 1.5(e)
EC 2-23	None
EC 2-24	Rule 6.1
EC 2-25	Rules 6.1, 6.2
EC 2-26	None
EC 2-27	Rule 6.2(a) & (c)
EC 2-28	Rule 6.2(a)
EC 2-29	Rule 6.2
EC 2-30	Rules 1.16(a)(1) & (2), 1.16(b)(4), 4.2, 6.2(b) & (c)
EC 2-31	Rules 1.3, 1.16(a) & (b)
EC 2-32	Rule 1.16
EC 2-33	Rules 5.4, 6.3, 6.4
DR 2-101(A)	Rule 7.1
DR 2-101(B)	Rules 7.1, 7.2(a)
DR 2-101(C)	Rule 7.1
DR 2-101(D)	None
DR 2-101(E)	Rule 7.1
DR 2-101(F)	Rule 7.1
DR 2-101(G)	Rule 7.1
DR 2-101(H)	Rule 7.2
DR 2-101(I)	Rule 7.2(b)
DR 2-102(A)	Rules 7.2(a), 7.2(c)
DR 2-102(B)	Rules 7.2(a), 7.1 (Comment)
DR 2-102(C)	Rule 7.1 (Comment)
DR 2-102(D)	Rule 7.1 (Comment)
DR 2-102(E)	Rules 7.1, 7.2(c)
DR 2-103(A)	Rule 7.3
DR 2-103(B)	Rule 7.2(a) & (b)
DR 2-103(C)	Rules 5.4(a), 7.2(b), 7.3
DR 2-103(D)	Rules 1.16(a)(1), 5.4(a), 7.2(b), 7.3
DR 2-103(E)	Rules 1.16(a), 7.2(a), 7.3
DR 2-104	Rules 1.16(a), 7.3
DR 2-105	Rule 7.2(c)
DR 2-106(A)	Rule 1.5(a)

APPENDIX B: CORRELATION TABLES

ABA MODEL CODE	ABA MODEL RULES
DR 2-106(B)	Rule 1.5(a)
DR 2-106(C)	Rule 1.5(d)
DR 2-107(A)	Rule 1.5(e)
DR 2-107(B)	Rule 5.4(a)(1)
DR 2-108(A)	Rule 5.6
DR 2-108(B)	Rule 5.6
DR 2-109(A)	Rules 1.16(a)(1), 3.1
DR 2-110(A)	Rule 1.16(b)(1), (c), & (d)
DR 2-110(B)	Rules 1.16(a), 3.1, 4.4(a)
DR 2-110(C)	Rules 1.4(a)(5), 1.16(a) & (b)

Canon 3: Unauthorized Practice

EC 3-1	None
EC 3-2	None
EC 3-3	Rule 8.4(e)
EC 3-4	None
EC 3-5	None
EC 3-6	Rule 5.3(a)
EC 3-7	None
EC 3-8	Rule 5.4(a), (b), & (d)
EC 3-9	Rule 8.4(d)
DR 3-101(A)	Rule 5.5(a)
DR 3-101(B)	Rules 5.5(a), 8.4(d)
DR 3-102	Rule 5.4(a)
DR 3-103	Rule 5.4(b)

Canon 4: Confidences and Secrets

EC 4-1	Rules 1.6(a), 1.18
EC 4-2	Rules 1.6(a) & (b)(1), 5.3(a)
EC 4-3	Rule 1.6(a)
EC 4-4	Rules 1.6(a), 1.13(g)
EC 4-5	Rules 1.8(b), 1.9(b), 1.10(a) & (b), 5.1(a) & (c), 5.3(a)
EC 4-6	Rule 1.9(b)
DR 4-101(A)	Rule 1.6(a)
DR 4-101(B)	Rules 1.6(a), 1.8(b), 1.9(b)
DR 4-101(C)	Rule 1.6(a) & (b)
DR 4-101(D)	Rules 5.1(a) & (b), 5.3(a) & (b)

ABA **MODEL CODE**	**ABA** **MODEL RULES**
Canon 5: Independent Judgment	
EC 5-1	Rules 1.7(a), 1.8(c), (d), (e), (f), (g), & (i)
EC 5-2	Rules 1.7(a), 1.8(c)
EC 5-3	Rules 1.7, 1.8(a), (d), & (e)
EC 5-4	Rule 1.8(d)
EC 5-5	Rule 1.8(a) & (c)
EC 5-6	Rules 1.8(c), 7.3
EC 5-7	Rules 1.5(c), 1.8(e) & (i), 1.15
EC 5-8	Rule 1.8(e)
EC 5-9	Rules 1.7(a), 3.7
EC 5-10	Rule 3.7(a)
EC 5-11	Rules 1.7(a), 2.1
EC 5-12	Rule 1.2(a)
EC 5-13	Rule 1.7(a)
EC 5-14	Rule 1.7(a)
EC 5-15	Rule 1.7
EC 5-16	Rules 1.7(b), 1.13(f) & (g)
EC 5-17	Rule 1.7
EC 5-18	Rule 1.13(a), (b), & (c)
EC 5-19	Rule 1.7(b)
EC 5-20	Rules 1.12(a) & (b), 2.4
EC 5-21	Rule 1.7
EC 5-22	Rule 1.7
EC 5-23	Rules 1.7(a), 1.8(f), 5.4(c)
EC 5-24	Rules 1.13(a), (b), & (c), 5.4(a)
DR 5-101(A)	Rules 1.7, 1.8(i), 6.3, 6.4
DR 5-101(B)	Rules 1.7, 3.7
DR 5-102(A)	Rules 1.7, 3.7
DR 5-102(B)	Rules 1.7(b), 3.7
DR 5-103(A)	Rules 1.8(i), 1.15
DR 5-103(B)	Rule 1.8(e)
DR 5-104(A)	Rules 1.7, 1.8(a)
DR 5-104(B)	Rule 1.8(d)
DR 5-105(A)	Rules 1.7, 1.10(c)
DR 5-105(B)	Rules 1.7, 1.13(g)
DR 5-105(C)	Rules 1.7(b), 1.13(g), 1.9(a)
DR 5-105(D)	Rules 1.10(a), 1.12(c), 1.13(c)
DR 5-106	Rule 1.8(g)
DR 5-107(A)	Rules 1.7(b), 1.8(f)

ABA MODEL CODE	ABA MODEL RULES
DR 5-107(B)	Rules 1.7(a), 1.8(f), 1.13(b) & (c), 2.1, 5.4(c)
DR 5-107(C)	Rule 5.4(a) & (d)

Canon 6: Competence

EC 6-1	Rule 1.1
EC 6-2	Rules 1.1, 5.1(a) & (b), 6.1
EC 6-3	Rule 1.1
EC 6-4	Rules 1.1, 1.3
EC 6-5	Rule 1.1
EC 6-6	Rule 1.8(h)
DR 6-101	Rules 1.1, 1.3, 1.4(a)
DR 6-102	Rule 1.8(h)

Canon 7: Zeal Within the Law

EC 7-1	Rules 1.2(d), 1.3, 3.1
EC 7-2	Rule 1.2(d)
EC 7-3	Rule 2.1
EC 7-4	Rules 3.1, 3.3(a)(1)
EC 7-5	Rules 1.2(d), 3.1, 3.3(a)(3) & (b), 4.1
EC 7-6	Rule 3.4(a) & (b)
EC 7-7	Rule 1.2(a)
EC 7-8	Rules 1.2(a) & (c), 1.4, 2.1
EC 7-9	Rule 1.2(c)
EC 7-10	Rule 4.4(a)
EC 7-11	Rules 1.14(a), 3.8(a), (b), (c), & (d), 3.9
EC 7-12	Rule 1.14
EC 7-13	Rule 3.8
EC 7-14	Rules 3.1, 3.8(a) & (f), 4.4(a)
EC 7-15	Rule 3.9
EC 7-16	Rule 3.9
EC 7-17	Rule 1.2(b)
EC 7-18	Rules 3.8(c), 4.2, 4.3
EC 7-19	None
EC 7-20	Rules 3.2, 3.5(a) & (d)
EC 7-21	Rule 4.4(a)
EC 7-22	Rules 1.2(d), 3.4(c)
EC 7-23	Rule 3.3(a)(2)
EC 7-24	Rules 3.3(d), 3.4(e)
EC 7-25	Rules 3.1, 3.4(c) & (e), 3.5(d), 3.6, 4.4(a)
EC 7-26	Rule 3.3(a)(3) & (b)

ABA MODEL CODE	ABA MODEL RULES
EC 7-27	Rules 3.3(b) & (d), 3.4(a) & (f)
EC 7-28	Rules 3.4(b), 5.3(a)
EC 7-29	Rules 3.5(a) & (c), 4.4(a)
EC 7-30	Rules 3.5(c), 4.4(a)
EC 7-31	Rule 3.5(a) & (c)
EC 7-32	Rules 3.3(a)(1) & (b), 3.5(a) & (c)
EC 7-33	Rule 3.6
EC 7-34	Rules 3.5(a), 8.4(f)
EC 7-35	Rule 3.5(b)
EC 7-36	Rule 3.5(d)
EC 7-37	Rules 3.5(d), 4.4(a)
EC 7-38	Rules 1.3, 3.4(c)
EC 7-39	None
DR 7-101(A)	Rules 1.2(a), 1.3, 3.2, 3.5(d), 4.4(a)
DR 7-101(B)	Rules 1.2(b), 1.16(b)
DR 7-102(A)(1)	Rules 3.1, 4.4(a)
DR 7-102(A)(2)	Rule 3.1
DR 7-102(A)(3)	Rules 3.3(a)(1), (a)(3), & (b), 4.1
DR 7-102(A)(4)	Rules 3.3(a) & (b), 4.1
DR 7-102(A)(5)	Rules 3.3(a)(1), 4.1
DR 7-102(A)(6)	Rules 1.2(d), 3.3(b), 3.4(b)
DR 7-102(A)(7)	Rules 1.2(d), 3.3(a)(3) & (b), 4.1
DR 7-102(A)(8)	Rules 1.2(d), 8.4(a) & (b)
DR 7-102(B)	Rules 1.6(b)(1), 3.3(b) & (c), 4.1
DR 7-103(A)	Rule 3.8(a)
DR 7-103(B)	Rule 3.8(d)
DR 7-104	Rules 3.4(f), 4.2, 4.3
DR 7-105	None
DR 7-106(A)	Rules 1.2(d), 3.4(c) & (d), 3.5(a)
DR 7-106(B)	Rules 3.3(a)(2), 3.9
DR 7-106(C)	Rules 3.4(a), (c), (d), & (e), 3.5(d), 4.4(a)
DR 7-107(A)–(I)	Rule 3.6
DR 7-107(D)–(F)	Rule 4.4(a)
DR 7-107(J)	Rules 5.1(a) & (b), 5.3(a) & (b)
DR 7-108(A)	Rule 3.5(a), (b), & (c)
DR 7-108(B)	Rules 3.5(a), (b), & (c), 5.3(b)
DR 7-108(C)	Rule 3.5(a), (b), & (c)
DR 7-108(D)	Rules 3.5(c)(3), 4.4(a)
DR 7-108(E)	Rules 3.5(a), (b), & (c), 4.4(a), 5.1(c), 5.3(b)

ABA MODEL CODE	ABA MODEL RULES
DR 7-108(F)	Rules 3.5(a), (b), & (c), 4.4(a)
DR 7-108(G)	Rules 3.3(b), 3.5(c)
DR 7-109(A)	Rules 3.3(a)(1), (a)(3), & (b), 3.4(a)
DR 7-109(B)	Rules 3.3(b), 3.4(a) & (f)
DR 7-109(C)	Rule 3.4(b)
DR 7-110(A)	Rules 3.5(a), 8.4(f)
DR 7-110(B)	Rule 3.5(a) & (b)

Canon 8: Improving Legal System

EC 8-1	Rule 6.1
EC 8-2	Rule 6.1
EC 8-3	Rules 6.1, 6.2(a), 8.4(d)
EC 8-4	Rule 3.9
EC 8-5	Rules 3.3(a)(1), (a)(3), & (b), 3.9
EC 8-6	Rule 8.2(a)
EC 8-7	Rule 6.1
EC 8-8	Rule 1.11(d)
EC 8-9	Rule 6.1
DR 8-101	Rules 3.5, 8.4(b), (c), & (f)
DR 8-102	Rule 8.2(a)
DR 8-103	Rule 8.2(b)

Canon 9: Appearance of Impropriety

EC 9-1	Rule 8.4(f)
EC 9-2	Rules 1.4(a), 8.4(e)
EC 9-3	Rules 1.11(a), 1.12(a) & (b)
EC 9-4	Rule 8.4(c) & (e)
EC 9-5	Rule 1.15
EC 9-6	Preamble, Rule 8.4(e)
EC 9-7	Rule 1.15
DR 9-101(A)	Rule 1.12(a) & (b)
DR 9-101(B)	Rules 1.11(a), 1.12(a) & (b)
DR 9-101(C)	Rules 1.4(a)(5), 3.9, 8.4(e)
DR 9-102	Rules 1.4(a), 1.15

ABA STANDING COMMITTEE ON ETHICS AND PROFESSIONAL RESPONSIBILITY

COMPOSITION AND JURISDICTION

The Standing Committee on Ethics and Professional Responsibility, which consists of ten members, may:

(1) by the concurrence of a majority of its members, express its opinion on proper professional or judicial conduct, either on its own initiative or when requested to do so by a member of the bar or the judiciary;

(2) periodically publish its issued opinions to the profession in summary or complete form and, on request, provide copies of opinions to members of the bar, the judiciary and the public;

(3) provide under its supervision informal responses to ethics inquiries the answers to which are substantially governed by applicable ethical codes and existing written opinions;

(4) on request, advise or otherwise assist professional organizations and courts in their activities relating to the development, modification and interpretation of statements of the ethical standards of the profession such as the Model Rules of Professional Conduct, the predecessor Model Code of Professional Responsibility and the Model Code of Judicial Conduct;

(5) recommend amendments to or clarifications of the Model Rules of Professional Conduct or the Model Code of Judicial Conduct; and

(6) adopt rules relating to the procedures to be used in issuing opinions, effective when approved by the Board of Governors.

[The above Composition and Jurisdiction statement is found at §31.7 of the Bylaws of the Association. The Rules of Procedure are not incorporated into the Bylaws.]

RULES OF PROCEDURE

1. The Committee may express its opinion on questions of proper professional and judicial conduct. The Model Rules of Professional Conduct and the Model Code of Judicial Conduct, as they may be amended or superseded, contain the standards to be applied. For as long as a significant number of jurisdictions continue to base their professional standards on the predecessor Model Code of Professional Responsibility, the Committee will continue to refer also to the Model Code in its opinions.

2. The Committee may issue an opinion on its own initiative or upon a request from a member of the bar or the judiciary or from a professional organization or a court.

3. The Committee may issue opinions of two kinds: Formal Opinions and Informal Opinions. Formal Opinions are those upon subjects the Committee determines to be of widespread interest or unusual importance. Other opinions are Informal Opinions. The Committee will assign to each opinion a non-duplicative identifying number, with distinction between Formal Opinions and Informal Opinions.

4. The Committee will not usually issue an opinion on a question that is known to be pending before a court in a proceeding in which the requestor is involved. The Committee's published opinions will not identify the person who was the requestor or whose conduct is the subject of the opinion. The Committee will not issue an opinion on a question of law.

5. The Committee may invite or accept written information relevant to a particular opinion from a person or persons interested in such an opinion before the Committee begins its work on an opinion. Ordinarily, the Committee will not invite anyone to make an oral presentation or argument in support of that position.

6. When a Committee or staff member receives an inquiry about the status of a draft opinion from anyone outside the Committee, the member may inform the inquirer that the Committee is considering the question. Draft opinions may, in appropriate circumstances, be shown to other interested ABA Committees and entities. Committee and staff members shall not, absent unusual circumstances, discuss the substance of pending opinions with the public, but may mention topics related to pending opinions in a general fashion.

7. Before issuing an opinion with respect to judicial conduct the Committee will submit the proposed opinion to the Judges' Advisory Committee and consider any objection or comment from the Judges' Advisory

Committee and any member of it. The Committee may assume that the Judges' Advisory Committee and its members have no objection or comment if none is received by the Committee within 30 days after the submission.

8. If the Committee decides not to issue a requested opinion the requestor will be promptly notified.

9. The Committee will issue an opinion only with the concurrence of six members in a vote taken at a meeting or in a telephone conference call. When a Committee member votes against a position declaring a Committee policy, that vote may be recorded in the minutes, which may include the name of the dissenting Committee member. The minutes shall not reflect the names of Committee members voting for or against any non-Committee policy question except that a member's vote shall be recorded and identified at the member's request. When drafting an opinion, policy statement or other document to be publicly disseminated, the Committee shall make every effort to reach a consensus. When, after a full examination of the issue and an exchange of views, the Committee cannot reach a consensus, a dissenting opinion may be appropriate to express the views of a Committee member or members. A member may place a statement of dissent in the Committee file or request that the dissent be published with the opinion.

10. The Chair may assign to one or more members the responsibility of preparing a proposed opinion for consideration by the Committee. The Committee will issue a requested opinion as promptly as feasible.

11. A Formal Opinion overrules an earlier Formal Opinion or Informal Opinion to the extent of conflict. An Informal Opinion overrules an earlier Informal Opinion to the extent of conflict but does not overrule an earlier Formal Opinion.

12. Opinions of the Committee issued before the effective dates of the Model Rules of Professional Conduct, the predecessor Model Code of Professional Responsibility and the Model Code of Judicial Conduct continue in effect to the extent not inconsistent with those standards and not overruled or limited by later opinions.

13. The Committee will make opinions and/or summaries of opinions available for publication in the American Bar Association journal. The Committee will cause Formal Opinions and Informal Opinions to be published in looseleaf form.

14. The Committee may through its staff arrange to provide informal responses to ethics inquiries the answers to which are substantially gov-

erned by applicable ethical codes and opinions of this Committee or other ethics committees. The staff will maintain a log of such inquiries that will periodically be reviewed by the Committee.

15. Information contained in Committee files relating to requests for opinions that would disclose the identity of the inquirer or the person whose conduct is the subject of the opinion will not voluntarily be disclosed by the Association without the consent of the affected persons.

ABA SPECIAL COMMITTEE ON IMPLEMENTATION OF THE MODEL RULES OF PROFESSIONAL CONDUCT (1983–1987)

MICHAEL FRANCK, *Chair*
Lansing, Michigan

EDWARD L. BENOIT
Twin Falls, Idaho

W. STELL HUIE
Atlanta, Georgia

ROGER BROSNAHAN
Minneapolis, Minnesota

JAMES T. JENNINGS
Roswell, New Mexico

WAYNE A. BUDD
Boston, Massachusetts

CAROLYN B. LAMM
Washington, D.C.

RICHARD M. COLEMAN
Los Angeles, California

LLOYD LOCHRIDGE
Austin, Texas

JOHN C. ELAM
Columbus, Ohio

LEON SILVERMAN
New York, New York

JOSEPH E. GALLAGHER
Scranton, Pennsylvania

E.C. WARD
Natchez, Mississippi

ROBERT O. HETLAGE
St. Louis, Missouri

BEN J. WEAVER
Indianapolis, Indiana

AMENDMENTS TO THE MODEL RULES OF PROFESSIONAL CONDUCT (BY RULE)

Preamble
Amended 2002 per Midyear Meeting Report 401.

Scope
Amended 2002 per Midyear Meeting Report 401.

Rule 1.0
Amended 2002 per Midyear Meeting Report 401.
Amended 2009 per Midyear Meeting Report 109.
Amended 2012 per Annual Meeting Report 105A.

Rule 1.1
Amended 2002 per Midyear Meeting Report 401.
Amended 2012 per Annual Meeting Reports 105A and C.

Rule 1.2
Amended 2002 per Midyear Meeting Report 401.

Rule 1.3
Amended 2002 per Midyear Meeting Report 401.

Rule 1.4
Amended 2002 per Midyear Meeting Report 401.
Amended 2012 per Annual Meeting Report 105A.

Rule 1.5
Amended 2002 per Midyear Meeting Report 401.

Rule 1.6
Amended 2002 per Midyear Meeting Report 401.
Amended 2003 per Annual Meeting Report 119A.
Amended 2012 per Annual Meeting Reports 105A and F.

Rule 1.7
Amended 1987 per Midyear Meeting Report 121.
Amended 2002 per Midyear Meeting Report 401.

Rule 1.8
Amended 1987 per Midyear Meeting Report 121.
Amended 2002 per Midyear Meeting Report 401.

Rule 1.9
Amended 1987 per Midyear Meeting Report 121.
Amended 1989 per Midyear Meeting Report 120A.
Amended 2002 per Midyear Meeting Report 401.

Rule 1.10
Amended 1989 per Midyear Meeting Report 120A.
Amended 2002 per Midyear Meeting Report 401.
Amended 2009 per Midyear Meeting Report 109.
Amended 2009 per Annual Meeting Report 109.

Rule 1.11
Amended 1987 per Midyear Meeting Report 121.
Amended 2002 per Midyear Meeting Report 401.

Rule 1.12
Amended 1987 per Midyear Meeting Report 121.
Amended 2002 per Midyear Meeting Report 401.

Rule 1.13
Amended 2002 per Midyear Meeting Report 401.
Amended 2003 per Annual Meeting Report 119B.

Rule 1.14
Amended 1997 per Midyear Meeting Report 113.
Amended 2002 per Midyear Meeting Report 401.

Rule 1.15
Amended 2002 per Midyear Meeting Report 401.

Rule 1.16
Amended 2002 per Midyear Meeting Report 401.

Rule 1.17
Added 1990 per Midyear Meeting Report 8A.
Amended 2002 per Midyear Meeting Report 401.
Amended 2012 per Annual Meeting Report 105F.

Rule 1.18
Added 2002 per Midyear Meeting Report 401.
Amended 2012 per Annual Meeting Report 105B.

Rule 2.1
Amended 2002 per Midyear Meeting Report 401.

Rule 2.2
Deleted 2002 per Midyear Meeting Report 401.

Rule 2.3
Amended 2002 per Midyear Meeting Report 401.

Rule 2.4
Added 2002 per Midyear Meeting Report 401.

Rule 3.1
Amended 2002 per Midyear Meeting Report 401.

Rule 3.2
Amended 2002 per Midyear Meeting Report 401.

Rule 3.3
Amended 2002 per Midyear Meeting Report 401.

Rule 3.4
Amended 2002 per Midyear Meeting Report 401.

Rule 3.5
Amended 2002 per Midyear Meeting Report 401.

Rule 3.6
Amended 1994 per Annual Meeting Report 100.
Amended 2002 per Midyear Meeting Report 401.

Rule 3.7
Amended 2002 per Midyear Meeting Report 401.

Rule 3.8
Amended 1990 per Midyear Meeting Report 118.
Amended 1994 per Annual Meeting Report 100.
Amended 1995 per Annual Meeting Report 101.
Amended 2002 per Midyear Meeting Report 401.
Amended 2008 per Midyear Meeting Report 105B.

Rule 3.9
Amended 2002 per Midyear Meeting Report 401.

Rule 4.1
Amended 2002 per Midyear Meeting Report 401.

Rule 4.2
Amended 1995 per Annual Meeting Report 100.
Amended 2002 per Midyear Meeting Report 401.

Rule 4.3
Amended 2002 per Midyear Meeting Report 401.

Rule 4.4
Amended 2002 per Midyear Meeting Report 401.
Amended 2012 per Annual Meeting Report 105A.

Rule 5.1
Amended 2002 per Midyear Meeting Report 401.

Rule 5.3
Amended 2002 per Midyear Meeting Report 401.
Amended 2012 per Annual Meeting Report 105C.

Rule 5.4
Amended 1990 per Midyear Meeting Report 8A.
Amended 2002 per Midyear Meeting Report 401.

Rule 5.5
Amended 2002 per Annual Meeting Report 201B.
Amended 2007 per Midyear Meeting Report 104.
Amended 2012 per Annual Meeting Reports 105 B and C.
Amended 2013 per Midyear Meeting Report 107A.
Amended 2016 per Midyear Meeting Report 103.

Rule 5.6
Amended 1990 per Midyear Meeting Report 8A.
Amended 2002 per Midyear Meeting Report 401.

Rule 5.7
Added 1994 per Midyear Meeting Report 113.
Amended 2002 per Midyear Meeting Report 401.

Rule 6.1
Amended 1993 per Midyear Meeting Report 8A.
Amended 2002 per Midyear Meeting Report 401.

Rule 6.3
Amended 1987 per Midyear Meeting Report 121.

Rule 6.5
Added 2002 per Midyear Meeting Report 401.

Rule 7.1
Amended 2002 per Midyear Meeting Report 401.
Amended 2012 per Annual Meeting Report 105B.
Amended 2018 per Annual Meeting Report 101.

Rule 7.2
Amended 1989 per Midyear Meeting Report 120B.
Amended 1990 per Midyear Meeting Report 8A.
Amended 2002 per Midyear Meeting Report 401.
Amended 2002 per Annual Meeting Report 114.
Amended 2012 per Annual Meeting Report 105B.
Amended 2018 per Annual Meeting Report 101.

Rule 7.3
Amended 1989 per Midyear Meeting Reports 115 and 120B.
Amended 2002 per Midyear Meeting Report 401.
Amended 2012 per Annual Meeting Report 105B.
Amended 2018 per Annual Meeting Report 101.

Rule 7.4
Deleted 2018 per Annual Meeting Report 101.

Rule 7.5
Deleted 2018 per Annual Meeting Report 101.

Rule 7.6
Added 2000 per Midyear Meeting Report 110.

Rule 8.1
Amended 2002 per Midyear Meeting Report 401.

Rule 8.3
Amended 1991 per Midyear Meeting Report 108C.
Amended 2002 per Midyear Meeting Report 401.

Rule 8.4
Amended 1998 per Annual Meeting Report 117.
Amended 2002 per Midyear Meeting Report 401.
Amended 2016 per Annual Meeting Report 109.

Rule 8.5
Amended 1993 per Annual Meeting Report 114.
Amended 2002 per Annual Meeting Report 201C.
Amended 2013 per Midyear Meeting Report 107D.

AMENDMENTS TO THE
MODEL RULES OF PROFESSIONAL
CONDUCT (BY DATE)

1987 Midyear Meeting
Rules 1.7, 1.8, 1.9, 1.11, 1.12 and 6.3

1989 Midyear Meeting
Rules 1.9, 1.10, 7.2, 7.3 and 7.4

1990 Midyear Meeting
Rules 1.17, 3.8, 5.4, 5.6 and 7.2

1991 Midyear Meeting
Rule 8.3

1992 Annual Meeting
Rule 7.4

1993 Midyear Meeting
Rule 6.1

1993 Annual Meeting
Rule 8.5

1994 Midyear Meeting
Rule 5.7

1994 Annual Meeting
Rules 3.6, 3.8 and 7.4

1995 Annual Meeting
Rules 3.8 and 4.2

1997 Midyear Meeting
Rule 1.14

1998 Annual Meeting
Rule 8.4

2000 Midyear Meeting
Rule 7.6

2002 Midyear Meeting
Preamble, Scope, Rules 1.0, 1.1, 1.2, 1.3, 1.4, 1.5, 1.6, 1.7, 1.8, 1.9, 1.10, 1.11, 1.12, 1.13, 1.14, 1.15, 1.16, 1.17, 1.18, 2.1, 2.2, 2.3, 2.4, 3.1, 3.2, 3.3, 3.4, 3.5, 3.6, 3.7, 3.8, 3.9, 4.1, 4.2, 4.3, 4.4, 5.1, 5.3. 5.4, 5.6, 5.7, 6.1, 6.5, 7.1, 7.2, 7.3, 7.4, 7.5, 8.1, 8.3 and 8.4

2002 Annual Meeting
Rules 5.5, 7.2, 7.5 and 8.5

2003 Annual Meeting
Rules 1.6 and 1.13

2007 Midyear Meeting
Rule 5.5

2008 Midyear Meeting
Rule 3.8

2009 Midyear Meeting
Rules 1.0 and 1.10

2009 Annual Meeting
Rule 1.10

2012 Annual Meeting
Rules 1.0, 1.1, 1.4, 1.6, 1.17, 1.18, 4.4, 5.3, 5.5, 7.1, 7.2 and 7.3

2013 Midyear Meeting
Rules 5.5 and 8.5

2016 Midyear Meeting
Rule 5.5

2016 Annual Meeting
Rule 8.4

2018 Annual Meeting
Rules 7.1, 7.2, 7.3, 7.4, and 7.5

FORMAL ETHICS OPINIONS

AMERICAN BAR ASSOCIATION
STANDING COMMITTEE ON ETHICS AND PROFESSIONAL RESPONSIBILITY

Formal Opinion 485   **February 14, 2019**

Judges Performing Same-Sex Marriages

A judge for whom performing marriages is a mandatory obligation of judicial office may not decline to perform marriages of same-sex couples. A judge for whom performing marriages is a discretionary judicial function may not decline to perform marriages of same-sex couples if the judge agrees to perform opposite-sex marriages. A judge's refusal to perform same-sex marriages while performing opposite-sex marriages calls into question the judge's integrity and impartiality and reflects bias and prejudice in violation of Rules 1.1, 2.2, 2.3(A), and 2.3(B) of the Model Code of Judicial Conduct. In a jurisdiction in which a judge is not obligated to perform marriages but has the discretion to do so, a judge may refuse to perform marriages for members of the public. A judge who declines to perform marriages for members of the public may still perform marriages for family and friends. If a judge chooses to perform marriages for family and friends, however, the judge may not decline to perform same-sex marriages for family and friends.

Introduction

The Committee has been asked whether a judge subject to the Model Code of Judicial Conduct[1] may perform marriages of opposite-sex couples but refuse to perform marriages for same-sex couples. The Committee concludes that such a refusal violates the Model Code. A judge for whom performing marriages is a discretionary function may, however, decline to perform any marriages for members of the public. A judge who declines to perform any marriages for members of the public may still perform marriages for family and friends. If a judge chooses to perform marriages for family and friends, though, the judge may not decline to perform same-sex marriages for family and friends.

Background

The laws of all fifty states and the District of Columbia authorize one or more categories of judicial officers to perform marriages. This opinion cov-

---

1. MODEL CODE OF JUDICIAL CONDUCT (2011) [hereinafter MODEL CODE].

ers judges for whom performing marriages is either a mandatory obligation of judicial office or a discretionary function.[2] The conclusions stated here are based solely on the Model Code.

The Model Code

Canon I of the Model Code articulates the bedrock principle that "[a] judge shall uphold and promote the independence, integrity, and impartiality of the judiciary, and shall avoid impropriety and the appearance of impropriety."[3] Rule 1.1 provides that "[a] judge shall comply with the law, including the Code of Judicial Conduct."[4] Accordingly, a judge must "act at all times in a manner that promotes public confidence in the independence, integrity, and impartiality of the judiciary, and shall avoid impropriety and the appearance of impropriety."[5] The term "impartiality" as used in this context means "the absence of bias or prejudice in favor of, or against, particular parties or classes of parties."[6]

Canon II expresses another fundamental principle: "A judge shall perform the duties of judicial office impartially, competently, and diligently."[7] Although a judge's performance of a marriage typically is a discretionary function rather than a mandatory function, it is nonetheless a duty of judicial office within the meaning of the Model Code.[8] Correspondingly, Model

---

2. A judge, within the meaning of [the Model] Code, is anyone who is authorized to perform judicial functions, including an officer such as a justice of the peace, magistrate, court commissioner, special master, referee, or member of the administrative law judiciary." *Id.* at Application I(B).

3. *Id.* at Canon I.

4. *Id.* at R. 1.1. The Model Code defines the term "law" to include constitutional provisions, court rules, decisional law, and statutes. *Id.* Terminology.

5. *Id.* at R. 1.2.

6. *Id.* at Terminology.

7. *Id.* at Canon II.

8. *See, e.g., In re* Day, 413 P.3d 907, 950 (Or. 2018) (concluding that the act of solemnizing marriages, once a judge has chosen to do so, qualifies as a judicial duty within the meaning of judicial ethics rules), *cert. denied,* 139

S. Ct. 324 (2018); Ariz. Sup. Ct., Judicial Ethics Advisory Comm. Op. 15-01, 2015 WL 1530659, at *1 (2015) ("Although the performance of a marriage by a judge is a 'discretionary function' rather than a mandatory function . . . it is based on statutory authority granted by the legislature. Because of this specific grant of authority . . . the performance of a marriage by a judicial officer is performance of a 'judicial duty' as contemplated by the Code [of Judicial Conduct]."); Sup. Ct. of Ohio, Bd. of Prof'l Conduct Adv. Op. 15-001, 2015 WL 4875137, at *1 (2015) ("When a judge performs a civil marriage ceremony . . . the judge is performing a judicial duty and is thus required to follow the Code of Judicial Conduct in the performance of that duty."); Wis. Sup. Ct., Judicial Conduct Advisory Comm. Op. No. 15-1, 2015 WL 5928528, at *2 (2015) (discussing judges' discretionary functions in connection with the performance of marriages); Elizabeth A. Flaherty, *Impartiality in Solemnizing Marriages,* JUDICIAL CONDUCT BD. OF PA. NEWSLETTER, Summer 2014, at 18, 25 ("When a judge chooses to conduct a wedding ceremony, s/he acts in an official judicial capacity, authorized by statute.").

Rule 2.2 requires a judge to "uphold and apply the law" and to "perform all duties of judicial office fairly and impartially."[9] Although judges come to the bench with different backgrounds and personal views or philosophies, judges "must interpret and apply the law, without regard to whether the judge approves or disapproves of the law" or principle or rule in question.[10] Model Rule 2.3(A) mandates that judges perform the duties of judicial office without bias or prejudice.[11]

Most importantly for present purposes, Model Rule 2.3(B) prohibits a judge who is performing judicial duties from manifesting bias or prejudice based on people's sex, gender, sexual orientation, or marital status.[12] A judge who manifests such bias or prejudice threatens to undermine public confidence in the judiciary and to bring it into disrepute.[13] Indeed, because impartiality and unbiased decision-making and conduct are critical to our justice system and to the public's faith in the judiciary, the Model Code emphasizes in several places that judges must avoid even conduct that may be *perceived* as biased or prejudiced.[14]

State Judicial Ethics Opinions

Several states have analyzed judges' obligations to perform same-sex marriages. In a leading opinion, the Supreme Court of Ohio Board of Professional Conduct was asked by judges and a judicial association on behalf of its members (1) whether a judge who is authorized to perform marriages may refuse to marry same-sex couples on personal, moral, or religious grounds, but still marry opposite-sex couples; and (2) whether a judge may decline to perform all marriages to avoid marrying same-sex couples.[15] Relying on the oath of office to which all Ohio judges swear, and provisions of the Ohio Code of Judicial Conduct, which track the Model Code, the Board concluded that "[a] judge who performs civil marriages may not refuse to perform same-sex marriages while continuing to perform opposite-sex marriages, based upon his or her personal, moral, and religious beliefs."[16] The

---

9. MODEL CODE R. 2.2, *supra* note 1.

10. *Id.* at cmt. [2].

11. *Id.* at R. 2.3(A).

12. *See id.* at R. 2.3(B) (prohibiting bias, prejudice, or harassment "based upon attributes including but not limited to race, sex, gender, religion, national origin, ethnicity, disability, age, sexual orientation, marital status, socioeconomic status, or political affiliation").

13. *Id.* at cmt. [1].

14. *See, e.g., id.* at Preamble cmt. [2] ("Judges should maintain the dignity of judicial office at all times, and avoid both impropriety and the *appearance of impropriety* in their professional and personal lives.") (emphasis added); *Id.* at R. 1.2 cmt. [3] ("Conduct that compromises or *appears to compromise the independence, integrity, and impartiality of a judge* undermines public confidence in the judiciary. . . . (emphasis added)).

15. Sup. Ct. of Ohio, Bd. of Prof'l Conduct Advisory Op. 15-001, 2015 WL 4875137, at *1 (2015).

16. *Id.* at *5.

Board further concluded that "[a] judge who takes the position that he or she will discontinue performing all marriages in order to avoid marrying same-sex couples based on his or her personal, moral, or religious beliefs may be interpreted as manifesting an improper bias or prejudice toward a particular class."[17] Thus, Ohio judges may not decline to perform all marriages to avoid marrying same-sex couples on personal, moral, or religious grounds.[18] Other authorities have disagreed on this final point, however, and have held that judges may decline to perform all marriages without manifesting bias or prejudice toward same-sex couples.[19]

The Arizona Supreme Court Judicial Ethics Advisory Committee concluded that judges may not (1) distinguish between same-sex and opposite-sex couples when deciding whether to perform marriage ceremonies; (2) decline to perform same-sex marriage ceremonies even if the judge refers would-be spouses to other courts or individuals; (3) decline to perform same-sex marriages if they perform other marriages in court facilities; or (4) decline to perform same-sex marriages even if they conduct all opposite-sex weddings outside of court facilities.[20] These principles hold true even if a judge's decision not to conduct same-sex marriages reflects the judge's sincerely-held religious beliefs.[21]

Because performing marriages is a discretionary function, an Arizona judge may choose to perform no marriages.[22] An Arizona judge may also choose to perform marriages exclusively for family and friends without violating judicial conduct rules because the judge's practice is unrelated to the celebrants' sexual orientation.[23] If judges opt to perform marriages only for friends and relatives, however, they cannot ethically refuse to perform same-sex marriages for friends and relatives.[24] To do so would violate Arizona Rule of Judicial Conduct 2.3(B), which prohibits judges who are performing judicial duties from manifesting bias or prejudice based on sexual orientation.[25]

The Nebraska Judicial Ethics Committee reached essentially the same conclusion. In Opinion 15-1, the Nebraska Committee held that judges may not refuse to perform same-sex marriages notwithstanding their personal

---

17. *Id.*

18. *Id.* at *1, *5.

19. *See, e.g.*, Wis. Sup. Ct., Judicial Conduct Advisory Comm. Op. 15-1, 2015 WL 5928528, at *1 (2015) (stating that judicial officers may not decline to officiate at same-sex weddings because of their religious or personal beliefs, but that judicial officers may decline to perform marriages at all, regardless of whether the parties seeking to be married are of the same or opposite genders, because officiating at weddings is a discretionary duty).

20. Ariz. Sup. Ct., Judicial Ethics Advisory Comm. Op. 15-01, 2015 WL 1530659, at *1 (2015).

21. *Id.*

22. *Id.*

23. *Id.* at *2.

24. *Id.* (citing Rule 2.3(B)).

25. *Id.*

or sincerely-held religious beliefs that marriage is limited to the union of one man and one woman.[26] Nor may a judge refuse to perform a same-sex wedding if he or she refers the couple to a judge who is willing to perform same-sex marriages because the refusal to perform the ceremony manifests bias or prejudice based on the couple's sexual orientation notwithstanding the referral.[27] A judge may choose to avoid such personal or religious conflicts by refusing to perform marriages altogether.[28] Judges may also choose to perform marriages exclusively for close friends and relatives, but if they do so, they may not refuse to perform same-sex marriages for close friends and relatives.[29]

Analysis

The public is entitled to expect that judges will perform their activities and duties fairly, impartially, and free from bias and prejudice.[30] Further, while actual impartiality is necessary, it is not sufficient; the public must also *perceive* judges to be impartial.[31]

If state law authorizes or obligates a judge to perform marriages, a judge's refusal to perform same-sex marriages while agreeing to perform marriages for opposite-sex couples is improper under Rules 1.1, 2.2, 2.3(A), and 2.3(B) Model Code. This conclusion would have been true in any state that recognized same-sex marriages before the Supreme Court decided *Obergefell v. Hodges*,[32] but it is broadly correct now. In *Obergefell*, the Supreme Court held that the Fourteenth Amendment to the U.S. Constitution prohibits states from refusing to license marriages between individuals of the same sex. As the Court explained, the U.S. Constitution "does not permit the State to bar same-sex couples from marriage on the same terms as accorded to couples of the opposite sex."[33] The Court further determined that "there is no

---

26. Neb. Judicial Ethics Comm. Op. 15-1, at 2 (2015), *available at* https://supremecourt. nebraska.gov/sites/default/ files/ethics-opinions/Judicial/15-1_0.pdf.

27. *Id.*

28. *Id.*

29. *Id.*

30. *See generally* Liteky v. United States, 510 U.S. 540, 558 (1994) (Kennedy, J., concurring) (noting that judicial impartiality in both fact and appearance is "one of the very objects of law"); Alexander v. Primerica Holdings, 10 F.3d 155, 162 (3d Cir. 1993) (noting the importance of "'the public's confidence in the judiciary, which may be irreparably harmed if a case is allowed to proceed before a judge who appears to be tainted'") (citations omitted); United States v. CBS, 497 F.2d 107, 109 (5th Cir. 1974) (observing that "the protection of the integrity and dignity of the judicial process from any hint or appearance of bias is the palladium of our judicial system").

31. *See* Caperton v. A.T. Massey Coal Co., 556 U.S. 868, 888–89 (2009).

32. 135 S. Ct. 2584 (2015).

33. *Id.* at 2607; *see also id.* at 2604–2605 (stating that "the right to marry is a fundamental right inherent in the liberty of the person, and under the Due Process and Equal Protection Clauses of the Fourteenth Amendment couples of the same-sex may not be deprived of that right and that liberty").

lawful basis for a State to refuse to recognize a lawful same-sex marriage performed in another State on the ground of its same-sex character."[34]

Model Rule 1.1 obligates judges to comply with the law. *Obergefell* makes clear that the U.S. Constitution prohibits state officials from engaging in discrimination and bias toward gays and lesbians in decisions related to same-sex marriage; in short, the decision establishes law with which judges must comply. Model Rule 2.2 requires judges to "uphold and apply [this] law," and further directs that judges "perform all duties of judicial office fairly and impartially."[35] As noted earlier, the term "impartiality" as used in this context means "the absence of bias or prejudice in favor of, or against, particular parties or classes of parties."[36]

Furthermore, Model Rule 2.3(A) specifically requires judges to perform their duties free from bias and prejudice. Model Rule 2.3(B) prohibits a judge who is performing judicial duties from manifesting bias or prejudice based on sex, gender, sexual orientation, or marital status. Indeed, we are aware of no state judicial ethics opinion concluding that similar judicial code provisions permit judges who perform marriage ceremonies for opposite sex couples to refuse to perform marriage ceremonies for same-sex couples.

A judge may choose to perform no marriages, or to perform marriages exclusively for family and friends. If judges opt to perform marriages only for friends and relatives, however, they cannot refuse to perform same-sex marriages for friends and relatives. Again, to refuse to perform same-sex marriages for friends and relatives while performing marriages of opposite-sex friends and relatives would violate Model Rules 2.2, 2.3(A), and 2.3(B). The fact that the judge's conduct affects a smaller group of people—that is, friends and family versus the public at large—does not change the judge's ethical obligations.

---

34. *Id.* at 2607–2608. We recognize that a judge's refusal to perform a same-sex marriage may be based on the judge's sincerely-held beliefs regarding the concept of marriage. As the Supreme Court noted in *Obergefell*, "[m]any who deem same-sex marriage to be wrong reach that conclusion based on decent and honorable religious or philosophical principles, and neither they nor their beliefs are disparaged here." *Id.* at 2602. We also recognize, as the Supreme Court observed in *Masterpiece Cakeshop, Ltd. v. Colorado Civil Rights Comm'n*, 138 S. Ct. 1719 (2018), that the First Amendment ensures that people receive proper protection as they seek to live according to the principles of their religious faith. *Id.* at 1727. *Masterpiece Cakeshop* also underscored the fundamental importance of impartiality on the part of all officials vested by the state with adjudicative authority. *Id.* at 1721 (noting that biased comments and differential treatment on the part of a state agency "cast doubt on the fairness and impartiality of the Commission's adjudication"). But as noted earlier and reiterated here, this opinion addresses the obligations of judicial officers under the Model Code.

35. MODEL CODE R. 2.2, *supra* note 1.

36. *Id.* at Terminology.

Our conclusions are reinforced by the Oregon Supreme Court's decision in *In re Day*.[37] The respondent in that case, Judge Vance Day, was appointed to the Oregon trial court bench in 2011 and re-elected in 2012. He made himself available to solemnize marriages upon becoming a judge in 2011.

After an Oregon federal judge invalidated Oregon's constitutional ban on same-sex marriage in 2014, Day's judicial assistant and clerk asked him about possibly performing weddings going forward given Day's religious belief that marriage should be confined to a man and a woman.[38] Judge Day "instructed [his clerk and judicial assistant] that, when his chambers received any marriage request, [they] should obtain" personal gender information available in the Oregon Judicial Information Network (OJIN)—which they had never done before—to try to determine whether the request involved a same-sex couple.[39] If it did, they were to inform the couple that the judge was not available on the desired date or otherwise notify him, so that he could decide how to proceed.[40] If the request came from an opposite-sex couple, however, his judicial assistant and clerk were to schedule the wedding.[41] On one occasion Day's judicial assistant checked OJIN and determined that the requesters might be a same-sex couple. Day had a genuine scheduling conflict, so the judicial assistant truthfully told the couple that the judge was unavailable. Day stopped performing marriages soon thereafter.

The Oregon Commission on Judicial Fitness and Disability charged Day with violating Rule 3.3(B) of the Oregon Code of Judicial Conduct, which provides: "A judge shall not, in the performance of judicial duties, by words or conduct, manifest bias or prejudice . . . against parties, witnesses, lawyers, or others based on attributes including but not limited to, sex, gender identity, race, national origin, ethnicity, religion, sexual orientation, marital status, disability, age, socioeconomic status, or political affiliation and shall not permit court staff, court officials, or others subject to the judge's direction and control to do so."[42] The *In re Day* court easily concluded that the act of solemnizing marriages, once a judge has chosen to do so, constitutes a judicial duty

---

37. 413 P.3d 907 (Or. 2018), *cert. denied*, 139 S. Ct. 324 (2018); *see also In re* Neely, 390 P.3d 728, 753 (Wyo. 2017) ("Judge Neely must perform her judicial functions, including performing marriages, with impartiality. She must either commit to performing marriages regardless of the couple's sexual orientation, or cease performing all marriage ceremonies. This does not mean . . . that no judge can now turn down any request to perform a marriage. What it means is that no judge can turn down a request to perform a marriage for reasons that undermine the integrity of the judiciary by demonstrating a lack of independence and impartiality."), *cert. denied*, 138 S. Ct. 639 (2018).

38. *In re Day*, 413 P.3d at 921, 949.

39. *Id.* at 921–22, 949.

40. *Id.* at 922, 949.

41. *Id.*

42. *Id.* at 950 (quoting OREGON CODE OF JUDICIAL CONDUCT R. 3.3(B) (2013)).

under Oregon Rule 3.3(B).[43] That led the court to the question of whether Day had manifested bias or prejudice against same-sex couples. Day argued that he had not done so because he never actually refused to marry any same-sex couple as a result of his short-lived screening process.[44] According to Day, Oregon Rule 3.3(B) could not authorize punishment "for discrimination that did not occur against unknown parties."[45]

The *In re Day* court reasoned that to "manifest" bias or prejudice, "the act in question must be undertaken such that it is obvious to others" or "must be capable of perception."[46] To be sure, Day's screening process was not displayed or made known in a manner that was capable of perception by anyone outside his chambers. But that factor did not resolve the issue because his "chosen course of action—motivated by his intention to marry only opposite-sex couples—was evident to his staff."[47] His instructions to his staff in implementing his plan to avoid marrying same-sex couples "indisputably communicated to his staff his intention to treat same-sex couples who requested a marriage officiant differently from opposite-sex couples."[48] Furthermore, he instructed his staff to implement "that differential treatment, which included providing inaccurate information to same-sex couples. Those actions 'manifest[ed]' prejudice in the performance of judicial duties, within the meaning of [Oregon] Rule 3.3(B)."[49]

Next, Day contended that because no same-sex couple was denied the opportunity to marry by virtue of his screening process, he did not discriminate or manifest prejudice "against" any such couple as required for a violation of Oregon Rule 3.3(B).[50] While it was true that he never actually refused to marry a same-sex couple, the *In re Day* court nevertheless concluded that Day's conduct manifested prejudice against others within the meaning of the rule.

> We reiterate that, in prohibiting a judge from manifesting prejudice against court participants or others based on personal attributes, [Oregon] Rule 3.3(B) seeks to prevent judicial actions that impair the fairness of a proceeding or prompt an unfavorable view of the judiciary Most commonly, problematic conduct likely would involve a judge's overt and prejudicial treatment of a particular person involved in a proceeding before the court—such as a litigant, juror, witness, or lawyer. . . . However, a judge could manifest prejudice against others based on personal attributes in a more general way that still

---

43. *Id.*
44. *Id.* at 951.
45. *Id.*
46. *Id.*
47. *Id.* at 952.
48. *Id.*
49. *Id.*
50. *Id.*

could affect perceptions of fairness or prompt an unfavorable view of the judiciary. . . . Given the fundamental objective of [Oregon] Rule 3.3(B)—ensuring the public's trust in an impartial and fair judiciary— we conclude that that rule is not limited to a manifestation of prejudice against an identified, particular person. Rather, it may encompass an expression of bias against an identifiable group, based on personal characteristics, in the performance of judicial duties.[51]

Day crafted a screening process that was intended to ensure that he married only opposite- sex couples. The screening process demonstrated to his staff that, in exercising his judicial duty to solemnize marriages, he would not treat all couples fairly. That conduct, in turn, manifested prejudice against same-sex couples based on their sexual orientation in violation of Oregon Rule 3.3(B).[52]

Conclusion

A judge for whom performing marriages is either a mandatory part of his or her official duties or an optional exercise of judicial authority violates the Model Code of Judicial Conduct by refusing to perform marriages for same-sex couples while agreeing to perform marriages of opposite-sex couples. In a jurisdiction where a judge is not obligated to perform marriages, the judge may decline to perform all marriages for members of the public. A judge who chooses not to perform any marriages for the public may still perform marriages for family and friends, so long as the judge does not discriminate between same-sex and opposite-sex couples when performing marriages for family and friends.

---

51. *Id.* at 952–53 (citations omitted).

52. *Id.* at 953. Although the Court found that Day violated Rule 3.3(B), it did not consider this violation in calculating the three-year suspension it imposed, explaining that "[i]n light of the other, notably serious misconduct that the commission has proved by clear and convincing evidence, we conclude that—whether respondent's constitutional challenges are meritorious or not—our ultimate conclusion to impose a lengthy, three-year suspension remains the same." *Id.* at 954.

AMERICAN BAR ASSOCIATION
STANDING COMMITTEE ON ETHICS AND PROFESSIONAL RESPONSIBILITY
321 N. Clark Street, Chicago, Illinois 60654-4714 Telephone (312) 988-5328
CHAIR: Barbara S. Gillers, New York, NY
■ John M. Barkett, Miami, FL ■ Robert Hirshon, Ann Arbor, MI ■ Thomas B. Mason, Washington, DC
■ Michael H. Rubin, Baton Rouge, LA ■ Douglas R. Richmond, Chicago, IL
■ Lynda Shely, Scottsdale, AZ ■ Norman W. Spaulding, Stanford, CA
■ Elizabeth Tarbert, Tallahassee, FL ■ Lisa D. Taylor, Parsippany, NJ

CENTER FOR PROFESSIONAL RESPONSIBILITY
Dennis A. Rendleman, Ethics Counsel
©2019 by the American Bar Association. All rights reserved.

Formal Opinion 486   **May 9, 2019**

Obligations of Prosecutors in Negotiating Plea Bargains for Misdemeanor Offenses

Model Rules 1.1, 1.3, 3.8(a), (b), and (c), 4.1, 4.3, 5.1, 5.3, and 8.4(a), (c) and (d) impose obligations on prosecutors when entering into plea bargains with persons accused of misdemeanors. These obligations include the duty to ensure that each charge incident to a plea has an adequate foundation in fact and law, to ensure that the accused is informed of the right to counsel and the procedure for securing counsel, to avoid plea negotiations that jeopardize the accused's ability to secure counsel, and, irrespective of whether an unrepresented accused has invoked the right to counsel, to avoid offering pleas on terms that knowingly misrepresent the consequences of acceptance or otherwise pressure or improperly induce acceptance on the part of the accused.[1]

I. Introduction

This opinion addresses a prosecutor's obligations under Model Rules 1.1, 1.3, 3.8(a), (b), and (c), 4.1, 4.3, 5.1, 5.3, and 8.4(a), (c), and (d) when negotiating with an unrepresented individual who is or may be entitled to counsel at the time the prosecutor initiates the plea bargaining process for a misdemeanor charge. The opinion also addresses a prosecutor's duties when plea bargaining with an unrepresented accused on a misdemeanor charge irrespective of whether the accused has invoked the right to counsel. These ethical obligations exist independently of any constitutional or statutory obligations prosecutors may have to an accused.

Part I emphasizes the unique role that prosecutors play in the administration of justice and highlights (i) the expansion of misdemeanor criminal enforcement and (ii) the displacement of trial by plea bargaining. Part II identifies evidence of practices that have developed in some jurisdictions to

---

1. This opinion is based on the ABA Model Rules of Professional Conduct as amended by the ABA House of Delegates through August 2018. The laws, court rules, regulations, rules of professional conduct and opinions promulgated in individual jurisdictions are controlling.

manage misdemeanor pleas. Part III turns to Model Rule 3.8, addressing first the need for guidance and then examining the text and scope of Rules 3.8(a)-(c) and related rules as they apply to misdemeanor plea bargaining. Part IV identifies the specific obligations of a prosecutor under Rules 3.8(b) and (c) with respect to the accused's right to counsel. Part V interprets Rules 4.1, 4.3, and 8.4 as they apply to negotiation and entry of plea bargains.

A. The Special Role of Prosecutors

The professional integrity of prosecutors is essential to the administration of criminal justice.[2] Their special role is reflected in a distinctive standard of professional responsibility. Under the Model Rules, a prosecutor "has the responsibility of a minister of justice and not simply that of an advocate."[3] Canon 5 of the 1908 American Bar Association Canons of Professional Ethics stated that "[t]he primary duty of a lawyer engaged in public prosecution is not to convict, but to see that justice is done."[4] The ABA Model Code of Professional Responsibility also emphasized a categorical difference between the responsibility of a public prosecutor and "that of the usual advocate."[5] A prosecutor's duty

> is to seek justice, not merely to convict. This special duty exists because: (1) the prosecutor represents the sovereign and therefore should use restraint in the discretionary exercise of governmental powers, such as in the selection of cases to prosecute; (2) during trial the prosecutor is not only an advocate but he may also make deci-

---

2. *See* JOHN JAY DOUGLASS, NATIONAL COLLEGE OF DISTRICT ATTORNEYS, ETHICAL ISSUES IN PROSECUTION 36 (1988) ("The first, best, and most effective shield against injustice for an individual accused, or society in general, must be found not in the persons of defense counsel, trial judge, or appellate jurist, but in the integrity of the prosecutor.") (quoting former prosecutor Carol Corrigan, Commentary, *Prosecutorial Ethics*, 13 HASTINGS CONST. L.Q. 537, 537 (1986)).

3. MODEL RULES OF PROF'L CONDUCT R. 3.8 cmt. [1]. *See also* ABA Comm. on Ethics & Prof'l Responsibility, Formal Op. 454 at 3 n.10 (2009) (a prosecutor's interest "in a criminal prosecution is not that it shall win a case, but that justice shall be done") (quoting Berger v. United States, 295 U.S. 78, 88 (1935)); ABA Comm. on Ethics & Prof'l Responsibility, Formal Op. 467 at 4 (2014) (same).

4. Specific references to the American prosecutor as a minister of justice date to the nineteenth century. *See, e.g.*, People v. Davis, 18 N.W. 362, 363 (Mich. 1884) (the prosecutor is a "sworn minister of justice, whose duty it was, while endeavoring to bring the guilty to punishment, to take care that the innocent should be protected"); Hurd v. People, 25 Mich. 405, 416 (1872) ("The prosecuting officer represents the public interest, which can never be promoted by the conviction of the innocent. His object like that of the court, should be simply justice; and he has no right to sacrifice this to any pride of professional success."), *superseded on other grounds by statute*, 1986 Mich. Pub. Acts 114, *as stated in* People v. Koonce, 648 N.W.2d 153, 155-56 (Mich. 2002).

5. MODEL CODE OF PROF'L RESPONSIBILITY EC 7-13 (1980).

sions normally made by an individual client, and those affecting the public interest should be fair to all; and (3) in our system of criminal justice the accused is to be given the benefit of all reasonable doubts.[6]

As this Committee has emphasized in prior opinions, there are "many excellent prosecutors who scrupulously follow or exceed the mandates of the Rules of Professional Conduct."[7] This opinion focuses on the distinctive challenges and obligations of prosecutors when negotiating pleas in misdemeanor cases.

B. Background on Misdemeanor Enforcement

Misdemeanors make up approximately 80 percent of state criminal dockets.[8] The number of misdemeanor prosecutions is estimated to have doubled since 1972.[9] The expansion has had a "concentrated impact on communities of color."[10] Most misdemeanor arrests result in charges – declination rates

---

6. *Id.*

7. ABA Comm. on Ethics & Prof'l Responsibility, Formal Op. 14-467 at 6 (2014) (on the supervisory and managerial responsibilities of prosecutors); *id.* at 1 ("We believe that most prosecutors know and follow the rules of professional conduct. Indeed, the laudable efforts of such prosecutors have provided good examples" for this and other opinions of the Committee.).

8. *See* Ben Kempinen, *The Ethics of Prosecutor Contact with the Unrepresented Defendant*, 19 Geo. J. Legal Ethics 1147, 1148 n.3 (2006) (citing Wisconsin data showing that in 2002, 79 percent of criminal cases filed in the state were for "criminal traffic or misdemeanor" offenses); ROBERT C. LAFOUNTAIN ET AL., EXAMINING THE WORK OF STATE COURTS: AN ANALYSIS OF 2008 STATE COURT CASELOADS 47 (2010) (listing data from study of 11 state dockets). A more recent study estimates that "there are three times as many misdemeanor cases as felony cases filed nationally each year." Megan Stevenson & Sandra Mayson, *The Scale of Misdemeanor Justice*, 98 B.U. L. REV. 731, 764 (2017).

Although there is variation in the exact classification of low-level offenses across state and federal jurisdictions, in this opinion we use the term "misdemeanor" in its generic sense to refer to any criminal offense less serious than a felony according to the law of the relevant jurisdiction.

9. *See* ROBERT C. BORUCHOWITZ ET AL., MINOR CRIMES, MASSIVE WASTE: THE TERRIBLE TOLL OF AMERICA'S BROKEN MISDEMEANOR COURTS 11 (2009) ("Most people who go to court in the United States go to misdemeanor courts," describing growth of misdemeanor prosecutions since 1972); Alexandra Natapoff, *Misdemeanors, in* 1 REFORMING CRIMINAL JUSTICE 71 (Erik Luna, ed. 2017) ("Most criminal convictions in this country are misdemeanors, and most Americans experience criminal justice through the petty offense process."). *But see* Stevenson & Mayson, *supra* note 8, at 747, 764 (estimating a seventeen percent decline in state misdemeanor filings over the last decade while reporting that the total number of misdemeanor cases remains substantial: 13.2 million in 2016).

10. *See* ISSA KOHLER-HAUSMANN, MISDEMEANORLAND: CRIMINAL COURTS AND SOCIAL CONTROL IN AN AGE OF BROKEN WINDOWS POLICING 51 & fig.1.10 (2018) (an empirical study of New York City courts, describing data showing that "the dramatic expansion of misdemeanor arrests has been hyperconcentrated on . . . black, and . . . Latino individuals"); Stevenson & Mayson, *supra* note 8, at 737 (finding a "profound . . . remarkably constant" racial disparity in the misdemeanor arrest rate over the last thirty-seven years); CIVIL RIGHTS DIV., U.S. DEP'T OF JUSTICE, INVESTIGATION OF THE BALTIMORE CITY POLICE DEPARTMENT 55-56 (2016) (reporting data showing that while African Americans make up 63 percent of

are low in many states, sometimes as low as 3 or 4 percent.[11] And "the vast majority of defendants plead guilty" at their initial appearance.[12] The result is a significant increase in the pre-trial dockets of state and local courts, and daunting legal and administrative burdens for both judges and prosecutors.[13] Collateral consequences for misdemeanor convictions have also expanded.[14] A misdemeanor conviction can lead to denial of employment, expulsion from school, deportation, denial of a professional license, and loss of eligibility for a wide range of public services including food assistance, public housing, health care, and federal student loans.[15]

To realize the legitimate law enforcement objectives of plea bargaining, a practice that has become "an essential component of the administration of

---

the population of Baltimore, for "misdemeanor street offense[s], unconnected to a more serious charge" between 2010 and 2015, they comprised 91 percent of trespassing charges, 91 percent of failure to obey charges, 88 percent of hindering charges, 84 percent of disorderly conduct charges, and 90 percent of people charged with resisting arrest where no other charge supported the resisting charge); Sean Webby, *Policing in San Jose: Strict Enforcement of "Conduct Crimes," Are Latinos Targeted?*, THE MERCURY NEWS (Apr. 4, 2009), https://www.mercurynews.com/2009/04/04/policing-in-san-jose-strict-enforcement-of- conduct-crimes-are-latinos-targeted/ (reporting that 70 percent of arrests for disturbing the peace, 57 percent of charges for resisting arrest, and 57 percent of arrests for public drunkenness were of Latinos, even though this group comprises less than a third of San Jose residents).

11. *See* Natapoff, *supra* note 9, at 78.

12. *Id.*; *see also* BORUCHOWITZ ET AL., *supra* note 9, at 8 ("In New York City in 2000, almost 70 percent of misdemeanor cases were disposed of at the first appearance—most through a guilty plea."); *Protecting the Constitutional Right to Counsel for Indigents Charged with Misdemeanors: Hearing Before the S. Comm. on the Judiciary*, 114th Cong. (2015) [hereinafter *Hearing*] (statement of Prof. Erica J. Hashimoto at 3), https://www.judiciary.senate.gov/imo/media/doc/05-13-15%20Hashimoto%20Testimony.pdf.

13. Hearing times in some jurisdictions run as short as three minutes. *See* ALISA SMITH ET AL., NAT'L ASS'N OF CRIMINAL DEF. LAWYERS, RUSH YO JUDGMENT: HOW SOUTH CAROLINA'S SUMMARY COURTS FAIL TO PROTECT CONSTITUTIONAL RIGHTS 19 (2017) (reporting that in South Carolina courts the hearings for misdemeanors and other minor crimes average 3.29 minutes and just two minutes long if a few outlier cases are excluded); ALISA SMITH & SEAN MADDAN, NAT'L ASS'N OF CRIMINAL DEF. LAWYERS, THREE-MINUTE JUSTICE: HASTE AND WASTE IN FLORIDA'S MISDEMEANOR COURTS 14-15 (2011); BORUCHOWITZ ET AL., *supra* note 9, at 32

14. *See National Inventory of the Collateral Consequences of Conviction*, JUSTICE CENTER, COUNCIL OF STATE GOVERNMENTS; JAMES B. JACOBS, THE ETERNAL CRIMINAL RECORD 225-300 (2015); Michael Pinard, *Collateral Consequences of Criminal Convictions: Confronting Issues of Race and Dignity*, 85 N.Y.U. L. REV. 457, 489-94 (2010); BORUCHOWITZ ET AL., *supra* note 9, at 12-13 (listing collateral consequences); People v. Suazo, 118 N.E.3d 168, 178 (N.Y. 2018) (requiring a jury trial where a misdemeanor conviction carries the potential penalty of deportation; "even if deportation is technically collateral, it is undoubtedly a severe statutory penalty that flows from the federal government as the result of a state criminal conviction"). A misdemeanor conviction can also result in sentence enhancements should the person re-offend. *See* Nichols v. United States, 511 U.S. 738, 746-48 (1994) (upholding use of misdemeanor DUI conviction to add 25 months to a subsequent felony drug sentence).

15. *See* sources gathered *supra* note 14.

justice,"[16] there must be "fairness in securing agreement between an accused and a prosecutor."[17] This is particularly so in the misdemeanor setting where, as the Supreme Court has warned, "the volume of . . . cases, far greater in number than felony prosecutions, may create an obsession for speedy dispositions, regardless of the fairness of the result."[18] Observance of the special obligations of prosecutors under the Rules of Professional Conduct is critical to achieving fair guilty pleas.

II. Evidence of Plea Bargaining Practices in Misdemeanor Cases

Notwithstanding the commitment of most prosecutors to high professional standards, there is evidence that in misdemeanor cases where the accused is or may be legally entitled to counsel, methods of negotiating plea bargains have been used in some jurisdictions that are inconsistent with the duties set forth in the Rules of Professional Conduct. As the report of a comprehensive five-year study chaired by a distinguished group of former prosecutors and judges summarized, "[w]hether because of a desire to move cases through the court system, a desire to keep indigent defense costs down, or ignorance, pervasive and serious problems exist in misdemeanor courts across the country because counsel is oftentimes either not provided, or provided late, to those who are lawfully eligible to be represented."[19] Methods of negotiating pleas documented in this report and other studies include:

(i)   requiring or encouraging plea negotiation with a prosecutor before the right to counsel has been raised;[20]

---

16. Santobello v. New York, 404 U.S. 257, 260 (1971); *see also id.* at 261 (the plea bargain "leads to prompt and largely final disposition of most criminal cases[,] . . . and, by shortening the time between charge and disposition, it enhances whatever may be the rehabilitative prospects of the guilty"). Counting both misdemeanors and felonies, "[n]inety-seven percent of federal convictions and ninety-four percent of state convictions are the result of guilty pleas." Missouri v. Frye, 566 U.S. 134, 143 (2012); *see also* Lafler v. Cooper, 566 U.S. 156, 170 (2012) ("[C]riminal justice today is for the most part a system of pleas, not a system of trials.").

17. *Santobello*, 404 U.S. at 261.

18. Argersinger v. Hamlin, 407 U.S. 25, 34 (1972) (citation omitted).

19. Nat'l Right to Counsel Comm., Constitution Project, Justice Denied: America's Continuing Neglect of Our Constitutional Right to Counsel 85 (2009) [hereinafter Justice Denied]. The Committee added that "when counsel is not provided, all too often, the defendant's waiver of legal representation is inadequate under Supreme Court precedents. As a result, there is a shocking disconnect between the system of justice envisioned by the Supreme Court's right-to-counsel decisions and what actually occurs in many of this nation's courts." *Id.* (citation omitted). The Committee's co-chairs included a former director of the Federal Bureau of Investigations, a former state attorney general, a former district attorney and chair of the National District Attorney's Association, two former United States Attorneys, and a former state district and state supreme court judge.

20. *See* Thomas B. Harvey et al., *Right to Counsel in Misdemeanor Prosecutions After Alabama v. Shelton*, 29 Crim. Just. Pol'y Rev. 688, 699 (2018) (reporting from court observations

(ii)　using delay or the prospect of a harsher sentence to dissuade the accused from invoking the right to counsel;[21]

(iii)　gathering arrestees into court *en masse* and instructing them, prior to any advice regarding the right to counsel or other rights, that they must tell the clerk of the court how they intend to plead;[22]

(iv)　using forms to obtain waivers of the right to counsel and other rights either as a condition of negotiating a plea or following a

---

in St. Louis, Missouri "that mention of a defendant's right to counsel occurred after the defendant, prosecutor, and judge have discussed sentencing and have decided that the defendant will enter a formal guilty plea. . . . [P]roceedings usually lasted only a few minutes."); STEPHEN F. HANLON ET AL., SECTION ON CIVIL RIGHTS AND SOCIAL JUSTICE, AMERICAN BAR ASS'N, DENIAL OF THE RIGHT TO COUNSEL IN MISDEMEANOR CASES: COURT WATCHING IN NASHVILLE, TENNESSEE 8-9 (2017); SIXTH AMENDMENT CTR., ACTUAL DENIAL OF COUNSEL IN MISDEMEANOR COURTS 6 (2015) [hereinafter ACTUAL DENIAL]; SIXTH AMENDMENT CTR., THE CRUCIBLE OF ADVERSARIAL TESTING: ACCESS TO COUNSEL IN DELAWARE'S CRIMINAL COURTS 29-33 (2014); JUSTICE DENIED, *supra* note 19, at 89 ("In several courts, the Committee's investigators found that defendants were encouraged to negotiate with prosecutors without the assistance of counsel, and in one court they were required to do so."); *see also* BORUCHOWITZ ET AL., *supra* note 9, at 9, 16-17.

This opinion addresses only the ethical obligations of prosecutors, including obligations under Rules 5.1, 5.3, and 8.4(a) toward lawyers and non-lawyers directed or supervised by the prosecutor. The opinion does not address the obligations of courts and court staff. While the Committee recognizes that courts and court staff are involved in some of the practices discussed in this opinion, prosecutors have independent and specific obligations in these circumstances, as discussed in this opinion.

21. *See* STANDING COMMITTEE ON LEGAL AID AND INDIGENT DEFENDANTS, AM. BAR ASS'N, *GIDEON'S* BROKEN PROMISE: AMERICA'S CONTINUING QUEST FOR EQUAL JUSTICE 25 (2004) [hereinafter *GIDEON'S* BROKEN PROMISE] (describing Rhode Island judge who "told the defendant that by requesting a lawyer, the defendant likely would receive three years of jail time instead" of six months, and California judges who told defendants "If you plead guilty today, you'll go home. If you want an attorney, you'll stay in jail for two more days" and noting that the judicial encouragement of waivers of fundamental rights is "especially acute" with regard to juvenile defendants); *see also* JUSTICE DENIED, *supra* note 19, at 85-86, 87 (noting that in Mississippi "[m]onths may pass before counsel is appointed, causing many people charged with non-violent offenses to serve more time in pretrial custody than warranted for the offenses themselves") (citations omitted); *see also id.* at 85-86, 89; BORUCHOWITZ ET AL., *supra* note 9, at 18-19.

22. *See* SMITH ET AL., *supra* note 13, at 8 (reporting from court observation in Richland County that defendants in a "packed courtroom" were told in an address that took less than two minutes that "everyone needed to form a line and come to the front of the room to tell the clerk how they intended to handle their case today. . . . No mention was made of the right to counsel. . . . Over the next hour or so, the defendants formed a line and the clerk worked through the [cases]. This process, though technically in open court, was a secret to observers who were present—whatever conversations the clerk had with those facing charges were not on the record and were inaudible to those in the seating area.").

negotiation absent proper confirmation that the defendant understands the forms and the rights being waived;[23]

(v)   permitting police officers involved in the investigation of a crime or arrest to act as prosecutors and negotiate pleas;[24]

(vi)   advising defendants of the right to counsel but failing to provide any procedure for asserting or validly waiving that right before requiring plea negotiation with a prosecutor;[25] and

---

23. *See* Harvey et al., *supra* note 20, at 700 (describing process of signing waivers after judge accepted uncounseled guilty plea); BORUCHOWITZ ET AL, *supra* note 9, at 16 (describing forms presented with instructions simply to sign); GIDEON'S BROKEN PROMISE, *supra* note 21, at 25 (reporting witness testimony that "in many Georgia courts, the clerk provides defendants with a complicated form that, if signed, serves as a waiver of counsel and guilty plea. Defendants are told that their case will not be called unless they sign the form.").

Forms are sometimes used after displaying a video describing the right to counsel and other important rights. *See* ACTUAL DENIAL, *supra* note 20, at 15-16 n.17 (describing use of video recordings to advise defendants of rights); SMITH & MADDAN, *supra* note 13, at 15, 23 tbl.8 (describing use of video advisements and written forms). However, in some jurisdictions no effort is made to ensure that all the defendants gathered in the screening area have seen the full video or understand its contents (e.g., a video may begin before some defendants arrive or end after others have been called to appear or have to step out of court). *See* ACTUAL DENIAL, *supra* note 20, at 15- 16 n.17; SMITH ET AL., *supra* note 13, at 8.

24. SMITH ET AL, *supra* note 13, at 19 (In South Carolina's minor crimes courts, police officers "were the majority of prosecutors in all counties, and nearly the sole prosecutor of defendants in [four]. . . . [T]hey negotiated directly with the defendants who they accused of violating the law. . . . Defendants were almost three times more likely to enter a plea of guilty or no contest when confronted by a police-officer-prosecutor. . . ."). *See also* State ex rel McLeod v. Seaborn, 244 S.E.2d 317, 319 (S.C. 1978) (holding that practice of arresting officers acting as prosecutors in certain misdemeanor cases does not constitute unauthorized practice of law); State v. Messervy, 187 S.E.2d 524, 525 (S.C. 1972) (noting that this practice in the state's magistrates courts has "been followed under a ruling of the attorney general since 1958"). For evidence of the practice in another jurisdiction, see State v. Aberizk, 345 A.2d 407 (N.H. 1975) (dismissing challenge of misdemeanor defendant to arresting officer serving as both prosecutor and witness). *Cf.* N.J. Supreme Court Advisory Comm. on Prof'l Ethics, Op. 672 *Conflict of Interest: Municipal Police Officer Serving as Municipal Prosecutor*, (1993), 1993 WL 137686, at *1 ("[T]he specter of an appearance of impropriety so permeates this situation as to preclude the dual service."); Ohio Bd. of Comm'rs on Grievances and Discipline, Advisory Op. No. 89-23 (1989), 1989 WL 535028, at *1-2 (advising that an impermissible conflict of interest arises from county prosecutor serving simultaneously as city police officer within same county if "one position is a check on, or subordinate to the other," if the officer acting as a prosecutor is "aware of the possibility of being called as a witness in the same case," or if there would otherwise be an "appearance of impropriety").

25. *See* GIDEON'S BROKEN PROMISE, *supra* note 21, at 24-25 (describing observation of Georgia court "mass arraignment of defendants charged with jailable misdemeanors during which the judge informed defendants of their rights and then left the bench. Afterwards, three prosecutors told defendants to line up and follow them one by one into a private room. When the judge reentered the courtroom, each defendant approached with the prosecutor, who informed the judge that the defendant intended to waive counsel and plead guilty to the charges.") (citations omitted).

(vii) failing to inform indigent defendants of the procedure for requesting a waiver of court application fees associated with as-
signment of a state subsidized defense lawyer.[26]

A prosecutor's use or endorsement of practices such as these would violate
the Model Rules of Professional Conduct, as discussed in Parts III through V
below.

III. The Prosecutor's Responsibilities Under Model Rule 3.8 and Related Rules

A. The Need for Guidance

Model Rules 3.8(a), (b), and (c) provide the foundation for analysis. Yet
more than thirty years after their adoption by the American Bar Association
there is still relatively little interpretive authority.[27] We address each of these

---

26. *See* ACTUAL DENIAL, *supra* note 20, at 6 (noting that a county in Michigan charges
$240 for all misdemeanor representation, a practice that contributes to 95% of defendants
waiving counsel and 50% "pleading guilty at first appearance"); BORUCHOWITZ ET AL., *supra*
note 9, at 19 (describing pressure to waive right to counsel arising from the amount of application fees in New Jersey, South Carolina, and Washington).

27. Rule 3.8(d) is discussed in detail in an earlier opinion of this Committee, *see* ABA
Comm. on Ethics & Prof'l Responsibility, Formal Op. 454 (2009). However, as the Illinois
State Bar Association has summarized, "[t]here is a dearth of legal opinions, not only in Illinois but in other states, on prosecutors seeking to obtain a waiver of an important pretrial
right from a pro se defendant." Ill. State Bar Ass'n, Advisory Op. 14-02, 2014 WL 2434672,
at *2 (2014); *see id.* at *3 (concluding nonetheless that "a prosecutor may convey a plea offer
to a pro se defendant prior to a court proceeding, regardless of who initiates the contact" as
long as the prosecutor does "not recommend the plea or otherwise force, threaten or coerce
the person to waive any important pretrial right," and the prosecutor "clearly identif[ies]
that he or she is not disinterested, clarif[ies] any misconception the person may have about
the prosecutor's role and advise[s] the person about the right to secure counsel."). *See also*
Pa. Bar Ass'n Comm. on Legal Ethics and Prof'l Responsibility, Formal Op. 2014-500, 2014
WL 10383870, at *7 (2014) (concluding that prosecutor may not condition guilty plea and
eligibility for favorable deferred adjudication program on defendant's waiver of right to
discovery because practice violates Rule 3.8(d), constitutes a "coercive practice" in violation of Rules 8.4(a) and (d) and "abdicat[es] his responsibility as a minister of justice by not
according the defendant procedural justice"; explaining that "[a] *pro se* defendant would
have little or no understanding of the importance of his procedural right of discovery; and
even if he had some understanding, the prosecution threat of facing increased penalties,
including incarceration, if he does not accept [the program] and its conditions, negates any
voluntary waiver of such procedural rights"); *see also* Va. State Bar Legal Ethics Advisory
Op. 1876, 2015 WL 4977834, at *4-6 (2015) (identifying duty of prosecutor who knows defendant is a noncitizen to include reference to immigration consequences in the plea or request
the court to include such consequences in the plea colloquy under the state version of Rule
3.8(b), which prohibits "knowingly tak[ing] advantage of an unrepresented defendant";
prohibiting a prosecutor from offering legal advice under Rule 4.3 to an unrepresented
non-citizen defendant). Wisconsin amended its rules for prosecutors in the wake of United
States v. Acosta, 111 F.Supp. 2d 1082, 1092-97 (E.D. Wis. 2000), *aff'd sub nom.* United States

sections of Rule 3.8 and its relationship to other provisions of the Rules of Professional Conduct below. At the outset, however, we note that faithful interpretation of the special responsibilities of a prosecutor under the Model Rules demands sensitivity to the higher calling of the role.[28] In some respects a prosecutor's duties exceed the requirements of statutory and constitutional law.[29]

B. Model Rule 3.8(a) and the Duty to Ascertain the Existence of Probable Cause to Charge

Rule 3.8(a) prohibits the prosecution of "a charge that the prosecutor knows is not supported by probable cause." The provision avoids undue interference with the exercise of prosecutorial discretion.[30] As Comment [1] emphasizes, however, the prosecutor has a "specific obligation [] to see that the defendant is accorded procedural justice [and] that guilt is decided upon the basis of sufficient evidence."[31] Read together with the duty of competence under Rule 1.1, the duty of diligence under Rule 1.3, and the prohibition on conduct "prejudicial to the administration of justice" in Rule 8.4(d), it is axiomatic that a prosecutor must actually exercise informed discretion with respect to the selection and prosecution of each charge. Thus, a prosecutor may not negotiate pleas without first making an independent assessment of the relevant facts and law for each charge.[32] While it is common for prosecutors

---

v. Olson, 450 F.3d 655, 681-82 (7th Cir. 2006). *See* WIS. SUP. CT. R. 20:3.8 (creating, inter alia, affirmative duty to inform an unrepresented person of the prosecutor's "role and interest in the matter" and of the person's right to counsel; specifying terms upon which prosecutor may negotiate a plea bargain with an unrepresented person); *see also* Wis. Bar Ass'n, Formal Op. E-09-02, slip op. at 3-4 (2009).

28. *See In re* Swarts, 30 P.3d 1011, 1031 (Kan. 2001) ("A prosecutor is a servant of the law and a representative of the people of Kansas. When one undertakes the responsibility of prosecution we must view his or her conduct by an enhanced standard.") (internal quotation marks and citation omitted).

29. *See, e.g.,* ABA Comm. on Ethics & Prof'l Responsibility, Formal Op. 454 at 4 (2009) ("Courts as well as commentators have recognized that the ethical obligation [of a prosecutor under Rule 3.8(d)] is more demanding than the constitutional obligation."); *see also* ABA/BNA LAWYER'S MANUAL ON PROF'L CONDUCT, *Prosecutors* 61:601 (ABA/BNA 2019) ("Model Rule 3.8 goes beyond what constitutional guarantees require of prosecutors on the subject of pretrial responsibilities to the unrepresented accused.").

30. *See also* MODEL CODE OF PROF'L RESPONSIBILITY DR 7-103(A) (1980).

31. MODEL RULES OF PROF'L CONDUCT R. 3.8 cmt. [1].

32. *See* MODEL RULES OF PROF'L CONDUCT R. 1.1 cmt. [5] ("Competent handling of a particular matter includes inquiry into and analysis of the factual and legal elements of the problem, and use of methods and procedures meeting the standards of competent practitioners."). *See also* CRIMINAL JUSTICE STANDARDS FOR THE PROSECUTION FUNCTION 3-5.6(c) (AM. BAR ASS'N 2015) ("The prosecutor should not enter into a disposition agreement before having information sufficient to assess the defendant's actual culpability."); *id.* at 3-5.6(g) ("A prosecutor should not agree to a guilty plea if the prosecutor reasonably believes that sufficient admissible evidence to support conviction beyond reasonable doubt would be lacking if the matter went to trial.").

to make a careful assessment of evidence compiled incident to a decision to offer a plea, in some jurisdictions the volume of misdemeanor cases and their relatively lower stakes may dispose a prosecutor to rely uncritically on a police report or citation and a criminal background check.[33] Unless the prosecutor has reasonable confidence in the thoroughness of the fact finding and the evenhandedness of the judgment of other law enforcement officers who prepare the supporting documents and investigation, reliance on them is likely to be misplaced and the very discretion the Rule is designed to protect may be abused.

If a prosecutor's workload is too heavy to permit the independent assessment of each charge as required by Rule 3.8(a) and the supervision of other state actors and their work product relevant to each case as required by Rules 5.1(b) and (c) and 5.3(b) and (c), the prosecutor may not be able to provide the competent representation required by Rule 1.1, nor act with the diligence required by Rule 1.3. A supervising prosecutor is responsible, under Rules 5.1(a), 5.3(a), and 8.4(a), for establishing policies, practices, and methods of monitoring prosecutors and non-lawyers that give "reasonable assurance" of compliance with prosecutors' ethical obligations, including the obligation to be diligent and perform competent work.[34] In the words of Comment [2] to

---

33. *See* State v. Young, 863 N.W.2d 249, 253 (Iowa 2015) ("Given the pressures of docket management, there is a risk that the ability of the system to function efficiently and at low cost, rather than the reliability of fact-finding, will shape judicial outcomes. . . . [T]he risk of an inaccurate verdict in uncounseled misdemeanor cases is higher than in most felony prosecutions."); *see also* KOHLER-HAUSMANN, *supra* note 10, at 131 (noting from lengthy New York City court observations and interviews with district attorneys, judges, and public defenders that "arraignment plea offers are based largely on prosecutorial practice and policy, and only minimally on factual or legal investigation"); *id.* at 125, 133, 138 (same). Evidence that misdemeanor convictions are not always tied to factual guilt can be found in studies going back to the 1950s. *See id.* at 62. On increases in misdemeanor dockets over the last three decades, see *id.* at 110, 111 fig 3.1, 119.

34. On the prosecutor's managerial and supervisory responsibilities, see ABA Comm. on Ethics & Prof'l Responsibility, Formal Op. 467 (2014). *See also* MODEL RULES OF PROF'L CONDUCT R. 3.8 cmt. [6] ("Like other lawyers, prosecutors are subject to Rules 5.1 and 5.3, which relate to responsibilities regarding lawyers and nonlawyers who work for or are associated with the lawyer's office."); N.Y. State Bar Ass'n Comm. on Prof'l Ethics Op. No. 2, 2018 WL 3019993, at *2 (discussing prosecutor's post-conviction duties regarding potential wrongful conviction, "[t]he Rules apply not only to individual prosecutors but also to their offices."); *id.* at *2 n.3 (referencing both state analogue to Model Rule 3.8 cmt. [6] and Rule 5.1(a)); Or. State Bar Ass'n Bd. of Governors, *Trial Publicity*, Formal Op. 2007-179, 2007 WL 7261223, at *8 (2007) (a prosecutor's level of responsibility under state analogues to Model Rule 5.1 and 5.3 "depends on the level of the prosecutor's authority over the investigator" with whom she works); *id.* *8 n.8 (describing circumstances under state analogue to Model Rule 5.1 in which a supervising prosecutor would be responsible for impermissible pre-trial publicity). *See also* MODEL RULES OF PROF'L CONDUCT R. 8.4(a) & R. 8.4 cmt. [1] (2019) ("Lawyers are subject to discipline when they . . . knowingly assist or induce another to [violate or attempt to violate the Rules of Professional Conduct] or do so through the acts of another, as when they request or instruct an agent to do so on the lawyer's behalf.").

Rule 1.3, a lawyer's workload "must be controlled so that each matter can be handled competently."

In Formal Opinion 441, the Committee addressed the ethical obligations of lawyers representing indigent criminal defendants when caseloads interfere with competent and diligent representation.[35] The same analysis applies to prosecutors. If workloads interfere with competent and diligent representation, appropriate remedial steps must be taken by the prosecutor and/or the supervising attorney to whom the prosecutor reports by, for example, reassigning cases or limiting other duties.[36]

C. Model Rule 3.8(b) and the Right to Counsel

Rule 3.8(b) requires the prosecutor to "make reasonable efforts to assure that the accused has been advised of the right to, and the procedure for obtaining, counsel and has been given reasonable opportunity to obtain counsel." This opinion does not address constitutional issues, but our analysis of a prosecutor's responsibilities under Rule 3.8(b) is aided by identifying circumstances in which the right to counsel applies. In a series of cases beginning with *Argersinger v. Hamlin*, the Supreme Court has held that the Sixth Amendment right to state subsidized counsel applies to misdemeanors if the punishment includes either actual imprisonment or a suspended sentence that may result in imprisonment.[37] Federal courts are divided over the test to determine when the Sixth Amendment right to state subsidized counsel attaches,[38] but there is no doubt that it can attach as early as an ini-

---

35. *See* ABA Comm. on Ethics & Prof'l Responsibility, Formal Op. 441 at 1, 7 (2006) ("[L]awyer supervisors must, working closely with the lawyers they supervise, monitor the workload of the supervised lawyers to ensure that the workloads do not exceed a level that may be competently handled by the individual lawyers"; possible ameliorative measures might include, for example, reassigning cases to others, refusing new cases, or reassigning non- representational work to others).

36. *Id*. at 1, 7.

37. *See* Argersinger v. Hamlin, 407 U.S. 25, 37 (1972) (extending right to counsel to misdemeanors and petty offenses involving imprisonment); *see also* Alabama v. Shelton, 535 U.S. 654, 658 (2002) ("a suspended sentence that may 'end up in the actual deprivation of a person's liberty' may not be imposed unless the defendant was accorded 'the guiding hand of counsel' in the prosecution of the crime charged") (quoting *Argersinger*, 407 U.S. at 40); Scott v. Illinois, 440 U.S. 367, 373-74 (1979) (clarifying that the Sixth Amendment right to counsel does not apply where state law provides both for fines and imprisonment, and a defendant is sentenced only to a fine).

38. Compare Turner v. United States, 885 F.3d 949, 953 (6th Cir. 2018) (en banc) (holding that Sixth Amendment right to counsel attaches "only at or after the time that adversary judicial proceedings have been initiated" and therefore does not extend to pre-indictment plea negotiations) (quoting United States v. Gouveia, 467 U.S. 180, 187 (1984)), *with* United States v. Larkin, 978 F.2d 964 (7th Cir. 1992) (holding that although Sixth Amendment right presumptively attaches only at or after the initiation of adversary judicial criminal proceedings . . . . [a] defendant may rebut this presumption by demonstrating that . . . the government had crossed the constitutionally significant divide from fact-finder to adversary" at an earlier stage) (internal quotations and citations omitted).

tial appearance,[39] that plea bargaining is a "critical phase" of the representation during which the assistance of counsel is important to ensure fair and accurate outcomes,[40] and that the Sixth Amendment protects against interference with the right to counsel whether counsel is subsidized by the state, appointed, or independently retained.[41] As importantly, a right to state subsidized counsel in misdemeanor cases may exist in circumstances not covered by the U.S. Constitution.[42] An accused person also has a constitutional right to proceed *without* the assistance of counsel, but the waiver of such assistance must be knowing, voluntary, and intelligent.[43]

---

39. *See* Brewer v. Williams, 430 U.S. 387, 398 (1977).

40. *See* Padilla v. Kentucky, 559 U.S. 356, 373 (2010) ("[W]e have long recognized that the negotiation of a plea bargain is a critical phase of litigation for purposes of the Sixth Amendment right to effective assistance of counsel"); Missouri v. Frye, 566 U.S. 134, 143-44 (2012). The right may attach even before a prosecutor decides formally to proceed with charges. *See* Rothgery v. Gillespie Cty., Tex., 554 U.S. 191, 207-08 (2008) (rejecting claim that the Sixth Amendment right to counsel attaches only after a prosecutor has formally decided to prosecute; the government's commitment is "sufficiently concrete" once an accusation is "filed with a judicial officer" by the police incident to arrest and incarceration, triggering an initial appearance). The key for attachment of the Sixth Amendment right is initiation of "adversary judicial proceedings." *Gouveia*, 467 U.S. at 187.

41. *See* Johnson v. Zerbst, 304 U.S. 458, 460, 469 (1938) (holding right to counsel violated where defendant allegedly invoked right in discussion with prosecutor and jailer but was not permitted by either to contact a lawyer and was tried and convicted); Powell v. Alabama, 287 U.S. 45, 58 (1932) (gathering state cases finding violation of right to counsel where accelerated pre-trial and trial process compromised appointed counsel's preparation of defense); *In re* Motz, 136 N.E.2d 430, 433 (Ohio Ct. App. 1955) (right to counsel violated where court refused a continuance to permit counsel retained by defendant to prepare, counsel withdrew, court refused to appoint new counsel, and defendant forced to trial pro se). Although we do not address how Rule 3.8 applies to the right to counsel in custodial interrogations, we note that the Fifth Amendment right to counsel can apply to misdemeanor defendants. *See* Miranda v. Arizona, 384 U.S. 436, 469-70 (1966); *cf. infra* notes 45 & 47.

42. State law frequently guarantees a right to subsidized counsel in circumstances in which the federal constitution does not. *See* State v. Young, 863 N.W.2d 249, 272 (Iowa 2015) (citing 2009 study showing that a majority of states provide a right to subsidized counsel broader than the Sixth Amendment "actual imprisonment" standard); DeWolfe v. Richmond, 76 A.3d 1019, 1031 (Md. 2013) (state constitutional right to due process requires right to state subsidized counsel at initial appearance). *See also Pretrial Right to Counsel*, NATIONAL CONFERENCE OF STATE LEGISLATURES, http://www.ncsl.org/research/civil-and-criminal-justice/pretrial-right-to-counsel.aspx (offering 50 state survey of state constitutional and statutory provisions establishing right to counsel) (last visited Apr. 30, 2019).

43. *See* Faretta v. California, 422 U.S. 806, 835 (1975); *see also* Godinez v. Moran, 509 U.S. 389, 390 (1993) ("[W]hen a defendant seeks to waive his right to counsel, a determination that he is competent to stand trial is not enough; the waiver must also be intelligent and voluntary before it can be accepted."). "[T]he law ordinarily considers a waiver knowing, intelligent, and sufficiently aware if the defendant fully understands the nature of the right and how it would likely apply *in general* in the circumstances—even though the defendant may not know the *specific detailed* consequences of invoking it." United States v. Ruiz, 536 U.S. 622, 629 (2002) (emphasis in original). Whether a waiver is knowing, intelligent and voluntary is a question of law on which we do not opine.

The first draft of the Model Rules addressed the accused's right to counsel, enjoining a prosecutor to "advise the defendant of the right to counsel and provide assistance in obtaining counsel."[44] The language of the current rule is more precise in several respects. First, rather than simply enjoin the prosecutor to "provide assistance," it specifies that the lynchpin to assistance is ensuring (i) that the accused is advised of the procedure for obtaining counsel and (ii) that the nature and timing of prosecution does not interfere with this procedure. Second, it replaces the restrictive term of art "defendant" with the more flexible term "accused," thus clarifying that the assistance obligations of the Rule apply before the filing of an indictment. Third, the shift to passive voice makes the prosecutor responsible for ensuring that the accused is aware of the state's procedure for obtaining counsel and has adequate time and access to the necessary administrative assistance to invoke it, irrespective of whether another state actor (e.g., the judge, the court clerk, the public defender office) is legally charged with providing counsel, making indigence determinations, or soliciting and recording waivers of the right. Fourth, the modifier "reasonable" in "reasonable efforts" clarifies that a prosecutor is not required to suffer undue delay or otherwise compromise legitimate law enforcement objectives in order to meet the obligations of the Rule. The prosecutor is therefore charged with specific responsibilities to ensure that those who are or may be entitled to counsel are afforded the information and reasonable time necessary to retain a lawyer.[45]

D. Model Rule 3.8(c) and the Duty Not to Seek Waivers of Important Pretrial Rights

Rule 3.8(c) provides that a prosecutor "shall not seek to obtain from an unrepresented accused a waiver of important pretrial rights, such as the right to a preliminary hearing." As with Rule 3.8(b), there is no direct analogue to this provision in the 1908 Canons or the 1969 Code. The first draft of the Model Rules provided that a prosecutor "shall not induce an unrepresented defendant to surrender important procedural rights, such as the right to a preliminary hearing."[46] The Rule as adopted is broader for several reasons. First, it prohibits seeking a waiver from an unrepresented "accused" and is therefore not limited to someone who is formally a "defendant." Second, "inducement" implies efforts to persuade, whereas "seek to obtain" reaches even a bare request. Finally, the replacement of "procedural rights" with

---

44. MODEL RULES OF PROF'L CONDUCT R. 3.10(b) (Discussion Draft 1980).

45. Although the Rule applies broadly to the right to counsel, this opinion is limited to its application in the context of misdemeanor plea bargaining. For guidance on the right to counsel under the Fifth Amendment in custodial interrogation, see ABA/BNA LAWYER'S MANUAL ON PROF'L CONDUCT, *Prosecutors* 61:616 (ABA/BNA 2019) (citing CRIMINAL JUSTICE STANDARDS FOR THE PROSECUTION FUNCTION 3-2.7, 3-3.2, 3-3.6 (AM. BAR ASS'N 1992)).

46. MODEL RULES OF PROF'L CONDUCT R. 3.10(c) (Discussion Draft 1980).

"pretrial rights" broadens the scope of the Rule by extending its application to all "important" rights (whether classified as substantive or procedural) and by explicitly targeting the pretrial stage—a particularly delicate phase of prosecution where judges exercise minimal or only intermittent supervision, the leverage of a prosecutor is extraordinary, and the risks and consequences of improper waiver by an unrepresented accused person are correspondingly acute.[47] As the Comment makes clear, the Rule does not apply to individuals who have elected to proceed pro se "with the approval of the tribunal," or to "the lawful questioning of an uncharged suspect who has knowingly waived the rights to counsel and silence."[48]

IV. Duties Arising from the Accused's Right to Counsel

As discussed in Parts III.C through III.D above, Model Rules 3.8(b) and (c) provide that the "prosecutor in a criminal case shall:

(b) make reasonable efforts to assure that the accused has been advised of the right to, and the procedure for obtaining, counsel and has been given reasonable opportunity to obtain counsel;

(c) not seek to obtain from an unrepresented accused a waiver of important pretrial rights, such as the right to a preliminary hearing."[49]

---

47. The example of a preliminary hearing indicates, as the Comment notes, that in jurisdictions where waiver can lead to the loss of a chance to challenge probable cause or use the preliminary hearing to ascertain relevant facts about the prosecution's case, prosecutors should not seek to deprive defendants of those opportunities. *See* MODEL RULES OF PROF'L CONDUCT R. 3.8 cmt. [2]. The contemporaneous ABA Standards of Criminal Justice, Prosecution Function, noted these features of the preliminary hearing in some jurisdictions. *See* CRIMINAL JUSTICE STANDARDS FOR THE PROSECUTION, Standard 3-5.1 (AM. BAR ASS'N 1980). But in its general reference to "important pretrial rights" the Rule as adopted plainly sweeps beyond that illustration. *See* ABA/BNA LAWYER'S MANUAL ON PROF'L CONDUCT 61:617 ("the phrase is broad enough to cover pretrial rights grounded on federal or state constitutions, statutes, or case law"). As the Comment emphasizes, "prosecutors should not seek to obtain waivers of preliminary hearings *or other important pretrial rights* from unrepresented accused persons." MODEL RULES OF PROF'L CONDUCT R. 3.8 cmt. [2] (emphasis added). *See also* ABA/BNA LAWYER'S MANUAL ON PROF'L CONDUCT 61:617 (ABA/BNA 2019) ("Rule 3.8(c) precludes prosecutors from seeking a waiver of important pretrial rights from an unrepresented accused, even when this conduct maybe permissible as a matter of constitutional law."). The Rule's reference to other "important pretrial rights" is particularly relevant to misdemeanor plea bargaining because there is often no requirement of a preliminary hearing or grand jury to provide an external check on prosecutors in misdemeanor cases and there are many important pretrial rights (among them not only the right to counsel but the right to disclosure of exculpatory evidence, the right to inspect evidence, and other discovery rights). This opinion addresses the right to counsel.

48. MODEL RULES OF PROF'L CONDUCT R. 3.8 cmt. [2].

49. MODEL RULES OF PROF'L CONDUCT R. 3.8 (b) & (c).

Rule 3.8(b) and (c) are of central importance to misdemeanor prosecutions because many people accused of misdemeanors are issued citations and notices to appear rather than arrested and brought in for questioning. Alternatively, they may be questioned in the field by police, arrested, and, particularly for the indigent, held if they cannot make bail. In these circumstances, they functionally become "unrepresented accused" persons either upon receipt of a citation and notice to appear, or as a consequence of an arrest. And yet, this early in the proceedings they may not be aware of their right to state subsidized counsel, the process for exercising it, or the fact that they have the right to retain a lawyer not paid for by the state. As importantly, a prosecutor may control whether the right to state subsidized counsel attaches because the Sixth Amendment right to counsel may hinge on the classification of the underlying offense and the prosecutor's decision about what kind of plea to offer.[50] Under these circumstances, a prosecutor must scrupulously conform to Rules 3.8(b) and (c), as well as Rule 4.3, which prohibits giving legal advice to an unrepresented person whose interests in defending herself may conflict with the prosecutor's interest in securing a conviction.[51] A prosecutor must also take steps to be reasonably sure that the conduct of her subordinates and agents is "'compatible with the professional obligations of the [prosecutor].'"[52]

Accordingly, if the charge associated with a plea offer triggers the right to counsel under *Argersinger* or where the circumstances of the offense, arrest, or initial appearance otherwise indicate that the accused has or may have a right to counsel under state or federal law, the prosecutor may not make a plea offer or seek a waiver of the right to counsel before complying with Rule 3.8(b). The prosecutor must make reasonable efforts to assure that the accused has been advised of the right to counsel and the procedure for obtaining counsel, and has been given a reasonable opportunity to exercise that right and obtain counsel. If the prosecutor delegates authority to or otherwise relies upon police officers or other state actors to discuss waivers of rights in misdemeanor cases, pursuant to Rules 5.1(b) and (c), 5.3(b) and (c), and 8.4(a), the prosecutor is responsible for ensuring that Rules 3.8 and 4.3 are not violated during those discussions. As noted earlier in this opinion, under Rules 5.1(a) and 5.3(a) a supervising prosecutor is responsible for es-

---

50. A plea offer of release for time served, for instance, triggers *Argersinger* because it is a sentence of actual imprisonment. Of course, state law, federal statutes, and the requirements of due process may create a legal right to subsidized counsel even though the Sixth Amendment does not. *See* note 42 *supra*. And the unrepresented accused has a core Sixth Amendment right to retain counsel at her own expense unless she elects to proceed pro se on terms approved by the court or by the laws and rules of the jurisdiction.

51. For a prosecutor's duties under Rule 4.3 when negotiating pleas in misdemeanor cases, see Part V *infra*.

52. ABA Comm. on Ethics & Prof'l Responsibility, Formal Op. 467 at 3 (2014) (quoting Rule 5.3(b)).

tablishing policies, practices, and methods of monitoring that give "reasonable assurance" of compliance with prosecutors' ethical obligations.

Moreover, under Rule 3.8(b) and (c), a prosecutor may not pressure, advise, or induce acceptance of a plea or waiver of the right to counsel after an unrepresented accused has been informed of the right to counsel and is deciding whether to invoke or has initiated the process to invoke that right.[53] Even asking an unrepresented accused if she wishes to waive the right to counsel or accept a plea is improper if it is clear from the circumstances that the accused does not understand the consequences of acceding to the request. This is so because legal advice may be necessary to clarify any such misunderstanding, and, consistent with Rules 3.8(b), 3.8(c), and as required by Rule 4.3, a prosecutor is precluded from offering legal advice other than to seek counsel.

On the other hand, if the accused has independently elected to proceed pro se on terms approved by the court or by the laws and rules of the jurisdiction, the prosecutor may negotiate a plea, but any negotiations must comply with the Rules discussed in Part V below.

V. Duties When Plea Bargaining with an Unrepresented Accused

Irrespective of whether an unrepresented accused has invoked the right to counsel, Model Rules 4.1, 4.3 and 8.4(c) constrain a prosecutor's conduct when negotiating a plea bargain with, e.g., (i) persons who are ineligible under state and federal law for state subsidized defense counsel and cannot afford or otherwise cannot secure private counsel, (ii) those who elect to proceed pro se even though they are eligible for subsidized counsel or could retain private counsel, and (iii) those who have invoked the right to counsel but are still in the process of securing counsel or deciding whether to do so.

Rule 4.1 prohibits a lawyer from knowingly making "a false statement of material fact or law to a third person." The rule "was intended to incorporate the law of misrepresentation by recognizing that the failure to disclose can amount to a misrepresentation in some circumstances. . . ."[54] Comment [1] emphasizes that misrepresentations can "occur by partially true but misleading statements or omissions that are the equivalent of false statements."[55] Rule 4.3 states that "[i]n dealing on behalf of a client with a person who is not represented by counsel" a lawyer "shall not give legal advice to an unrepre-

---

53. This is so whether the unrepresented accused intends to pursue counsel subsidized by the state or retain counsel at the accused's expense.

54. CTR. FOR PROF'L RESPONSIBILITY, AM. BAR ASS'N, A LEGISLATIVE HISTORY OF THE DEVELOPMENT OF THE ABA MODEL RULES, 1982-2005, at 522 (2006) [hereinafter LEGISLATIVE HISTORY] (discussion at February 1983 Midyear Meeting). Rules 4.1 and 8.4(c) also apply when the accused has retained counsel, as does Rule 4.2.

55. The comment was amended in 2002 according to the recommendations of the Ethics 2000 Commission. The amendment explicitly expanded emphasis on misrepresentation by omission, substituting the current language for the prior, more vague, reference to misrepresentation by "failure to act." See id. at 527-28.

sented person, other than the advice to secure counsel, if the lawyer knows or reasonably should know that the interests of such a person are or have a reasonable possibility of being in conflict with the interests of the client."[56] Finally, Rule 8.4(c) prohibits a lawyer from engaging "in conduct involving dishonesty, fraud, deceit or misrepresentation."[57]

In the context of plea negotiations, these rules circumscribe the terms on which a prosecutor may deal with an unrepresented accused. An unrepresented accused, particularly one who lacks experience with the intricacies of the criminal justice system, is in an acutely vulnerable position.[58] The accused faces the vast array of resources at the prosecutor's disposal as well as the prosecutor's legal expertise at a moment in which, even in misdemeanor cases, substantial liberty interests and financial security are in jeopardy.[59] Moreover, once a prosecutor has committed to pursue a misdemeanor charge in plea negotiations, the interests of the prosecutor and the unrepresented accused are adverse, so the prosecutor must take particular care to avoid giving the impression that she is "disinterested" and to correct any misunderstanding regarding the prosecutor's role in the matter. From the moment of arrest there is already, within the meaning of Rule 4.3, "a reasonable possibility of . . . conflict with the interests of" the unrepresented accused. Accordingly, a prosecutor is prohibited by Rule 4.3 from offering legal advice regarding the substance of the plea, the process of its negotiation and entry, or the consequences incident to conviction.[60] As discussed below, however, a prosecutor can and sometimes must disclose material information regarding the substance of the plea, the process of its negotiation and entry, and known consequences of a conviction to an unrepresented person.

Comment [2] to Rule 4.3 states that a lawyer is not generally prohibited from "settling a dispute with an unrepresented person," but a plea bargain

---

56. Amendments approved in 2002 on the recommendation of the Ethics 2000 Commission elevated the prohibition on giving advice from the comments to the rule in response to reports that "in negotiations between lawyers and unrepresented parties, the giving of legal advice (often misleading or overreaching) is not uncommon." *Id.* at 550. The Commission recognized that "although the line may be difficult to draw, it is important to discourage lawyers from overreaching in their negotiations with unrepresented persons." *Id.* at 549-50. On the law of misrepresentation by omission, see RESTATEMENT (SECOND) OF TORTS § 551 (AM. LAW INST. 1977).

57. Comment [1] to Rule 4.1 states that for "dishonest conduct that does not amount to a false statement or for misrepresentations by a lawyer other than in the course of representing a client, see Rule 8.4."

58. Comment [2] to Rule 4.3 emphasizes that "[w]hether a lawyer is giving impermissible advice may depend on the experience and the sophistication of the unrepresented person, as well as the setting in which the behavior and comments occur."

59. *See* Part IB *supra.*

60. *See* Ill. State Bar Ass'n, Advisory Op. No. 02, 2014 WL 2434672, at *3 ("It would be a violation of Rule 4.3 . . . should the communication [with a person who has elected to proceed pro se] give value to the plea offer or in any way advise the pro se defendant ('It is a good offer' or 'Take the deal.').").

is no ordinary arms-length transaction or settlement agreement. The stakes are often significantly higher than in civil matters and the terms must meet specific constitutional standards designed to ensure that the accused's acceptance is "voluntary, knowing, and intelligent."[61] Thus while a prosecutor may negotiate a plea bargain with a pro se litigant, the prosecutor's duties under Rules 4.1 and 8.4(c) are heightened in this setting. Assertions regarding the terms of a plea violate these rules if the prosecutor knows they are materially underinclusive. For example, statements regarding the value of a plea offer, particularly those which omit known collateral consequences of accepting a plea or the legal relevance of a plea to enhancement of a sentence in any subsequent case, can constitute prohibited misrepresentations under Rule 4.1 or deceptive conduct under Rule 8.4(c).[62] Thus, where a prosecutor knows from the charge selected, the accused's record, or any other information that certain collateral consequences or sentence enhancements apply to a plea on that charge, statements like the following would constitute prohibited misrepresentations:

> "Take this plea for time served and you are done, you can go home now."

> "This is a suspended sentence, so as long as you comply with its terms, you avoid jail time with this plea."

> "You only serve three months on this plea, that's the sentence."

A prosecutor will rarely know all of the potentially relevant collateral consequences of accepting a plea or the exact nature of any subsequent sentence enhancement. However, if the prosecutor knows the consequences of a plea—either generic consequences or consequences that are particular to the accused—the prosecutor must disclose them during the plea negotiation.[63]

Finally, a prosecutor's duties under these rules do not end once a plea has been accepted. If a prosecutor learns during the plea colloquy with the court or other interactions that the unrepresented accused's acceptance of a plea or waiver of the right to counsel is not in fact voluntary, knowing, and

---

61. *See* Part IIIB *supra*.

62. Furthermore, in the context of plea negotiations, violation of either rule is conduct prejudicial to the administration of justice under Rule 8.4(d).

63. Given the delicacy of balancing the need to disclose material information to avoid either misrepresentation or deception, on the one hand, and the prohibition on legal advice, on the other, the best practice is to carefully record and preserve plea negotiations with an unrepresented accused. *See* CRIMINAL JUSTICE STANDARDS FOR THE PROSECUTION FUNCTION 3-5.6(b) (AM. BAR ASS'N 2015) (encouraging record keeping where defendant waives right to counsel and proceeds pro se). Additional guidance is provided in the NAT'L PROSECUTION STANDARDS §§ 2-7.2, 2-7.4 and 2-7.5 (3d ed. 2009).

intelligent, or if the plea colloquy conducted by the court is inadequate to ascertain whether the plea or waiver of the right to counsel is in fact voluntary, knowing, and intelligent, the prosecutor is obliged to intervene. The prosecutor cannot, consistent with her role as a minister of justice under Rule 3.8 and the duty to avoid conduct prejudicial to the administration of justice under Rule 8.4(d), knowingly permit an unconstitutional plea to be entered by an unrepresented accused.[64]

VI. Conclusion

Under Model Rules 1.1, 1.3, 3.8(a), and 8.4(a) and (d), prosecutors have a duty to ensure that charges underlying a plea offer in misdemeanor cases have sufficient evidentiary and legal foundation. Under Model Rules 1.1, 5.1, 5.3, and 8.4(a) prosecutors must take appropriate steps to make reasonably sure that the work of their subordinates and agents is compatible with their professional obligations. Under Model Rule 3.8(b) prosecutors must make reasonable efforts to assure that unrepresented accused persons are informed of the right to counsel and the process for securing counsel, and must avoid conduct that interferes with that process. After an unrepresented accused has been informed of the right to counsel and is deciding whether to invoke that right or is in the process of attempting to secure counsel, a prosecutor may not, under Model Rules 3.8(b) and (c), pressure, advise, or induce acceptance of a plea or waiver of the right to counsel. Finally, irrespective of whether an unrepresented accused has invoked the right to counsel, a prosecutor must, under Model Rules 4.1, 4.3 and 8.4(c) and (d), avoid offering, negotiating, and entering pleas on terms that knowingly misrepresent the consequences of acceptance, or otherwise improperly pressure, advise, or induce acceptance on the part of the unrepresented accused.

---

64. *See also* ABA Comm. on Ethics & Prof'l Responsibility, Formal Op. 454 (2009).

AMERICAN BAR ASSOCIATION
STANDING COMMITTEE ON ETHICS AND PROFESSIONAL RESPONSIBILITY
321 N. Clark Street, Chicago, Illinois 60654-4714 Telephone (312) 988-5328
CHAIR: Barbara S. Gillers, New York, NY
■ John M. Barkett, Miami, FL ■ Robert Hirshon, Ann Arbor, MI ■ Thomas B. Mason, Washington, DC
■ Michael H. Rubin, Baton Rouge, LA ■ Douglas R. Richmond, Chicago, IL
■ Lynda Shely, Scottsdale, AZ ■ Norman W. Spaulding, Stanford, CA
■ Elizabeth Clark Tarbert, Tallahassee, FL ■ Lisa D. Taylor, Parsippany, NJ

CENTER FOR PROFESSIONAL RESPONSIBILITY
©2019 by the American Bar Association. All rights reserved.

AMERICAN BAR ASSOCIATION
STANDING COMMITTEE ON ETHICS AND PROFESSIONAL RESPONSIBILITY

Formal Opinion 487　　　　　　　　　　　　　　　　**June 18, 2019**

Fee Division with Client's Prior Counsel

In a contingent fee matter, when a counsel (successor counsel) from one firm replaces a counsel (predecessor counsel) from another firm as counsel for the client, Rules 1.5(b) and (c) require that the successor counsel notify the client, in writing, that a portion of any contingent fee earned may be paid to the predecessor counsel. The successor counsel may not be able to state at the beginning of the representation the specific amount or percentage of a recovery, if any, that may be owed to the predecessor counsel unless the amount or percentage has been agreed by the client and both predecessor and successor counsels. The successor counsel is not bound by the requirements of Rule 1.5(e), either at the time of engagement or upon a recovery, because Rule 1.5(e) addresses situations where two lawyers are working on a case together, not situations where one lawyer is replacing another. Upon a monetary recovery, the successor counsel may only disburse a portion of the overall attorney's fee to the predecessor counsel with client consent or pursuant to an order of a tribunal of competent jurisdiction. If there is a dispute as to the amount due to the predecessor counsel under Rule 1.15(e) the disputed amount may have to remain in a client trust account until the matter is resolved. If successor counsel negotiates with predecessor counsel on the client's behalf, successor counsel must explain to the client the potential conflict of interest in the dual roles pursuant to Rule 1.7, where successor counsel has a personal interest in the amount predecessor counsel may receive or in the timing of the release of funds held pursuant to Rule 1.15(e).[1]

I.　Introduction

A client has the right to terminate a lawyer's services at any time[2] but when the client terminates the services of a contingent fee counsel, without

---

1 This opinion is based on the ABA Model Rules of Professional Conduct as amended by the ABA House of Delegates through August 2018. The laws, court rules, regulations, rules of professional conduct and opinions promulgated in individual jurisdictions are controlling.

2 MODEL RULES OF PROF'L CONDUCT R. 1.16 cmt. 4 (2018) [hereinafter MODEL RULES]; RESTATEMENT (THIRD) OF THE LAW GOVERNING LAWYERS § 32(1) (2000) [hereinafter RESTATEMENT].

cause, prior to the occurrence of the contingency on which the parties' agreement is based, the counsel may be entitled to a fee for services performed before discharge under *quantum meruit* or, in some jurisdictions, pursuant to a so-called "conversion clause" or "termination clause" in the contingent fee agreement. This opinion addresses the successor counsel's obligations under the Model Rules of Professional Conduct after taking over the case when there is a monetary recovery. A counsel who subsequently takes over the case (the successor counsel) must advise the client, in writing, of the predecessor counsel's potential claim on a recovery.[3]

II. Analysis

A. The Successor Counsel's Obligation to Advise the Client that the Predecessor Counsel May Make a Claim Against Any Recovery

Just as in any contingent fee matter, the successor counsel must comply with both Model Rule 1.5(b) in describing the rate or basis of the fee and with Model Rule 1.5(c)'s requirement that the written fee agreement include the method of determining the fee. Paragraphs (b) and (c) of Rule 1.5 provide:

(b) The scope of the representation and the basis or rate of the fee and expenses for which the client will be responsible shall be communicated to the client, preferably in writing, before or within a reasonable time after commencing the representation, except when the lawyer will charge a regularly represented client on the same basis or rate. Any changes in the basis or rate of the fee or expenses shall also be communicated to the client.

(c) A fee may be contingent on the outcome of the matter for which the service is rendered, except in a matter in which a contingent fee is prohibited by paragraph (d) or other law. A contingent fee agreement shall be in a writing signed by the client and shall state the method by which the fee is to be determined, including the percentage or percentages that shall accrue to the lawyer in the event of settlement, trial or appeal; litigation and other expenses to be deducted from the recovery; and whether such expenses are to be deducted before or after the contingent fee is calculated. The agreement must

---

3 This opinion applies where the client terminates a lawyer without cause and hires a new lawyer to replace that lawyer to handle a contingent fee matter. The opinion does not apply when a client terminates a lawyer with cause, or the lawyer withdraws without cause. In such situations, a lawyer may forfeit some or all of her fee. RESTATEMENT § 37 (2000); David Hricik, *Dear Lawyer: If you decide it's not economical to represent me, you can fire me as your contingent fee client, but I agree I will still owe you a fee*, 64 MERCER L. REV. 363 (2012-2013).

clearly notify the client of any expenses for which the client will be liable whether or not the client is the prevailing party. Upon conclusion of a contingent fee matter, the lawyer shall provide the client with a written statement stating the outcome of the matter and, if there is a recovery, showing the remittance to the client and the method of its determination.

Although Rules 1.5(b) and 1.5(c) do not specifically address obligations when one counsel replaces another, both rules are designed to ensure that the client has a clear understanding of the total legal fee, how it is to be computed, when it is to be paid, and by whom. "[A]n understanding as to fees . . . must be promptly established."[4] A contingent fee agreement that fails to mention that some portion of the fee may be due to or claimed by the first counsel in circumstances addressed by this opinion is inconsistent with these requirements of Rule 1.5(b) and (c).[5] To avoid client confusion, making the disclosure in the fee agreement itself is the better practice, but this disclosure may be made in a separate document associated with the contingent fee agreement and provided to the client at the same time.

Assume, for example, that a client retains a lawyer in a matter and enters into a written fee agreement in which the lawyer is entitled to one-third of any recovery. The client then decides to terminate the lawyer, without cause, and hires new counsel. The successor counsel takes the matter on the same terms as the predecessor counsel (one-third of any recovery) but the successor counsel's written fee agreement is silent on whether that one-third is in addition to or in lieu of the one-third specified in the predecessor counsel's fee agreement, and no such disclosure is made in a separate document provided to the client. In these circumstances, the client may not know whether the client must pay one or both lawyers or the amount of the fees owed. The client may be aware of the right to terminate a lawyer's representation at any

---

4 MODEL RULES R. 1.5 cmt. 2.

5 ABA Comm. on Ethics & Prof'l Responsibility, Formal Op. 94-389, at 4 (1994) (explaining that "the nature (and details) of the compensation arrangement should be fully discussed by the lawyer and client before any final agreement is reached."); Joyce v. Elliott, 857 P.2d 549, 552 (Colo. App. 1993) (stating that "one of the principal purposes of the rules respecting contingency fee agreements is to assure that a client is fully advised at the time such agreement is executed of all of the financial obligations that such client is assuming by the establishment of the attorney-client relationship."); Shaw v. Manufacturers Hanover Trust Co., 499 N.E.2d 864, 866 (N.Y. 1986) ("The importance of an attorney's clear agreement with a client as to the essential terms of representation cannot be overstated. The client should be fully informed of all of the relevant facts and the basis of the fee charges, especially in contingent fee arrangements[.]"); In re Davenport, 522 S.W.3d 452, 458 (Tex. 2017) ("The goal of an attorney-client fee agreement is to ensure that the client is informed of its terms. . . . whether the lawyer was reasonably clear is determined from the client's perspective.") (footnotes omitted).

time but may not be aware that termination does not necessarily extinguish an obligation to pay prior counsel for the value of the work performed – the *quantum meruit* claim – or in some cases a termination amount specified in the predecessor counsel's fee agreement. If the predecessor counsel was not terminated for cause, that lawyer may be entitled to payment for the fair value contributed to the case before being terminated.[6] Under those circumstances, "a contingency client should be advised by the successor attorney of the existence and effect of the discharged attorney's claim for fees on the occurrence of the contingency as part of the terms and conditions of the employment by the successor attorney."[7]

Where a client hires successor counsel to handle an existing contingency fee matter, it does not pose an unreasonable burden on the successor counsel to advise the client that the predecessor counsel may have a claim to a portion of the legal fee if there is a recovery. In many instances, precision on this issue may be difficult as successor counsel may need to review the predecessor counsel's fee agreement and assess its enforceability. Similarly, successor counsel may not be fully familiar with the nature and extent of the prior lawyer's work on the matter. Successor counsel also will not know the amount of the recovery, if any, at the beginning of the representation. Nevertheless, Rules 1.5(b) and (c) mandate that successor counsel provide written notice that a portion of the fee may be claimed by the predecessor counsel.

Successor counsel must address with the client whether the client risks paying twice: one contingent fee to the predecessor counsel and another to the successor counsel. A client cannot be exposed to more than one contingent fee when switching attorneys, given that under the Rule 1.5(a) factors, each counsel did not perform all of the services required to achieve the result. Thus, neither the predecessor nor the successor counsel ordinarily would be entitled to a full contingent fee.

B. Rule 1.5(e) Fee Division Provisions Do Not Apply

There is some authority concluding that successor counsel replacing a client's prior counsel must comply with Rule 1.5(e);[8] however, this Rule is de-

---

6 *See generally* RESTATEMENT § 40 cmts. b & c (2000) (On discharge, a lawyer may be entitled to the fair value of the lawyer's services. Determination of fair value takes into account the proportion of work performed by the discharged lawyer, and the value of work contributed. The determination also may consider a contract amount prorated for work actually performed.).

7 San Francisco Bar Ass'n, Ethics Comm., Advisory Op. 1989-1 (1989).

8 These authorities focus on client consent to a fee division. *See, e.g.*, Statewide Grievance Comm. v. Dixon, 772 A.2d 160, 164-65 (Conn. App. Ct. 2001) (concluding that the lawyer violated Rule 1.5(e) by failing to inform the client of payment made from recovery to prior lawyer in a different firm); Conn. Bar Ass'n, Comm. on Prof'l Ethics Op. 01-10, 2001 WL 34004971, at *1 (2001) (involving a new lawyer replacing the original lawyer because of conflict). None discuss other provisions of the rule, for example, how "joint responsibility" works. As dis-

signed to regulate fee-sharing between lawyers in different firms who handle a case simultaneously. Comment 7 to Rule 1.5 underscores this reading. It states:

> A division of fee is a single billing to a client covering the fee of two or more lawyers who are not in the same firm. *A division of fee facilitates association of more than one lawyer in a matter in which neither alone could serve the client as well,* and most often is used when the fee is contingent and the division is between a referring lawyer and a trial specialist. Paragraph (e) permits the lawyers to divide a fee either on the basis of the proportion of services they render or if each lawyer assumes responsibility for the representation as a whole. In addition, the client must agree to the arrangement, including the share that each lawyer is to receive, and the agreement must be confirmed in writing. Contingent fee agreements must be in a writing signed by the client and must otherwise comply with paragraph (c) of this Rule. Joint responsibility for the representation entails financial and ethical responsibility for the representation as if the lawyers were associated in a partnership. A lawyer should only refer a matter to a lawyer whom the referring lawyer reasonably believes is competent to handle the matter. See Rule 1.1. (Emphasis added.)

Comment 7 thus clarifies that Rule 1.5(e) is limited to situations where two or more lawyers are working on a case simultaneously – not sequentially. Accordingly, Rule 1.5(e) was not meant to apply to the situation where one lawyer's services are terminated and the client retains a second lawyer to complete the matter.

Under Rule 1.5(e), fees must either be divided in proportion to the work performed or in some other specified division where both lawyers assume "joint responsibility" for the matter. Fee-sharing in proportion to the work performed by lawyers concurrently representing a client is similar to the *quantum meruit* analysis that is frequently used post-hoc to divide contingent fees between successive law firms. What differs where predecessor and successor counsel are involved in such fee issues before a recovery has been obtained is that the underlying case and the client's rights to discharge her lawyer may be adversely affected if the client is required to enter into a fee-sharing agreement under Rule 1.5(e). Requiring the predecessor and successor counsel and the client to agree on a proportional fee division may hinder the client's right to terminate a counsel by making the process of finding a replacement more difficult and protracted. A simple fee negotiation between the client and successor counsel would turn into a three-way debate.

---

cussed above, we agree that client consent to a payment by the successor lawyer to the predecessor lawyer is necessary, but reach that conclusion without reliance on Rule 1.5(e).

The other approach under Rule 1.5(e) to divide a fee among lawyers concurrently representing a client requires that all counsel assume "joint responsibility" for the related matter. Such responsibility entails financial and ethical responsibility for the representation as if the counsel were associated in a partnership.[9] A referring counsel is allowed to receive a greater portion of the fee than the counsel's own efforts would otherwise merit through the acceptance of joint responsibility.[10] When a client discharges a lawyer and hires a new one, there is no "referring counsel" and there is no simultaneous representation of the client. Joint responsibility in practice does not exist because predecessor counsel has been replaced. To require "joint responsibility" under Rule 1.5(e) in these situations as a pre-condition of paying the predecessor counsel's fee claim is not realistic and ultimately burdens the client's ability to discharge the first lawyer and find replacement counsel. If the successor counsel would be responsible for the errors or omissions of a discharged predecessor, he or she would at best be reluctant to accept the engagement.

C. Client Agreement on the Eventual Fee Allocation Between the Discharged Counsel and the Current Counsel and Conflict of Interest Waiver

Because the client approval requirement is explicit in Rule 1.5(e), some authorities have used it as the vehicle to mandate client consent to fee divisions in consecutive representations even though Rule 1.5(e) is limited to joint representations. Rule 1.5(a), however, alone supports the conclusion that client consent is required to divide the fee at the end of the case.

Rule 1.5(a) requires that any fee be reasonable, including the total fees of predecessor and successor counsel, and client consent is required for all disbursements, including all fees payable to predecessor and successor counsel.

A client always has the right to challenge the total fee charged or the separate fee claimed by the predecessor counsel. The successor counsel may not disburse fees claimed by that counsel absent the client's consent. Otherwise, the client's right to challenge the fee as unreasonable would be impaired, if not extinguished. Of course, there may be circumstances where client consent may be inferred. For example, consent may be inferred where successor counsel has repeatedly provided notice of a proposed payment to predecessor counsel and the client has not responded.[11]

---

9 MODEL RULES R. 1.5 cmt. 7; N.Y. Cnty. Lawyers' Ass'n, Comm. on Prof'l Ethics Op. 715, 1996 WL 592658, at *4 & n.2 (1996).

10 MODEL RULES R. 1.5(e)(1).

11 The fee must, of course, be within the total fee as authorized by the client in the successor lawyer's fee agreement. The successor lawyer must also have a reasonable basis to conclude that the client has received the communications and is not suffering from any mental or physical disorder that prevents the client from considering the successor lawyer's communications.

D. Role of Successor Counsel with Respect to Predecessor Counsel's Claim for a Share of the Fee

The role of the successor counsel in the process of addressing the predecessor counsel's claim for a share of the fee may vary. The successor counsel's work may include an assessment of the legitimacy of the predecessor counsel's fee claim to properly advise the client on the client's share of any recovery and the amount of funds, if any, that successor counsel must hold in trust under Rule 1.15. If the initial scope of successor counsel's representation of the client simply leaves the matter to be decided by the predecessor counsel and the client, the successor counsel should so indicate in the engagement agreement. But if the successor counsel offers to represent the client in the *client's* dispute (as opposed to the successor counsel's dispute) with the predecessor counsel, such scope of representation should be reflected either in the initial fee agreement or in a new or revised fee agreement. Typically, where successor counsel is negotiating on behalf of a client with predecessor counsel, successor counsel should review with the client the nature and extent of the predecessor counsel's entitlement to a fee, including whether the predecessor counsel has forfeited the right to a fee, in whole or in part.

Successor counsel's compensation for representing the client in the client's dispute with predecessor counsel must be reasonable, which in this context means, at a minimum, that the successor counsel cannot charge the client for work that only increases the successor counsel's share of the contingent fee and does not increase the client's recovery. Successor counsel must also obtain the client's informed consent to any conflict of interest that exists due to successor counsel's dual roles as counsel for the client *and* a party interested in a portion of the proceeds.

In many situations, the fees paid to predecessor and successor counsel may not affect the client's recovery. In these instances, successor counsel may obtain the client's consent to any fee split that does not alter the client's recovery. The client can, after consultation and adequate disclosure, decide that the matter should be worked out between counsel without further need for consent or consultation with the client. The client's consent should be informed and successor counsel may need to raise the possibility of protracted proceedings that could burden a client who may have nothing to gain and may be indifferent about the outcome.[12] Where the client is indifferent as to

---

12 Most disputes between lawyers about a fee will likely involve the client as a witness. The disputes may also involve disclosure of the client's confidential information under Rule 1.6. In many such circumstances, the client may wish simply to move on and not be involved in any dispute between her lawyers. In addition, where recoveries are obtained through settlement, many settlement agreements impose confidentiality obligations on the client as to the settlement terms. In adjudicating a fee dispute with predecessor counsel, the successor lawyer must take steps to ensure that any confidentiality term of a settlement is respected.

the fee allocation between the two counsel, both counsel must, in adjudicating their own dispute over their respective shares of the contingent fee, take adequate steps to protect client confidentiality under Rule 1.6, as well as any confidentiality provisions in any underlying settlement agreement.

The predecessor counsel may also seek client consent to a share of the fee. If the successor counsel represents the client in the fee dispute, then the predecessor counsel may not communicate about the fee directly with the former client without successor counsel's consent under Rule 4.2.

E. The Successor Counsel's Obligations with Respect to the Funds

Where a disagreement persists between the predecessor counsel and the client, or predecessor counsel and successor counsel, about the amount of the predecessor counsel's fees from the proceeds obtained by the successor counsel, the successor counsel must comply with Rule 1.15 and substantive law in notifying predecessor counsel of the receipt of the funds and in deciding how to handle the funds. In many jurisdictions, a counsel terminated without cause has the right to payment based on *quantum meruit*. If the client asserts that client terminated the predecessor counsel for cause, that counsel may not have any right to proceeds from the recovery.[13] If there is a dispute as to whether some or all of those funds should be paid to the predecessor counsel by the client but there is a claim to the proceeds by that counsel, the successor counsel must hold the disputed portion of the funds in a client trust account pursuant to Rule 1.15(e).[14]

III. Conclusion

Where a client has engaged successor counsel in a contingent fee matter to replace predecessor counsel, successor counsel must inform the client in writing that predecessor counsel may have a claim against the contingent fee. Successor counsel is not, however, bound by the fee-division procedures set forth in Model Rule 1.5(e) because such procedures are designed to address

---

13 Determination of what constitutes terminating a lawyer's services "for cause" or a lawyer withdrawing from a representation *without* "just cause" vary by state, but some examples of situations where a lawyer had justifiable cause to withdraw and may be entitled to a *quantum meruit* fee are: obligation to withdraw due to unforeseen conflict of interest (Smith & Burnetti, P.A. v. Faulk, 677 So. 2d 404 (Fla. Dist. Ct. App. 1996)); unanticipated costs and expenses of litigation (Smith v. R.J. Reynolds Tobacco Co., 630 A.2d 820 (N.J. Super. Ct. App. Div. 1993)); client refused to comply with discovery obligations (Ashford v. Interstate Trucking Corp. of America, Inc., 524 N.W.2d 500 (Minn. Ct. App. 1994)).

14 The statements in this section are general in nature and do not address substantive law issues that may vary from state to state regarding charging or retaining liens. The rights and claims of the predecessor lawyer may depend on whether the client terminated the lawyer for cause or without cause, whether the lawyer withdrew with or without cause, or whether the lawyer has an effective lien. These substantive law issues are not addressed in this Opinion.

situations where two lawyers from different firms handle a case concurrently. Upon a recovery, successor counsel must obtain the client's agreement before dividing any fee with predecessor counsel. In resolving any dispute, particularly a dispute solely between counsel, both successor and predecessor counsel remain bound by their confidentiality obligations to the client and any further confidentiality obligations undertaken by the client in a settlement of the underlying matter. In handling funds that are in dispute, the successor lawyer must follow the requirements of Model Rule 1.15.

AMERICAN BAR ASSOCIATION
STANDING COMMITTEE ON ETHICS AND PROFESSIONAL RESPONSIBILITY
321 N. Clark Street, Chicago, Illinois 60654-4714 Telephone (312) 988-5328
CHAIR: Barbara S. Gillers, New York, NY
■ John M. Barkett, Miami, FL ■ Robert Hirshon, Ann Arbor, MI ■ Thomas B. Mason, Washington, DC
■ Michael H. Rubin, Baton Rouge, LA ■ Douglas R. Richmond, Chicago, IL
■ Lynda Shely, Scottsdale, AZ ■ Norman W. Spaulding, Stanford, CA
■ Elizabeth Clark Tarbert, Tallahassee, FL ■ Lisa D. Taylor, Parsippany, NJ

CENTER FOR PROFESSIONAL RESPONSIBILITY
Dennis A. Rendleman, Ethics Counsel
©2019 by the American Bar Association. All rights reserved.

AMERICAN BAR ASSOCIATION
STANDING COMMITTEE ON ETHICS AND PROFESSIONAL RESPONSIBILITY

Formal Opinion 488   **September 5, 2019**

Judges' Social or Close Personal Relationships with Lawyers or Parties as Grounds for Disqualification or Disclosure

Rule 2.11 of the Model Code of Judicial Conduct identifies situations in which judges must disqualify themselves in proceedings because their impartiality might reasonably be questioned—including cases implicating some familial and personal relationships—but it is silent with respect to obligations imposed by other relationships. This opinion identifies three categories of relationships between judges and lawyers or parties to assist judges in evaluating ethical obligations those relationships may create under Rule 2.11: (1) acquaintanceships; (2) friendships; and (3) close personal relationships. In short, judges need not disqualify themselves if a lawyer or party is an acquaintance, nor must they disclose acquaintanceships to the other lawyers or parties. Whether judges must disqualify themselves when a party or lawyer is a friend or shares a close personal relationship with the judge or should instead take the lesser step of disclosing the friendship or close personal relationship to the other lawyers and parties, depends on the circumstances. Judges' disqualification in any of these situations may be waived in accordance and compliance with Rule 2.11(C) of the Model Code.[1]

I. Introduction

The Committee has been asked to address judges' obligation to disqualify[2] themselves in proceedings in which they have social or close personal relationships with the lawyers or parties other than a spousal, domestic partner, or other close family relationship. Rule 2.11 of the Model Code of Judi-

---

1 This opinion is based on the Model Code of Judicial Conduct as amended by the House of Delegates through February 2019. Individual jurisdictions' court rules, laws, opinions, and rules of professional conduct control. The Committee expresses no opinion on the applicable law or constitutional interpretation in a particular jurisdiction.

2 The terms "recuse" and "disqualify" are often used interchangeably in judicial ethics. *See* MODEL CODE OF JUDICIAL CONDUCT R. 2.11 cmt. 1 (2011) [hereinafter MODEL CODE] (noting the varying usage between jurisdictions). We have chosen to use "disqualify" because that is the term used in the Model Code of Judicial Conduct.

cial Conduct ("Model Code") lists situations in which judges must disqualify themselves in proceedings because their impartiality might reasonably be questioned—including cases implicating some specific family and personal relationships—but the rule provides no guidance with respect to the types of relationships addressed in this opinion.[3]

Public confidence in the administration of justice demands that judges perform their duties impartially, and free from bias and prejudice. Furthermore, while actual impartiality is necessary, the public must also perceive judges to be impartial. The Model Code therefore requires judges to avoid even the appearance of impropriety in performing their duties.[4] As part of this obligation, judges must consider the actual and perceived effects of their relationships with lawyers and parties who appear before them on the other participants in proceedings.[5] If a judge's relationship with a lawyer or party would cause the judge's impartiality to reasonably be questioned, the judge must disqualify himself or herself from the proceeding.[6] Whether a judge's relationship with a lawyer or party may cause the judge's impartiality to reasonably be questioned and thus require disqualification is (a) evaluated against an objective reasonable person standard;[7] and (b) depends on the facts of the case.[8] Judges are presumed to be impartial.[9] Hence, judicial disqualification is the exception rather than the rule.

Judges are ordinarily in the best position to assess whether their impartiality might reasonably be questioned when lawyers or parties with whom they have relationships outside of those identified in Rule 2.11(A) appear before them.[10] After all, relationships vary widely and are unique to the individuals involved. Furthermore, a variety of factors may affect judges' decisions whether to disqualify themselves in proceedings. For example, in smaller communities and relatively sparsely-populated judicial districts,

---

3 *See* MODEL CODE R. 2.11(A) (listing relationships where a judge's impartiality might reasonable be questioned, including where (1) the judge has "a personal bias or prejudice" toward a lawyer or party; (2) the judge's spouse, domestic partner, or a person within the third degree of relationship to the judge or the judge's spouse or domestic partner is a party or a lawyer in the proceeding; or (3) such person has more than a de minimis interest in the matter or is likely to be a material witness).

4 MODEL CODE R. 1.2.

5 *See* MODEL CODE R. 2.4(B) (stating that a judge shall not permit family or social interests or relationships to influence the judge's judicial conduct or judgment).

6 MODEL CODE R. 2.11(A).

7 Mondy v. Magnolia Advanced Materials, Inc., 815 S.E.2d 70, 75 (Ga. 2018); State v. Payne, 488 S.W.3d 161, 166 (Mo. Ct. App. 2016); Thompson v. Millard Pub. Sch. Dist. No. 17, 921 N.W.2d 589, 594 (Neb. 2019).

8 N.Y. Advisory Comm. on Judicial Ethics Op. 11-125, 2011 WL 8333125, at *1 (2011) [hereinafter N.Y. Jud. Adv. Op. 11-125].

9 Isom v. State, 563 S.W.3d 533, 546 (Ark. 2018); L.G. v. S.L., 88 N.E.3d 1069, 1073 (Ind. 2018); State v. Nixon, 254 So.3d 1228, 1235 (La. Ct. App. 2018); *Thompson*, 921 N.W.2d at 594.

10 N.Y. Jud. Adv. Op. 11-125, *supra* note 8, at *2.

judges may have social and personal contacts with lawyers and parties that are unavoidable. In that circumstance, too strict a disqualification standard would be impractical to enforce and would potentially disrupt the administration of justice. In other situations, the relationship between the judge and a party or lawyer may have changed over time or may have ended sufficiently far in the past that it is not a current concern when viewed objectively. Finally, judges must avoid disqualifying themselves too quickly or too often lest litigants be encouraged to use disqualification motions as a means of judge-shopping, or other judges in the same court or judicial circuit or district become overburdened.

Recognizing that relationships vary widely, potentially change over time, and are unique to the people involved, this opinion provides general guidance to judges who must determine whether their relationships with lawyers or parties require their disqualification from proceedings, whether the lesser remedy of disclosing the relationship to the other parties and lawyers involved in the proceedings is initially sufficient, or whether neither disqualification nor disclosure is required. This opinion identifies three categories of relationships between judges and lawyers or parties to assist judges in determining what, if any, ethical obligations Rule 2.11 imposes: (1) acquaintanceships; (2) friendships;[11] and (3) close personal relationships. Judges need not disqualify themselves in proceedings in which they are acquainted with a lawyer or party. Whether judges must disqualify themselves when they are friends with a party or lawyer or share a close personal relationship with a lawyer or party or should instead disclose the friendship or close personal relationship to the other lawyers and parties, depends on the nature of the friendship or close personal relationship in question. The ultimate decision of whether to disqualify is committed to the judge's sound discretion.

II. Analysis

Rule 2.11(A) of the Model Code provides that judges must disqualify themselves in proceedings in which their impartiality might reasonably be questioned and identifies related situations. Perhaps most obviously, under Rule 2.11(A)(1), judges must disqualify themselves when they have a personal bias or prejudice concerning a party or a party's lawyer, or personal

---

11 Social media, which is simply a form of communication, uses terminology that is distinct from that used in this opinion. Interaction on social media does not itself indicate the type of relationships participants have with one another either generally or for purposes of this opinion. For example, Facebook uses the term "friend," but that is simply a title employed in that context. A judge could have Facebook "friends" or other social media contacts who are acquaintances, friends, or in some sort of close personal relationship with the judge. The proper characterization of a person's relationship with a judge depends on the definitions and examples used in this opinion.

knowledge of facts that are in dispute in the proceeding. The parties may not waive a judge's disqualification based on personal bias or prejudice.[12]

Beyond matters in which the judge's alleged or perceived personal bias or prejudice is at issue, Rule 2.11(A) identifies situations in which a judge's personal relationships may call into question the judge's impartiality. Under Rule 2.11(A)(2), these include proceedings in which the judge knows that the judge, the judge's spouse or domestic partner, or a person within the third degree of relationship to either of them, or the spouse or domestic partner of such a person (a) is a party to the proceeding, or is a party's officer, director, general partner, or managing member; (b) is acting as a lawyer in the proceeding; (c) has more than a de minimis interest that could be affected by the proceeding; or (d) is likely to be a material witness in the proceeding. Under Rule 2.11(A)(4), a judge may further be required to disqualify himself or herself if a party, the party's lawyer, or that lawyer's law firm has made aggregate contributions to the judge's election or retention campaign within a specified number of years that exceed a specified amount or an amount that is reasonable and appropriate for an individual or entity. But, while Rule 2.11(A) mandates judges' disqualification in these situations, Rule 2.11(C) provides that a judge may disclose on the record the basis of the judge's disqualification and may ask the parties and their lawyers whether they waive disqualification. If the parties and lawyers agree that the judge should not be disqualified, the judge may participate in the proceeding.[13]

Apart from the personal relationships identified in Rule 2.11(A), a judge may have relationships with other categories of people that, depending on the facts, might reasonably call into question the judge's impartiality. These include acquaintances, friends, and people with whom the judge shares a close personal relationship.

A. Acquaintances

A judge and lawyer should be considered acquaintances when their interactions outside of court are coincidental or relatively superficial, such as being members of the same place of worship, professional or civic organization, or the like.[14] For example, the judge and the lawyer might both attend bar association or other professional meetings; they may have represented co-parties in litigation before the judge ascended to the bench; they may meet each other at school or other events involving their children or spouses; they may see each other when socializing with mutual friends; they may belong to the same country club or gym; they may patronize the same businesses and periodically encounter one another there; they may live in the same area or

---

12 MODEL CODE R. 2.11(C).

13 Disqualification may not be waived where the judge harbors a personal bias or prejudice toward a party or a party's lawyer. *See* MODEL CODE R. 2.11(A)(1) & (C).

14 N.Y. Jud. Adv. Op. 11-125, *supra* note 8, at *2.

neighborhood and run into one another at neighborhood or area events, or at homeowners' meetings; or they might attend the same religious services. Generally, neither the judge nor the lawyer seeks contact with the other, but they greet each other amicably and are cordial when their lives intersect.[15]

A judge and party should be considered acquaintances in the same circumstances in which a judge and lawyer would be so characterized. Additionally, a judge and party may be characterized as acquaintances where the party owns or operates a business that the judge patronizes on the same terms as any other person.

Evaluated from the standpoint of a reasonable person fully informed of the facts,[16] a judge's acquaintance with a lawyer or party, standing alone, is not a reasonable basis for questioning the judge's impartiality.[17] A judge therefore has no obligation to disclose his or her acquaintance with a lawyer or party to other lawyers or parties in a proceeding. A judge may, of course, disclose the acquaintanceship if the judge so chooses.

B. Friendships

In contrast to simply being acquainted, a judge and a party or lawyer may be friends. "Friendship" implies a degree of affinity greater than being acquainted with a person; indeed, the term connotes some degree of mutual affection. Yet, not all friendships are the same; some may be professional, while others may be social. Some friends are closer than others. For example, a judge and lawyer who once practiced law together may periodically meet for a meal when their busy schedules permit, or, if they live in different cities, try to meet when one is in the other's hometown. Or, a judge and lawyer who were law school classmates or were colleagues years before may stay in touch through occasional calls or correspondence, but not regularly see one another. On the other hand, a judge and lawyer may exchange gifts at holidays and special occasions; regularly socialize together; regularly communicate and coordinate activities because their children are close friends and routinely spend time at each other's homes; vacation together with their families; share a mentor-protégé relationship developed while colleagues before the judge was appointed or elected to the bench; share confidences and intimate details of their lives; or, for various reasons, be so close as to consider the other an extended family member.

---

15 *Id.*

16 *See* State v. Mouelle, 922 N.W.2d 706, 713 (Minn. 2019) ("In deciding whether disqualification is required, the relevant question is 'whether a reasonable examiner, with full knowledge of the facts and circumstances, would question the judge's impartiality.'" (quoting *In re* Jacobs, 802 N.W.2d 748, 753 (Minn. 2011)).

17 N.Y. Jud. Adv. Op. 11-125, *supra* note 8, 2011 WL 8333125, at *2; Va. Judicial Ethics Advisory Comm. Op. 01-08, 2001 WL 36352802, at *1, *2 (2001).

Certainly, not all friendships require judges' disqualification,[18] as the Seventh Circuit explained over thirty years ago:

> In today's legal culture friendships among judges and lawyers are common. They are more than common; they are desirable. A judge need not cut himself off from the rest of the legal community. Social as well as official communications among judges and lawyers may improve the quality of legal decisions. Social interactions also make service on the bench, quite isolated as a rule, more tolerable to judges. Many well-qualified people would hesitate to become judges if they knew that wearing the robe meant either discharging one's friends or risking disqualification in substantial numbers of cases. Many courts therefore have held that a judge need not disqualify himself just because a friend—even a close friend—appears as a lawyer.[19]

Judicial ethics authorities agree that judges need not disqualify themselves in many cases in which a party or lawyer is a friend.[20]

There may be situations, however, in which the judge's friendship with a lawyer or party is so tight that the judge's impartiality might reasonably be questioned. Whether a friendship between a judge and a lawyer or party reaches that point and consequently requires the judge's disqualification in

---

18 *See, e.g., In re* Complaint of Judicial Misconduct, 816 F.3d 1266, 1268 (9th Cir. 2016) (stating that "friendship between a judge and a lawyer, or other participant in a trial, without more, does not require recusal"); Schupper v. People, 157 P.3d 516, 520 (Colo. 2007) (reasoning that friendship between a judge and a lawyer is not a per se basis for disqualification; rather, a reviewing court should "look for those situations where the friendship is so close or unusual that a question of partiality might reasonably be raised"); *In re* Disqualification of Park, 28 N.E.3d 56, 58 (Ohio 2014) ("[T]he existence of a friendship between a judge and an attorney appearing before her, without more, does not automatically mandate the judge's disqualification . . . ."); *In re* Disqualification of Lynch, 985 N.E.2d 491, 493 (Ohio 2012) ("The reasonable person would conclude that the oaths and obligations of a judge are not so meaningless as to be overcome merely by friendship with a party's counsel."); State v. Cannon, 254 S.W.3d 287, 308 (Tenn. 2008) ("The mere existence of a friendship between a judge and an attorney is not sufficient, standing alone, to mandate recusal.").

19 United States v. Murphy, 768 F.2d 1518, 1537 (7th Cir. 1985).

20 U.S. Judicial Conf., Comm. on Codes of Conduct Advisory Op. No. 11, 2009 WL 8484525, at *1 (2009); Ariz. Supreme Ct., Judicial Ethics Advisory Comm. Op. 90-8, 1990 WL 709830, at *1 (1990) [hereinafter Ariz. Jud. Adv. Op. No. 11]; N.Y. Jud. Adv. Op. 11-125, *supra* note 8, 2011 WL 8333125, at *2. *But see* Fla. Supreme Ct., Judicial Ethics Advisory Comm. Op. No. 2012-37, 2012 WL 663576, at *1 (2012) (stating that a judge "must recuse from any cases in which the judge's [close personal] friend appears as a party, witness or representative" of the bank where the friend was employed).

the proceeding is essentially a question of degree.[21] The answer depends on the facts of the case.[22]

A judge should disclose to the other lawyers and parties in the proceeding information about a friendship with a lawyer or party "that the judge believes the parties or their lawyers might reasonably consider relevant to a possible motion for disqualification, even if the judge believes there is no basis for disqualification."[23] If, after disclosure, a party objects to the judge's participation in the proceeding, the judge has the discretion to either continue to preside over the proceeding or to disqualify himself or herself. The judge should put the reasons for the judge's decision to remain on the case or to disqualify himself or herself on the record.

C. Close Personal Relationships

A judge may have a personal relationship with a lawyer or party that goes beyond or is different from common concepts of friendship, but which does not implicate Rule 2.11(A)(2). For example, the judge may be romantically involved with a lawyer or party, the judge may desire a romantic relationship with a lawyer or party or be actively pursuing one, the judge and a lawyer or party may be divorced but remain amicable, the judge and a lawyer or party may be divorced but communicate frequently and see one another regularly because they share custody of children, or a judge might be the godparent of a lawyer's or party's child or vice versa.

A judge must disqualify himself or herself when the judge has a romantic relationship with a lawyer or party in the proceeding, or desires or is pursuing such a relationship. As the New Mexico Supreme Court has observed, "the rationale for requiring recusal in cases involving family members also applies when a close or intimate relationship [between a judge and a lawyer appearing before the judge] exists because, under such circumstances, the judge's impartiality is questionable."[24] A judge should disclose other intimate

---

21 *See Schupper*, 157 P.3d at 520 (explaining that friendship between a judge and a lawyer is not an automatic basis for disqualification; rather, a reviewing court should "look for those situations where the friendship is so close or unusual that a question of partiality might reasonably be raised"); Ariz. Jud. Adv. Op. No. 11, *supra* note 20, at *1 (suggesting that in weighing disqualification where a lawyer who is a friend appears in the judge's court, the judge should consider as one factor "the closeness of the friendship"); Charles G. Geyh et al., Judicial Conduct and Ethics § 4.07[4], at 4-27 (5th ed. 2013) ("Whether disqualification is required when a friend appears as a party to a suit before a judge depends on how close the personal . . . relationship is between the judge and the party.").

22 N.Y. Jud. Adv. Op. 11-125, *supra* note 8, at *1.

23 *See* Model Code R. 2.11 cmt. [5] ("A judge should disclose on the record information that the judge believes the parties or their lawyers might reasonably consider relevant to a possible motion for disqualification, even if the judge believes there is no basis for disqualification.").

24 *In re* Schwartz, 255 P.3d 299, 304 (N.M. 2011).

or close personal relationships with a lawyer or party to the other lawyers and parties in the proceeding even if the judge believes that he or she can be impartial.[25] If, after disclosure, a party objects to the judge's participation in the proceeding, the judge has the discretion to either continue to preside over the proceeding or to disqualify himself or herself. The judge should put the reasons for the judge's decision to remain on the case or to disqualify himself or herself on the record.

D. Waiver

In accordance and compliance with Rule 2.11(C), a judge subject to disqualification based on a friendship or close personal relationship with a lawyer or party may disclose on the record the basis for the judge's disqualification and may ask the parties and their lawyers to consider whether to waive disqualification.[26] If the parties and lawyers agree that the judge should not be disqualified, the judge may participate in the proceeding. The agreement that the judge may participate in the proceeding must be put on the record of the proceeding.

III. Conclusion

Judges must decide whether to disqualify themselves in proceedings in which they have relationships with the lawyers or parties short of spousal, domestic partner, or other close familial relationships. This opinion identifies three categories of relationships between judges and lawyers or parties to assist judges in determining what, if any, ethical obligations those relationships create under Rule 2.11: (1) acquaintances; (2) friendships; and (3) close personal relationships. In summary, judges need not disqualify themselves if a lawyer or party is an acquaintance, nor must they disclose acquaintanceships to the other lawyers or parties. Whether judges must disqualify themselves when a party or lawyer is a friend or shares a close personal relationship with the judge or should instead take the lesser step of disclosing the friendship or close personal relationship to the other lawyers and parties, depends on the circumstances. Judges' disqualification in any of these situations may be waived in accordance and compliance with Rule 2.11(C) of the Model Code.

---

25 *See* Model Code R. 2.11 cmt. [5]. A judge who prefers to keep such a relationship private may disqualify himself or herself from the proceeding.

26 Disqualification may not be waived if the judge has a personal bias or prejudice concerning a party or a party's lawyer. MODEL CODE R. 2.11(C).

AMERICAN BAR ASSOCIATION
STANDING COMMITTEE ON ETHICS AND PROFESSIONAL RESPONSIBILITY
321 N. Clark Street, Chicago, Illinois 60654-4714 Telephone (312) 988-5328
CHAIR: Barbara S. Gillers, New York, NY
■ John M. Barkett, Miami, FL ■ Robert Hirshon, Ann Arbor, MI ■ Thomas B. Mason, Washington, DC
■ Michael H. Rubin, Baton Rouge, LA ■ Douglas R. Richmond, Chicago, IL
■ Lynda Shely, Scottsdale, AZ ■ Norman W. Spaulding, Stanford, CA
■ Elizabeth Clark Tarbert, Tallahassee, FL ■ Lisa D. Taylor, Parsippany, NJ

CENTER FOR PROFESSIONAL RESPONSIBILITY
Dennis A. Rendleman, Ethics Counsel
©2019 by the American Bar Association. All rights reserved.

Formal Opinion 489   **December 4, 2019**

Obligations Related to Notice When Lawyers Change Firms

Lawyers have the right to leave a firm and practice at another firm. Likewise, clients have the right to switch lawyers or law firms, subject to approval of a tribunal, when applicable (and conflicts of interest). The ethics rules do not allow non-competition clauses in partnership, member, shareholder, or employment agreements. Lawyers and law firm management have ethical obligations to assure the orderly transition of client matters when lawyers notify a firm they intend to move to a new firm. Firms may require some period of advance notice of an intended departure. The period of time should be the minimum necessary, under the circumstances, for clients to make decisions about who will represent them, assemble files, adjust staffing at the firm if the firm is to continue as counsel on matters previously handled by the departing attorney, and secure firm property in the departing lawyer's possession. Firm notification requirements, however, cannot be so rigid that they restrict or interfere with a client's choice of counsel or the client's choice of when to transition a matter. Firms also cannot restrict a lawyer's ability to represent a client competently during such notification periods by restricting the lawyer's access to firm resources necessary to represent the clients during the notification period. The departing lawyer may be required, pre- or post-departure, to assist the firm in assembling files, transitioning matters that remain with the firm, or in the billings of pre-departure matters.[1]

I.   Introduction

As succinctly noted in ABA Op. 09-455, "Many lawyers change law firm associations during their careers." That opinion addressed the need to disclose to new firms information about clients of a departing lawyer in order to perform a conflict of interest analysis before the departing lawyer joins the new firm. This opinion discusses the ethical obligations of both a departing

---

1 This opinion is based on the ABA Model Rules of Professional Conduct as amended by the ABA House of Delegates through August 2019. The laws, court rules, regulations, rules of professional conduct, and opinions promulgated in individual jurisdictions are controlling.

lawyer and their former firm in protecting client interests during the lawyer's transition. Such ethical obligations include providing the firm with sufficient notice of the intended departure for the firm and departing lawyer to notify clients, work together to ensure that the transition of files as directed by clients is orderly and timely, return firm property, update remaining firm staff/lawyers, and organize files that clients authorize to remain with the firm.[2] A departing lawyer's and law firm's agreement to cooperate in these matters post-departure is relevant in determining whether notice provided by such lawyer to the firm is consistent with these obligations and with Rule 5.6(a) as further discussed below. Ideally the firm will have written policies to provide guidance to lawyers about the procedures the firm anticipates following when a lawyer leaves the firm. This affords everyone some uniform expectations about working together to facilitate transitioning clients.

Firm partnership/shareholder/member/employment agreements cannot impose a notification period that would unreasonably delay the diligent representation of the client or unnecessarily interfere with a lawyer's departure beyond the time necessary to address transition issues, particularly where the departing lawyer has agreed to cooperate post-departure in such matters. Nor may a firm penalize a client who wants to go with a departing lawyer by withholding firm resources the lawyer needs to continue to represent the client prior to departure. Departing lawyers also have a duty, pre- or post-departure to cooperate with the firm they are leaving to assist in the organization and updating of client files for clients remaining with the firm, including docketing of deadlines, updating lawyers at the firm who will take over the file and the like, and similarly to cooperate reasonably in billing. A departing partner may be required to return or account for firm property, such as intellectual property, proprietary information, and hardware/phones/computers, and to allow firm data to be deleted from all devices retained by the departing attorney, unless the data is part of the client files transitioning with the departing lawyer.[3]

---

2 *See* ABA Comm. on Ethics & Prof'l Responsibility, Formal Op. 99-414 (1999) at n. 1 (clients should be given the option to stay with a firm, go with a departing attorney, or choose another firm altogether).

3 *See* State Bar of Ariz., Formal Op. 10-02 (2010) ("When a lawyer's employment with a firm is terminated, both the firm and the departing lawyer have ethical obligations to notify affected clients, avoid prejudice to those clients, and share information as necessary to facilitate continued representation and avoid conflicts. These ethical obligations can best be satisfied through cooperation and planning for any departure.").

II. Analysis

A. The Lawyer's Obligation to Represent Clients Diligently

Lawyers must represent clients competently and diligently. Rule 1.3 provides:

A lawyer shall act with reasonable diligence and promptness in representing a client.

Rule 3.2 similarly requires:

A lawyer shall make reasonable efforts to expedite litigation consistent with the interests of the client.

In addition to the duty to represent clients diligently, lawyers have an obligation to communicate relevant information to clients in a timely manner, according to Rule 1.4. This would include promptly notifying a client if a lawyer is changing law firm affiliations.[4] Law firms may not restrict a lawyer's prompt notification of clients, once the law firm has been notified or otherwise learns of the lawyer's intended departure. As noted in ABA Op. 99-414, "informing the client of the lawyer's departure in a timely manner is critical to allowing the client to decide who will represent him."[5] While the departing lawyer and the firm each may unilaterally inform clients of the lawyer's impending departure at or around the same time that the lawyer provides notice to the firm, the firm and departing lawyer should attempt to agree on a joint communication to firm clients with whom the departing lawyer has had significant contact, giving the clients the option of remaining with the firm, going with the departing attorney, or choosing another attorney.[6] In the event that a firm and departing lawyer cannot promptly agree on the terms of a joint letter, a law firm cannot prohibit the departing lawyer from soliciting firm clients.[7]

Some states, such as Florida and Virginia, have a specific Rule of Professional Conduct regarding such situations. For instance, Florida Rule of Professional Conduct 4-5.8(c)(1) provides:

---

4 See D.C. Bar Op. 273 (1997) (A lawyer has an obligation under Rule 1.4 to notify a client "sufficiently in advance of the departure to give the client adequate opportunity to consider whether it wants to continue representation by the departing lawyer and, if not, to make other representation arrangements.").

5 See ABA Comm. on Ethics & Prof'l Responsibility, Formal Op. 99-414, *supra* note 2, at 2.

6 *Id.* at n. 2 & 5; State Bar of Ariz., Formal Op. 99-14 (1999).

7 See Ill. State Bar Ass'n, Advisory Op. 91-12 (1991); Iowa Bd. of Prof'l Ethics Op. 89-48 (1990); State Bar of Mich., Inf. Op. RI-86 (1991); Tex. Comm. on Prof'l Ethics Op. 422 (1985); Va. State Bar, Legal Ethics Op. 1403 (1991); Wash. State Bar Ass'n, Advisory Op. 2118 (2006); RESTATEMENT OF THE LAW THIRD, THE LAW GOVERNING LAWYERS § 9(3)(a) (2000).

Lawyers Leaving Law Firms. Absent a specific agreement otherwise, a lawyer who is leaving a law firm may not unilaterally contact those clients of the law firm for purposes of notifying them about the anticipated departure or to solicit representation of the clients unless the lawyer has approached an authorized representative of the law firm and attempted to negotiate a joint communication to the clients concerning the lawyer leaving the law firm and bona fide negotiations have been unsuccessful.

Under the Model Rules, departing lawyers need not wait to inform clients of the fact of their impending departure, provided that the firm is informed contemporaneously. Law firm management and lawyers remaining at the firm may also contact clients to inform them of the lawyer's impending departure. The preferred next step is for the departing lawyer and the firm to agree upon a joint communication sent to the clients requesting that the clients elect who will continue representing them.

Departing lawyers should communicate with all clients with whom the departing lawyer has had significant client contact that the lawyer intends to change firms. "Significant client contact" would include a client identifying the departing lawyer, by name, as one of the attorneys representing the client.[8] A departing attorney would not have "significant client contact," for instance, if the lawyer prepared one research memo on a client matter for another attorney in the firm but never spoke with the client or discussed legal issues with the client. Similarly, remaining members of the firm may communicate with these clients, offering for the client to be represented by the firm, another firm, or the departing lawyer. Neither the departing lawyer nor the firm may engage in false or misleading statements to clients.[9]

B. Clients Determine Who Will Represent Them

Clients are not property. Law firms and lawyers may not divide up clients when a law firm dissolves or a lawyer transitions to another firm. Subject to conflicts of interest considerations, clients decide who will represent them going forward when a lawyer changes firm affiliation.[10] Where the departing lawyer has principal or material responsibility in a matter, firms should not assign new lawyers to a client's matter, pre-departure, displacing

---

8 *See* State Bar of Ariz., Formal Op. 99-14 (1999), *see also* RESTATEMENT, *supra* note 7, at § 9(3)(a)(i) (limiting solicitation by departing lawyer to "firm clients on whose matters the lawyer is actively and substantially working").

9 *See, e.g.*, Va. Rules of Prof'l Conduct R. 5.8; MODEL RULES OF PROF'L CONDUCT R. 7.1.

10 *See* ABA Comm. on Ethics & Prof'l Responsibility, Formal Op. 99-414, *supra* note 2; *see also* Heller Ehrman LLP v. Davis Wright Tremaine LLP, 411 P.3d 548, 555 (Cal. 2018) (noting "the client's right to terminate counsel at any time, with or without cause" and that "[t]he client always owns the matter") (citations omitted).

the departing lawyer, absent client direction or exigent circumstances arising from a lawyer's immediate departure from the firm and imminent deadlines needing to be addressed for the client. Thus, clients must be notified promptly of a lawyer's decision to change firms so that the client may decide whether to go with the departing lawyer or stay with the existing firm and have new counsel at the firm assigned.

C. Firm and Departing Lawyer Obligations for Orderly Transitions

Law firm management also has obligations to establish reasonable procedures and policies to assure the ethical transition of client matters when lawyers elect to change firms.

Rule 5.1 provides:

(a) A partner in a law firm, and a lawyer who individually or together with other lawyers possesses comparable managerial authority in a law firm, shall make reasonable efforts to ensure that the firm has in effect measures giving reasonable assurance that all lawyers in the firm conform to the Rules of Professional Conduct.

Firms may require that departing lawyers notify firm management contemporaneously with the departing lawyer communicating with clients, employees of the firm, or others about the anticipated departure so that the firm and departing lawyer may work together to assure a professional transition of the client matters. The orderly transition of a client matter may require the firm to assess if it has the capacity and expertise to offer to continue to represent the clients. If a departing lawyer is the only lawyer at the firm with the expertise to represent a client on a specific matter, the firm should not offer to continue to represent the client unless the firm has the ability to retain other lawyers with similar expertise.[11]

The firm and departing lawyer must coordinate to assure that all electronic and paper records for client matters are organized and up to date so that the files may be transferred to the new firm or to new counsel at the existing firm, depending upon the clients' choices. A departing lawyer who does not continue to represent a client nevertheless has the obligation to take "steps to the extent reasonably practicable to protect a client's interests."[12] This duty includes the departing lawyer updating files and lawyers at the firm who take over the representation, when possible. If exigent circumstances cause a lawyer's immediate departure from the firm, either voluntarily or involuntarily, relevant clients of that lawyer still must be notified of

---

11 *See* MODEL RULES OF PROF'L CONDUCT R. 1.1.
12 *Id.* at R. 1.16(d).

the departure and the firm should provide the lawyer with a list of their current and former clients for conflict-checking purposes. The departed lawyer and firm should endeavor to coordinate after the departure, if necessary, to protect client interests.

Firm management should establish policies and procedures to protect the confidentiality of client information from inadvertent disclosure or misuse.[13] The duty of confidentiality requires that departing attorneys return and/or delete all client confidential information in their possession, unless the client is transferring with the departing attorney. The exception to this requirement is for a departing lawyer to retain names and contact information for clients for whom the departing lawyer worked while at the firm, in order to determine conflicts of interests at the departing lawyer's new firm and comply with other applicable ethical or legal requirements. Rule 1.6(b) (7) provides that a lawyer may disclose confidential information "to detect and resolve conflicts of interest arising from the lawyer's change of employment or from changes in the composition or ownership of a firm, but only if the revealed information would not compromise the attorney-client privilege or otherwise prejudice the client." Firms should have policies that require the deletion or return of all electronic and paper client data in a departing lawyer's possession, including on a departing lawyer's personal electronic devices, if the clients are remaining with the firm. Personal electronic devices may include, for instance, cell phones, laptop computers, tablets, home computers, jump drives, discs, cloud storage, and hard drives.

D. Reasonable Notice Periods Cannot Restrict Client's Choice of Counsel or the Right of Lawyers to Change Firms

Model Rule 5.6 prohibits restraints on a client's choice of counsel. The Rule provides:

A lawyer shall not participate in offering or making:
    (a) a partnership, shareholders, operating, employment, or other similar type of agreement that restricts the right of a lawyer to practice after termination of the relationship, except an agreement concerning benefits upon retirement . . .

Firms have an ethical obligation to assure that client matters transition smoothly and therefore, firm partnership/shareholder/member/employment agreements may request a reasonable notification period, necessary to assure that files are organized or updated, and staffing is adjusted to meet client needs. In practice, these notification periods cannot be fixed or rigidly

---

13 *Id*. at R. 1.6(c).

applied without regard to client direction, or used to coerce or punish a lawyer for electing to leave the firm, nor may they serve to unreasonably delay the diligent representation of a client. If they would affect a client's choice of counsel or serve as a financial disincentive to a competitive departure, the notification period may violate Rule 5.6. A lawyer who wishes to depart may not be held to a pre-established notice period particularly where, for example, the files are updated, client elections have been received, and the departing lawyer has agreed to cooperate post-departure in final billing. In addition, a lawyer who does not seek to represent firm clients in the future should not be held to a pre-established notice period because client elections have not been received.

Case law interpreting Rule 5.6 supports the conclusion that lawyers cannot be held to a fixed notice period and required to work at a firm through the termination of that period. Financial disincentives to a competitive departure have routinely been struck down by the courts and criticized in ethics opinions. In *Cohen v. Lord, Day & Lord*, 550 N.E.2d 410, 411 (N.Y. 1989), the Court of Appeals of New York held that any provision that imposes a "significant monetary penalty" on an attorney who remains in private practice is the functional equivalent of a restriction on the practice of law, even though there is no express prohibition on competitive activities imposed on the withdrawing partner.[14] Courts routinely refuse to enforce provisions in partnership agreements or the like that restrict the right of a lawyer to practice law by means of financial disincentives to competitive departures. "[C]ourts will not enforce contract terms that violate public policy . . . the foundation for Rule 5.6 rests on considerations of public policy, and it would be inimical to public policy to give effect" to provisions inconsistent with the rule.[15]

---

14 *See* Pettingell v. Morrison, Mahoney & Miller, 687 N.E.2d 1237, 1238 (Mass. 1997) (reduction in payments based on the net worth of the firm); Whiteside v. Griffis & Griffis, P.C., 902 S.W.2d 739, 741 (Tex. App. 1995) (same); Jacob v. Norris McLaughlin & Marcus, 607 A.2d 142, 146 (N.J. 1992) (reduced payments based on annual draws); Gray v. Martin, 663 P.2d 1285 (Or. Ct. App. 1983) (reduced share of future firm profits).

15 Dowd & Dowd, Ltd. v. Gleason, 693 N.E.2d 358, 370 (Ill. 1998); *see also* Stevens v. Rooks Pitts and Poust, 682 N.E.2d 1125, 1130 (Ill. App. Ct. 1997) ("courts have overwhelmingly refused to enforce provisions in partnership agreements which restrict the practice of law through financial disincentives to the withdrawing attorney"); *Pettingell*, 687 N.E.2d at 1239 ("[t]he strong majority rule . . . is that a court will not give effect to an agreement that greatly penalizes a lawyer for competing with a former law firm"); Pierce v. Hand, Arendall, Bedsole, Greaves & Johnston, 678 So.2d 765, 767 (Ala. 1996); *Gray*, 663 P.2d at 1290. *But see* Howard v. Babcock, 863 P.2d 150 (Cal. 1993). The Supreme Court of California reviewed a partnership agreement which provided that departing partners who competed in the Los Angeles area in the field of insurance defense during the year following their departure forfeited their entitlement to withdrawal benefits other than their capital accounts. The court upheld the forfeiture provision: "[a]n agreement that assesses a reasonable cost against a partner who chooses to compete with his or her former partners does not restrict the practice of law." *Id.* at 156. The *Babcock* decision has been rejected by courts outside of California

There is no meaningful distinction for the purposes of Rule 5.6 between an agreement provision that imposes a financial disincentive to a competitive departure irrespective of the pre-departure notice requirements and a provision that imposes a financial disincentive for the failure to comply with a fixed, pre-established notice period that extends beyond the time necessary, generally or in a particular case, to ensure an appropriate transition, as discussed above. "Although 'reasonable' notice provisions may be justified to ensure clients are protected when firm lawyers depart, what is 'reasonable' in any given circumstances can turn on whether it is truly the client's interest that is being protected or simply a thinly disguised restriction on the right to practice in violation of RPC 5.6(a)."[16] Moreover, to the extent that a firm routinely waives the full notice requirement, enforcement in a particular instance is problematic when used to penalize a lawyer who leaves to compete with the firm.[17]

E. Access to Firm Resources During Transition Period

After the firm knows that a lawyer intends to depart but such lawyer has not yet, in fact, left the firm, the lawyer must have access to adequate firm resources needed to competently represent the client during any interim period. For instance, the lawyer cannot be required to work from home or remotely, be deprived of appropriate and necessary assistance from support staff or other lawyers necessary to represent the clients competently, including access to research and drafting tools that the firm generally makes available to lawyers. A lawyer cannot be precluded from using associates or other lawyers, previously assigned to a client matter or otherwise normally available to lawyers at the firm to represent firm clients competently and diligently during the pre-departure period.

---

that have considered it. *Pettingell*, 687 N.E.2d at 1239 ("[c]ourts have not been attracted to the contrary view expressed in *Howard v. Babcock*"); *see also Stevens*, 682 N.E.2d at 1130–33; Zeldes, Needle & Cooper v. Shrader, 1997 WL 644908, at *6 n.6 (Conn. Super. Ct. 1997); *Whiteside*, 902 S.W.2d at 744 ("[w]e are unwilling to follow this distinctly minority position and abandon the concept of client choice that we believe remains the premise underlying DR 2-108"); RESTATEMENT, *supra* note 7, at § 13 RN to cmt. b. ("Only in California . . . are restrictive covenants in law-firm agreements enforced"); *but see* Capozzi v. Latasha & Capozzi, P.C., 797 A.2d 314, 320-322 (Pa. Sup. Ct. 2002) (holding that forfeiture for competition provisions were enforceable but striking down the clause at issue as unreasonable).

16 Mark J. Fucile, *Moving On: Duties Beyond the RPCs When Changing Law Firms*, OR. ST. B. BULL. (June 2013); *see also* Borteck v. Riker, Danzig, Scherer, Hyland & Perretti LLP, 179 N.J.246, 260–261 (N.J. 2004) ("firms must guard against provisions that unreasonably delay an attorney's orderly transition from one firm to another").

17 *See* Angela Morris, *Are Law Firms Invoking Obscure Contractual Clauses to Delay Lateral Moves? Or Does It Just Seem That Way?*, ABA J., Apr. 1, 2019.

Similarly, firms cannot prohibit or restrict access to email, voicemail, files, and electronic court filing systems where such systems are necessary for the departing attorney to represent clients competently and diligently during the notice period. Once the lawyer has left the firm, the firm should set automatic email responses and voicemail messages for the departed lawyer's email and telephones, to provide notice of the lawyer's departure, and offer an alternative contact at the firm for inquiries. A supervising lawyer at the firm should review the departed lawyer's firm emails, voicemails, and paper mail in accordance with client directions and promptly forward communications to the departed lawyer for all clients continuing to be represented by that lawyer.

F. New Matters Coming in During Transition Period
During the notification period the lawyer and firm should determine how any new matters or new clients coming into the departing attorney will be treated—as a new client (or matter) of the existing firm or the new firm. To avoid client confusion and disputes, the firm and departing lawyer should discuss and clarify how new client matters will be addressed at the time that the departing lawyer notifies the firm of the impending departure.

G. Conclusion
Lawyers have the right to leave a firm and practice at another firm. Likewise, clients have the right to switch lawyers or law firms, subject to the approval of a tribunal, when applicable (and conflicts of interest). The ethics rules do not allow non-competition clauses in partnership or employment agreements. Lawyers and law firm management have ethical obligations to assure the orderly transition of client matters when lawyers notify a firm they intend to move to a new firm. Firms may require some period of advance notice of an intended departure to provide sufficient time to notify clients to select who will represent them, assemble files, adjust staffing at the firm if the firm is to continue as counsel on matters previously handled by the departing attorney, and secure firm property in the departing lawyer's possession. Firm notification requirements, however, cannot be fixed or pre-determined in every instance, cannot restrict or interfere with a client's choice of counsel, and cannot hinder or unreasonably delay the diligent representation of a client. Firms also cannot restrict a lawyer's ability to represent a client competently during any pre-departure notification periods by restricting the lawyer's access to firm resources necessary to represent the clients during the notification period. Firms should not displace departing lawyers before departure by assigning new lawyers to a client's matter, absent client direction or exigent circumstances requiring protection of clients' interests. A firm's reliance on a fixed notice period set forth in an agreement either to attempt to require the lawyer to stay at the firm for that period or to impose a financial

penalty for an early departure must be justified by particular circumstances related to the orderly transition of client matters and must account for the departing lawyer's offer to cooperate post-departure in these and other matters. Otherwise, a firm's imposition of a fixed notice period may be inconsistent with Rule 5.6(a).

Abstaining: Hon. Goodwin Liu.

AMERICAN BAR ASSOCIATION
STANDING COMMITTEE ON ETHICS AND PROFESSIONAL RESPONSIBILITY
321 N. Clark Street, Chicago, Illinois 60654-4714 Telephone (312) 988-5328
CHAIR: Barbara S. Gillers, New York, NY
■ Lonnie T. Brown, Athens, GA ■ Robert Hirshon, Ann Arbor, MI ■ Hon. Goodwin Liu, San Francisco, CA
■ Thomas B. Mason, Washington, D.C. ■ Michael H. Rubin, Baton Rouge, LA
■ Lynda Shely, Scottsdale, AZ ■ Norman W. Spaulding, Stanford, CA
■ Elizabeth Clark Tarbert, Tallahassee, FL ■ Lisa D. Taylor, Parsippany, NJ

CENTER FOR PROFESSIONAL RESPONSIBILITY
Mary McDermott, Lead Senior Counsel
©2019 by the American Bar Association. All rights reserved.